Causal Inference for Traders

Moving Beyond Correlation in Financial Markets

Victor Trex

Published by NobleTrex Press

For permissions and other inquiries, write to:
P.O. Box 3132, Framingham, MA 01701, USA

Contents

Introduction

Financial markets reward decisions, not merely predictions. A backtest can glow with statistical significance and still lose money once transaction costs, regime shifts, and strategic feedback from other agents are accounted for. This book argues that the remedy is not more elaborate forecasting, but a shift in mindset: from correlational pattern-hunting to explicit, assumption-aware causal reasoning. Causal inference gives traders language and tools to ask the counterfactual questions that matter for capital allocation: What would have happened to P&L if we had changed exposure, execution timing, or eligibility rules? Which clients, assets, or time windows truly benefit from a policy, and which are harmed? How can we evaluate a strategy offline, safely, before risking live capital?

Causal Inference for Traders: Moving Beyond Correlation in Financial Markets is written for quantitative practitioners who operate close to the data and the decision. It embraces the uncomfortable fact that markets are adaptive, noisy, and interconnected. Signals beget trades; trades move prices; prices alter signals. Ignoring this loop can turn a predictive model into a self-defeating strategy. The book builds a bridge between modern causal methodology and the realities of market data engineering, microstructure, and risk constraints, offering a principled path from messy datasets to robust, auditable trading policies.

We begin with foundations that traders will recognize as decisive long before any estimator is chosen. Market & data plumbing-prices, returns, corporate actions, point-in-time integrity, survivorship control, and calendar alignment-determine whether a "treatment" precedes an "outcome" without leakage. Microstructure introduces spreads, depth, and latency that complicate identification through endogenous timing and interference across assets. Factor models such as CAPM and its multi-factor descendants are positioned as baseline controls, clarifying what should be attributed to systematic risk versus idiosyncratic causal impact. We close this groundwork by cataloging backtesting pitfalls-look-ahead bias, p-hacking, and sloppy benchmark conventions-and by proposing engineering checklists for reproducible research pipelines.

The mathematical and statistical pillars that follow are intentionally pragmatic. We review probability, Bayes' rule, and independence through the lens of ignorability and graphical separation; random variables and heavy-tailed distributions as they shape estimator variance; and estimation principles-MLE, method of moments, robust errors, and multiple-testing correction-because uncertainty quantification is nonnegotiable when capital is at stake. Linear algebra, convexity, and KKT conditions furnish the geometry of regression, synthetic control, and constrained policy optimization. We highlight linear models, regularization, bootstrap and cross-validation with time-series folds, and core machine-learning learners used as nuisance models inside causal estimators.

With this scaffolding, we transition from correlation to causation. The book formalizes treatments, outcomes, and assumptions via the Neyman-Rubin potential-outcomes model and directed acyclic graphs, introducing SUTVA and d-separation as workhorses for transparent identification arguments. We study back-door and front-door criteria, do-calculus, and instrumental-variable intuition, emphasizing how collider and selection biases arise in financial workflows. We also confront interference, mediation, and the limits of Granger predictability, showing why predictive precedence is neither necessary nor sufficient for causal impact.

We then define effect targets-ATE, ATT, and ATC-linking returns to P&L translation and overlap requirements. Heterogeneous effects and CATE frame allocation questions: who should receive a trade, when, and at what size? We treat local effects with instruments (LATE), clarifying compliance, monotonicity, and interpretability. Estimation proceeds through design-first matching and propensity weighting, stabilized weights in high dimensions, and doubly robust estimators such as

AIPW and TMLE. Orthogonalization, cross-fitting, and meta-learners (S/T/X/R) make modern ML an ally rather than a source of bias.

Because markets rarely hand out randomized experiments, we devote an entire part to quasi-experimental and panel time-series designs. Difference-in-differences and event studies are presented with parallel-trends diagnostics, staggered-adoption estimators, and cross-sectional correlation corrections. Regression discontinuity provides credible identification around thresholds, with applications such as index inclusions. Synthetic control and matrix completion enable donor-based counterfactuals with placebo inference and regularized extensions. Instrumental variables and two-stage least squares receive a trader's treatment-weak-IV diagnostics and the local nature of identified effects. We integrate these ideas with interrupted time-series, fixed-effects panels, and hybrids that accommodate dynamics and non-stationarity.

Finally, we move from effect estimation to decisions. Offline policy evaluation-IPS, DR, and self-normalized variants with variance clipping-supports safe valuation of strategies before deployment. Policy learning turns CATE into budget-constrained treatment rules, while mean-variance, CVaR, and robust optimization encode risk and operational limits such as turnover and exposure caps. We close with causal reinforcement learning, safe exploration, and sequential experimentation under interference, along with governance: sensitivity analysis, transportability, uncertainty bands, causal data engineering, cost monitoring, and model-risk controls for sustained performance.

Throughout, the emphasis is on clarity of assumptions, auditable workflows, and decisions that survive contact with the market. If you bring curiosity, skepticism, and an appetite for disciplined design, this book aims to help you turn correlations into causal insights-and causal insights into enduring trading policies.

Chapter 1

Market & Data Foundations for Causal Analysis

Causal inference in markets is only as good as the prices, timestamps, and benchmarks it stands on. This chapter strips trading data down to its moving parts-returns, corporate actions, order books, factor models, and backtests-to show how subtle implementation choices can completely change your estimated "causal" edge. By the end, you'll see why serious traders treat data engineering and microstructure as part of the model, not as a footnote.

1.1 Financial Returns and Instruments

Causal questions in markets are always about changing something and seeing how payoffs respond. To make those payoffs comparable across assets, strategies, and horizons, we need a common language for prices, returns, and instrument types. This section builds that language.

We will move step by step: from raw prices to different notions of return, then to how corporate actions modify price paths, and finally to how major instruments naturally define outcomes in different units (per dollar, per contract, per unit of risk). Throughout, keep one guiding principle in mind:

A causal effect is only as meaningful as the units of the outcome you use to measure it.

From Price Levels to Returns

Most market data arrive as *levels*: a stock trades at $100, an exchange rate is 1.25 dollars per euro, a futures contract price is 4200 index points. These levels are convenient for quoting, but they are not the most useful representation for causal analysis.

If you say "my signal increases the price of stock A by 2," that effect has very different meanings depending on whether the price was 10 or 200. In contrast, expressing changes in percentage terms makes effects more comparable.

Simple returns

The simplest way to measure how a price changes from one time to the next is the *simple return*. Suppose P_t is the price at time t and P_{t+1} is the price at the next observation. The simple return over that interval is

$$R_{t+1} = \frac{P_{t+1} - P_t}{P_t}.$$

You can read this as "profit per dollar invested at time t." If you bought one dollar of the asset at time t, your wealth at $t+1$ would be $1 + R_{t+1}$ dollars before costs.

Simple returns have several properties that matter for causal interpretation:

- They are **scale-free**: a 5% return is meaningful regardless of whether the stock costs $5 or $500.
- They are **aligned with investor intuition**: performance is typically reported as percentages.

- They are **bounded below** by -100% but **unbounded above**: you can lose at most your entire investment but can in principle make more than 100%.

When we later ask, "what is the average effect of treatment (signal, policy, regime) on one-period returns?", we will almost always be talking about simple returns.

Log returns

For some purposes, especially when modeling higher-frequency data or compounding over many periods, it is convenient to use *logarithmic* (or continuously compounded) returns:

$$r_{t+1} = \log\left(\frac{P_{t+1}}{P_t}\right).$$

Log returns have three attractive features:

- **Additivity over time**: if you have log returns $r_{t+1}, r_{t+2}, \ldots, r_{t+T}$, then the total log return over the whole horizon is just their sum. This simplifies modeling and inference over multiple periods.
- **Approximation to simple returns**: for small returns (say, within a few percent), r_{t+1} is very close to R_{t+1}. This means you can often switch between them without losing much economic meaning on short horizons.
- **Symmetry for up and down moves**: a +10% simple return and a -10% simple return do not cancel out in simple-return space, but the corresponding log returns do nearly cancel, which can make some statistical properties easier to reason about.

In this book, we will mainly interpret causal effects in terms of simple returns, because they map most directly to dollars earned or lost. However, we will sometimes use log returns for modeling and derivations. When we do, we will be explicit about the units.

Price vs. Return as Outcome Variables

Why insist on returns rather than prices as the basic outcome? There are three main reasons:

- **Comparability across assets**: a \$1 price move in a \$10 stock is very different from a \$1 move in a \$200 stock. A 10% return is directly comparable across both.
- **Portfolio aggregation**: a portfolio combines many assets. Portfolio returns are natural weighted averages of individual returns. Portfolio prices are not.
- **Risk interpretation**: risk is commonly measured by the variability of returns, not prices, because investors care about relative fluctuations in wealth.

When we define causal estimands such as "average treatment effect on daily returns," what we are really doing is standardizing the outcome to a per-period, per-dollar unit. This makes the same estimand interpretable across very different strategies, from equities to FX to futures.

Total Return vs. Price Return

So far, we have only talked about changes in the traded price. Many instruments also deliver income streams such as dividends (equities), coupons (bonds), or financing adjustments (futures). These cash flows are economically part of the payoff but may or may not be included in the quoted price series.

Price return

A *price return* only uses the change in the quoted price:

$$R_{t+1}^{price} = \frac{P_{t+1} - P_t}{P_t}.$$

This is what you get if you ignore dividends, coupons, and other distributions. It answers questions like, "how did the quoted price move?" but not, "how much did an investor actually earn?"

Total return

A *total return* includes both price changes and cash distributions received during the period:

$$R_{t+1}^{total} = \frac{P_{t+1} - P_t + D_{t+1}}{P_t},$$

where D_{t+1} is the cash amount per share (or per unit) paid out to holders between t and $t + 1$.

Schematically, total return is:

$$\text{Total return} = \text{price return} + \text{income yield}.$$

For causal work, it is usually total return that matters, because it reflects the full economic payoff to the position. If a dividend announcement causes the price to drop by almost the dividend amount on the ex-dividend date, a price-return-only outcome would misleadingly suggest a negative effect on investors, even though the dividend itself compensates them.

Total-return indices

Many databases construct a *total-return index* series, which represents the value of a hypothetical investment that reinvests all distributions back into the asset. You can think of this as a price series where dividends or coupons are immediately recycled into more units.

If I_t is the total-return index at time t, then its returns implicitly include both price and income. Using such an index as the basis for returns is a convenient way to avoid separately handling distributions in your causal estimands, as long as you understand how the index is constructed.

Corporate Actions and Adjusted Prices

Real-world price series are interrupted by *corporate actions* that change the number of units outstanding, the nominal price, or the way cash flows are distributed. Causal analysis that compares pre-

and post-treatment outcomes must use price and return series that are adjusted in a consistent way.

Splits and reverse splits

A stock split increases the number of shares while reducing the price per share proportionally. For example, in a 2-for-1 split, each share becomes two shares, and the price roughly halves. The economic value of your position does not change at the split moment.

If you ignore the split and look at a raw price chart, you will see a large artificial price drop on the split date. That drop is not an economic loss, but a change in units. For causal work, such artificial jumps must not contaminate returns.

Data vendors handle this by providing *split-adjusted* prices. Historical prices prior to the split are scaled down so that the price path is smooth, and the split itself does not appear as a jump. Returns computed from these adjusted prices reflect genuine economic moves.

Dividends and special distributions

Ordinary cash dividends are typically paid out on a schedule (quarterly, for example). On the ex-dividend date, the stock price tends to drop by roughly the amount of the dividend, because new buyers are no longer entitled to receive that payment. If you compute price returns without adjusting for this, you will see a negative move that is exactly offset by the cash payment.

Some datasets provide *dividend-adjusted* prices, where historical prices are scaled such that drops on ex-dividend dates are smoothed out, mimicking a total-return index. Others provide raw prices and separate dividend fields.

For causal analysis, you must decide whether your outcome is:

- a **price-return-only** series (using split-adjusted prices but treating dividends separately), or
- a **total-return** series (using dividend-adjusted prices or a total-return index).

Being explicit about this choice is crucial, because it changes the economic meaning of your causal estimand.

Symbol changes, mergers, and spin-offs

Other corporate events—such as ticker symbol changes, mergers and acquisitions, or spin-offs—also affect the continuity of price series. Vendors typically handle these through mapping tables and adjustment factors.

From a causal perspective, the key point is that your dataset should represent the value path of a well-defined *economic claim*. If the structure of that claim changes (for instance, a company splits into two, and you now hold both), you need to ensure your outcome variable tracks the combined position in a way that makes pre/post comparisons meaningful.

Simple vs. Log Returns and Adjusted Series: A Visual Comparison

To fix ideas, imagine a stock with a gradually rising adjusted price, punctuated by a split and some regular dividends. The price series will show smooth growth when properly adjusted for the split, while the total-return index will grow a bit faster as dividends are reinvested. Simple and log returns computed from these series will be close for small moves but will differ slightly during larger swings.

The following figure illustrates these relationships on a stylized example.

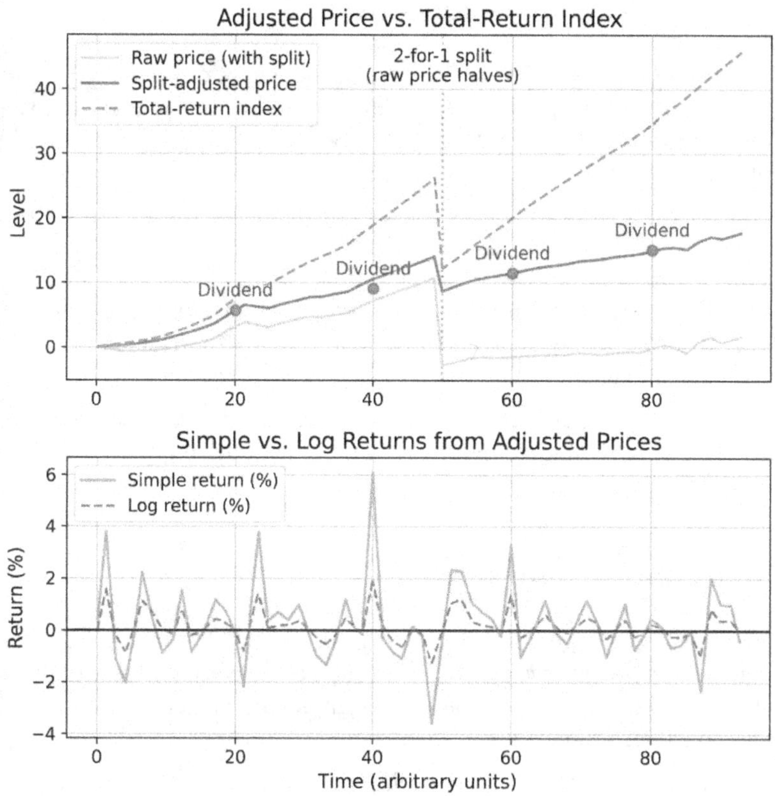

This kind of visualization is a useful sanity check: before estimating any causal effect, verify that your underlying price and return series behave as expected around corporate events.

Single Assets, Portfolios, and Units of Exposure

So far we have spoken as if there is a single asset. In practice, strategies hold many instruments with different weights. To keep causal effects interpretable, you must define clearly what one "unit" of treatment exposure means.

Per-asset vs. per-dollar outcomes

For a single asset, you can define returns per share or per contract, but these are always implicitly per dollar invested at the prevailing price. For a portfolio with weights $w_{i,t}$ in assets $i = 1, \ldots, N$ at time t, the portfolio return is

$$R_{t+1}^{port} = \sum_{i=1}^{N} w_{i,t} R_{i,t+1},$$

assuming the weights sum to one. This aggregation preserves the per-dollar interpretation: if $w_{i,t}$ is the fraction of wealth invested in asset i, then R_{t+1}^{port} is the overall percentage change in wealth.

When we later speak about "the effect of a signal on portfolio returns," we are implicitly talking about this kind of aggregated, per-dollar outcome.

Per-risk-unit outcomes

Some strategies equalize risk rather than capital. For example, a risk-parity portfolio sets weights so that each asset contributes equally to total portfolio volatility. In such a design, it can be meaningful to measure causal effects per unit of risk taken rather than per dollar.

While we will not insist on a specific risk unit here, it is important to understand that once you define your unit of exposure (dollar, share, contract, risk unit), you should stay consistent when reporting causal effects.

Instrument Types and Natural Outcome Definitions

Different instruments embed leverage, margining, and cash-flow structures that change how returns should be measured. A treatment might have the same effect on the underlying price, but very different effects on the actual payoff of a futures or options position. To avoid mixing apples and oranges, we briefly review the main instrument types and their natural return definitions.

Equities and ETFs

Equities. A common stock represents an ownership claim on a company. The natural outcome is the total return per share, including price changes and dividends. Split-adjusted, dividend-adjusted price series or total-return indices are standard.

ETFs. Exchange-traded funds are pooled vehicles that hold baskets of assets. Most equity ETFs aim to track an index; bond and commodity ETFs may use underlying securities or derivatives. For most purposes, ETF returns can be treated like stock returns: total return per share, including distributions.

For both equities and ETFs, your causal effect is often measured as the change in daily, weekly, or monthly total returns, per dollar invested.

Futures

A futures contract is a standardized agreement to buy or sell an underlying asset at a future date for a price agreed on today. Key features:

- Futures are typically traded on margin: you post a fraction of the notional value as collateral.
- They are marked to market daily: gains and losses are credited or debited to your account each day.
- The quoted price is in units natural to the underlying (index points, dollars per barrel, etc.), but your position size is in contracts, each representing a fixed notional.

Because of margining and leverage, there are two distinct notions of return:

- **Per-notional return**: percentage change in the futures price, similar to a spot return on the underlying.
- **Per-equity return**: percentage change in your account equity, which depends on margin, leverage, and financing.

For causal analysis that compares futures and spot positions, per-notional returns are often the right unit. For analyzing the effect of a strategy on an investor's P&L, per-equity returns matter more. Being explicit about which you use avoids confusion when interpreting effect sizes.

Options

Options are nonlinear claims: their payoff depends on the underlying asset price in a convex way. An at-the-money call option might double in value when the underlying rises by 5%, then fall to near zero if the underlying declines modestly.

Because of this convexity and embedded leverage, raw percentage returns on options can be enormous (hundreds of percent) and unstable. Causal questions around options are often better expressed in terms of:

- **Changes in implied volatility** (a model-based parameter),
- **Changes in option price per unit of vega** (sensitivity to volatility),
- **Delta-hedged P&L** (isolating certain risk exposures).

In any case, you should think carefully about the natural economic unit: is your causal effect about how treatments change the likelihood of an option finishing in the money, about the price per unit of volatility risk, or about the strategy-level P&L from an options portfolio?

Foreign exchange (FX)

In FX, "price" is an exchange rate: how many units of one currency for one unit of another. For example, EUR/USD = 1.25 means one euro costs 1.25 dollars. A long EUR/USD position gains when the euro appreciates against the dollar.

For causal work, define clearly:

- Which currency is the *base* (first) and which is the *quote* (second).
- In which currency you measure returns and P&L.

FX returns are naturally measured as percentage changes in the exchange rate, but if your investor reports wealth in a home currency, you may need to convert multi-currency positions into that common unit to define portfolio outcomes.

Fixed income

Bonds and other fixed-income instruments pay coupons and return principal at maturity. Their "price" is often quoted as a percentage of face value. Key notions:

- **Yield to maturity**: a summary measure of the bond's discount rate, given its price and cash-flow schedule.
- **Duration**: a measure of price sensitivity to changes in yield.

For causal questions about interest-rate policy or macro shocks, you might focus on changes in yields or duration-adjusted price moves, rather than naive percentage price changes. For investor-level questions ("what did my bond strategy earn?"), total returns including coupons are most relevant.

Ensuring Comparability of Causal Effects

We can now return to the guiding principle: to compare causal effects across assets and strategies, you must standardize both the outcome and the unit of exposure.

Before you run any causal estimation procedure in later chapters, it is good practice to write down explicitly:

- **Outcome variable**: Is it a simple or log return? Over what horizon (daily, weekly, monthly)? Is it price return or total return? Is it per-dollar, per-contract, or per-risk-unit?

- **Instrument treatment**: What is the instrument type (equity, ETF, future, option, FX pair, bond)? Which corporate actions and cash flows are included in the outcome?
- **Exposure unit**: When you say "the treatment increases returns by 0.5%," does that mean per day per dollar invested, per contract of notional, or something else?

Only after these definitions are in place does it make sense to interpret the magnitude of an estimated effect: whether an additional 10 basis points per day is trivial noise or a major improvement depends on the unit, the horizon, and the risk profile.

In the rest of the chapter we will build on this foundation, moving from the abstract definitions here to the concrete structure of market data, and then to the microstructure and backtesting practices that determine whether our causal conclusions can be trusted.

1.2 Market Data Structures and Corporate Actions

In the previous section we standardized how to talk about prices, returns, and instruments so that causal effects can be expressed in clear economic units. We now turn to an equally important question: *where do those numbers actually come from, and how must they be organized so that causal claims are not quietly corrupted by data bugs?*

Traders often think in terms of "the price of stock i at time t." In reality, that number is produced by a chain of systems: exchange feeds, internal databases, corporate-action processors, and research pipelines. At each step, choices about timestamps, identifiers, adjustments, and calendars can introduce subtle look-ahead or survivorship biases. This section makes that chain explicit.

Our goals are:

- To introduce the basic building blocks of market data: ticks, bars, and reference data.

- To explain *point-in-time integrity*: ensuring that data visible at time t use only information that was actually known at or before t.
- To show how corporate actions and survivorship are handled in well-designed research datasets.

By the end, you should be able to read a "clean" research table and understand how it relates back to raw exchange messages, and why that matters for causal inference.

From Exchange Feeds to Research Tables: The Layers

It is helpful to think of market data as being organized in layers, from raw to research-ready.

Raw exchange feeds

At the base are *raw feeds* from exchanges and trading venues. These feeds contain time-stamped messages such as:

- individual trades: executed quantity, price, and side,
- quotes: updates to the best bid and ask, or to deeper levels of the order book,
- administrative events: trading halts, resume messages, and so on.

Each message has a timestamp (sometimes multiple, such as exchange time and receipt time), an instrument identifier (exchange-specific symbol or code), and a payload (price, size, flags). These messages arrive at sub-second or microsecond frequencies for active securities.

For causal work, raw feeds are rarely used directly. They are too granular and too idiosyncratic. Instead, they are stored in *tick databases* and transformed.

Tick-level storage

A *tick* is a single event record: one trade, one quote update, one status change. Tick storage typically keeps each tick as a row with:

- precise timestamp,
- instrument identifier (often an internal ID rather than a raw symbol),
- message type (trade, quote, cancel, etc.),
- fields such as price, size, bid, ask, bid size, ask size,
- optional flags (e.g., off-exchange trade, auction, crossed market).

Tick data are the most faithful representation of the market's evolution, and they are essential when studying microstructure, execution, or very short-horizon causal effects. But they are also heavy: a single day of ticks for a liquid stock can contain hundreds of thousands of records. For many questions, we instead work with aggregated forms.

Bar data: time, tick, volume, and range bars

A *bar* aggregates many ticks into one record. Popular bar types include:

- **Time bars**: one record per fixed time interval, such as 1 minute or 5 minutes. Each bar records open, high, low, close (OHLC), and volume.
- **Tick bars**: each bar contains a fixed number of trades, such as 100 trades per bar, regardless of clock time.
- **Volume bars**: each bar aggregates trades until a target cumulative volume is reached.
- **Range bars**: each bar covers a fixed price range; a new bar starts when the price moves by more than a threshold.

Time bars are the most common in daily or intraday causal studies. They line up cleanly with calendar time, making it easy to define pre- and post-treatment windows ("one hour after the signal," "next trading day," and so on). Tick, volume, and range bars can be useful when the clock is a poor measure of market activity, but they complicate alignment across instruments.

Reference data (security master)

Alongside ticks and bars, you need *reference data* describing what each instrument is:

- static attributes: name, exchange, currency, instrument type (stock, ETF, future, option, bond),
- life-cycle dates: listing date, delisting date, maturity date for derivatives,
- identifiers: local symbols, global IDs (e.g., ISIN, CUSIP), internal keys,
- corporate actions: splits, dividends, symbol changes, mergers, spin-offs.

This collection is often called the *security master*. It tells you which rows in tick or bar tables correspond to which economic assets, and what happened to those assets over time.

At the end of the pipeline is a *research table*: a relatively compact table where each row usually corresponds to an instrument–date (or instrument–timestamp) combination, with columns for returns, volumes, features, and labels. A single row might look like:

> "Stock i, on 2022-05-03, had a total return of 0.8%, traded $10M of volume, and had factor exposures X, Y, Z."

The rest of this section explains how to move from raw feeds to such research tables without contaminating them with future information or by silently dropping "dead" instruments.

A Data-Flow View

To keep the layers straight, it is useful to visualize the flow from raw messages to the final research dataset.

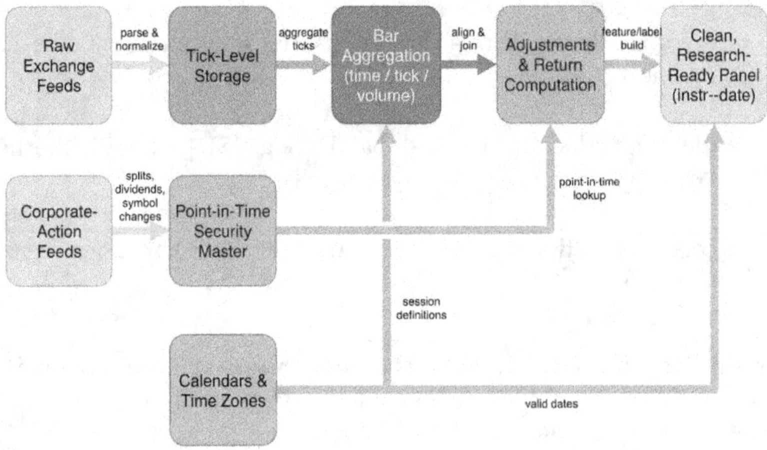

This diagram emphasizes three key ingredients:

- The main price and volume information flows from raw feeds to tick storage, then to bar data.
- Corporate actions and security master information feed into an adjustment layer that converts raw bars into meaningful returns.
- Calendars and time zones provide the scaffolding for aligning data across instruments and markets.

Causal questions live at the rightmost end of the diagram, but their validity depends on all the upstream layers being correct and truly *point-in-time.*

Point-in-Time Integrity

Point-in-time integrity means: if you simulate standing at time t and looking at your database, you see only information that was actually available at or before t. Nothing from the future has leaked backward.

This sounds obvious, but it is violated surprisingly often. Common failures include:

- Using the *latest* security description for historical periods (e.g., including a current industry classification for years before it was assigned).
- Applying corporate actions retroactively without tracking when the adjustment factors became known.
- Using survivorship-biased universes (e.g., "today's S&P 500 constituents back to 1990") that implicitly use future information about which firms survived.

To maintain point-in-time integrity, your data structures must carry effective dates:

- Each corporate action record should include the announcement date, ex-date, payable date, and record date, so you can tell which actions were known on a given trading day.
- Each security master attribute (sector, currency, instrument type) should be tagged with a "valid from" and "valid to" date.
- Your universe definitions (which instruments are eligible for trading at time t) must be based on information up to t, not on the full future history.

Conceptually, every query your backtest makes—"what is the return of stock i today?", "what is its market capitalization?", "is it in the universe?"—should be answered by looking up the state of the world as of that date, not by peeking at the full historical record.

Calendars and Alignment Across Markets

Calendars are the glue that holds multi-asset datasets together. Even if you only trade U.S. equities, you need to distinguish:

- trading days vs. calendar days,
- regular sessions vs. half-days or holidays,
- intraday session boundaries (open, close, auction periods).

When you incorporate other asset classes—European stocks, Asian futures, FX, crypto—you add more complexity: different time zones, overlapping but not identical trading hours, and different holiday rules.

For causal analysis, misalignment here can easily lead to look-ahead or mis-timed responses. Examples:

- You define a "one-day-ahead" effect, but because of time zones, your "next day" FX return partly overlaps with the period before your signal was actually observed.
- You join daily stock returns to macro data by calendar date, without realizing that some macro releases come out after the market close, so the "same day" stock move actually reacted to older information.

A robust approach is:

- Define a canonical time zone for your backtest (often UTC).
- For each instrument, map exchange timestamps into this canonical zone.
- Explicitly define the decision time (when your signal is computed) and the execution window (when trades happen) in this canonical time.
- Build your research table so that each outcome row (e.g., daily return from t to $t+1$) is anchored to those decisions and execution windows.

Only once calendars and time zones are handled carefully can you trust that "pre-treatment" and "post-treatment" windows mean what you think they mean.

Corporate Actions: Splits, Dividends, and More

Corporate actions modify the relationship between raw price series and economic value. We already met splits and dividends when defining returns; here we focus on how they are represented in data and how they can introduce biases.

Data representation of corporate actions

A corporate-action feed typically contains records like:

- split ratios and effective dates,
- cash dividend amounts, announcement dates, and ex-dates,
- stock dividends and spin-offs,
- symbol or identifier changes,
- mergers and acquisitions (including terms of exchange).

These records are used to compute *adjustment factors* that scale historical prices and volumes. For example, after a 2-for-1 split, past prices are often halved and past volumes doubled so that the series is continuous.

From a causal perspective, you want bar-level data where:

- artificial jumps due to splits are removed,
- ex-dividend drops are handled consistently with your choice of price vs. total return,
- mergers and spin-offs are treated so that you track the evolution of an economic claim rather than a raw symbol.

Look-ahead traps in adjustment

A subtle trap arises because data providers often represent adjusted prices as if the entire history had always been quoted in today's terms. For example, when a company executes a split in 2024, the data vendor immediately adjusts prices all the way back to the 1990s in the historical file.

If you naively use these adjusted prices in a backtest that purports to simulate the world as of 2010, you are implicitly using knowledge of a 2024 split to transform 2010 prices. In many cases this is benign, because splits represent pure renaming of units and do not carry economic information. But for more complex actions, such as spinoffs or special distributions, the choice of adjustment can embed assumptions about how you would have reinvested proceeds.

A careful causal researcher:

- Uses adjustment logic that can be reproduced using only corporate actions with ex-dates up to the simulation date.
- Documents whether prices are adjusted only for splits or also for dividends and other actions.
- Ensures that the mapping from raw to adjusted prices does not leak information that would not have been available to a trader at the time.

Security Master and Survivorship Bias

Survivorship bias occurs when your dataset includes only instruments that survive to some reference date, silently excluding those that delisted, merged, or went bankrupt. This can severely distort causal findings, especially when treatments are correlated with risk of failure.

The security master is your main defense against survivorship bias. It should:

- List all instruments that ever traded, including those that delisted or defaulted.
- Record listing and delisting dates, and preferably reasons (merger, bankruptcy, voluntary delisting).

- Allow you to construct universes at time t based on attributes known at or before t (e.g., market cap, exchange, country), not based on future survival.

When building a panel for, say, all U.S. equities from 2000 to 2020, the correct approach is:

- Start from the full set of instruments that met your inclusion criteria as of each date in the past, even if they later died.
- Include their returns up to their delisting date; after that, treat them as gone, not as having zero or missing returns while others continue.

A common but dangerous shortcut is to start from "today's" list of listed securities and go backward in time. This produces an unrealistically rosy picture of how strategies would have performed, since you are effectively discarding the worst failures.

From a causal perspective, survivorship bias means your estimands no longer apply to the population of *all* tradable instruments at the time of decision, but only to the subset that survives. If survival is affected by the same factors as your treatment or outcome, your effect estimates can be badly distorted.

Building the Clean Research Table

We can now tie the pieces together. A typical clean research table for cross-sectional daily equity strategies might have rows of the form:

instrument ID, date, universe flag, returns, volume, features, label

Constructing this table in a causally safe way involves several steps:

- **Define the calendar and decision times.** Choose the time zone and daily session definition. Specify when signals are computed (e.g., at the close of day t) and when trades are executed (e.g., at the close of t or the open of $t+1$).

- **Aggregate raw data into bars.** Starting from tick data, build daily or intraday bars with open, high, low, close, and volume, correctly aligned to the session calendar.
- **Apply corporate-action adjustments.** Using point-in-time corporate-action feeds, compute adjusted prices and total-return series, ensuring that only ex-dates up to day t influence the transformation used for returns from t to $t + 1$.
- **Join with point-in-time security master.** Attach attributes such as sector, country, market cap, and instrument type, using effective dates so that each row reflects only information known as of that date.
- **Define the universe flag.** For each instrument–date, decide whether it is eligible for trading based on criteria that use only past and present information (e.g., average volume over the prior month, price above a threshold, not halted).
- **Compute features and labels.** Build predictor variables (e.g., past momentum, valuation ratios) from historical data up to time t and define labels (e.g., next-day return, next-week return) from t to $t + 1$ or beyond, respecting your decision-execution timing.

At each step, the question to ask is: *could this operation be performed by a trader living at time t, using only information available up to t?* If the answer is "no," you have introduced look-ahead bias or data leakage.

Why This Matters for Causal Studies

Causal inference in markets is hard even with perfect data, because we rarely get to run true randomized experiments. We rely heavily on observational designs that adjust for confounders, control for risk exposures, and exploit quasi-experiments.

If the underlying data are compromised—by look-ahead-adjusted prices, survivorship-biased universes, or misaligned calendars—then even the most sophisticated causal method will be answering the wrong question. It might detect "effects" that vanish in live trading.

By understanding and controlling the entire data pipeline-from raw exchange feeds and tick storage, through bar aggregation, corporate-action processing, and point-in-time security master, all the way to the clean research table-you give your causal designs a solid empirical foundation. In the next section, we will move down one layer further into market microstructure, where the details of order books, liquidity, and execution introduce their own challenges for credible causal identification.

1.3 Market Microstructure and Liquidity

The previous sections treated returns and data structures at a relatively coarse level: daily or bar returns for well-defined instruments, cleaned for corporate actions and survivorship. That is the right scale for many causal questions. But as soon as your treatment or outcome involves intraday timing, trade execution, or high-frequency signals, another layer becomes critical: *market microstructure*.

Microstructure is the plumbing of markets. It governs how orders become trades, how quotes evolve, and how liquidity is supplied and withdrawn. For causal inference, microstructure matters because it determines:

- what "the price at time t" really means,
- how your own orders affect prices and other traders,
- how much noise contaminates short-horizon returns.

This section connects order-book mechanics, transaction costs, and execution timing to microstructural noise and interference, and explains how these forces can distort causal estimates if ignored.

The Limit Order Book: Where Prices Come From

In most modern electronic markets, trading is organized around a *limit order book*. Understanding its basic structure is essential.

Bids, asks, and the spread

At any instant, the book contains:

- **Bid orders**: standing offers to buy a certain quantity at a specified price or better.
- **Ask (offer) orders**: standing offers to sell a certain quantity at a specified price or better.

The highest bid price is called the *best bid.* The lowest ask price is the *best ask.* The difference between them is the *bid–ask spread.* The midquote, or *midprice,* is their average.

The spread is central for traders because it represents a basic friction. If you buy at the best ask and then immediately sell at the best bid, you lose the spread (ignoring fees). Any causal effect on "price" over a very short horizon is competing with this built-in cost.

Depth and the shape of the book

Besides best bid and ask, there are deeper levels:

- At each price level, the book records the total quantity available to buy or sell—this is *depth.*
- The distribution of depth across prices forms the *shape* of the order book.

Depth matters for causal analysis whenever your trades are large enough to move the market. If a small buy order consumes all the liquidity at the best ask and climbs to the next ask level, the execution price reflects both your action and the pre-existing state of the book.

Order types and execution priority

Traders submit different types of orders:

- **Limit orders**: specify a price and quantity; they provide liquidity if they rest in the book until someone trades against them.
- **Market orders**: specify a quantity to buy or sell at the best available prices; they consume liquidity immediately.

- Variants: stop orders, pegged orders, hidden orders, and others, which add complexity but follow the same basic logic.

The exchange uses a matching engine to determine which orders execute and at what prices. Typically, there is a priority rule (such as price-time priority: better price first, then earlier orders at the same price). These rules drive the dynamics of who trades when, at what prices, and how long orders rest in the book.

For our purposes, we can summarize: the limit order book is a constantly evolving summary of supply and demand. Quotes and trades are snapshots of that evolution.

Liquidity: More Than Just the Spread

Traders often use "liquidity" as a single word, but it has multiple dimensions. For causal analysis, it is important to distinguish them, because each affects how your treatment translates into executed outcomes.

Tightness: the cost of immediacy

Tightness refers to how close the best bid and ask are. A tight market has a small spread; a wide market has a large spread. All else equal, narrower spreads make it easier for small treatments (like a modest increase in trading intensity) to show up in observed returns without being swamped by trading costs.

If your strategy buys at the ask and later sells at the bid, you pay the spread twice. When you compute short-horizon returns, failing to account for this cost can produce an apparent negative "treatment effect" that is really just the cost of immediate execution.

Depth: the volume available at each price

Depth measures how much you can trade at a given price without moving it. A deep order book lets you execute large trades with little price impact; a shallow book forces you to walk the book and pay worse prices as your order consumes available liquidity.

For causal studies, depth matters because:

- If a strategy's treatment involves trading larger sizes, its causal effect on realized returns may be very different in deep vs. shallow markets.

- The same nominal "signal" might generate higher slippage in low-depth environments, biasing your estimate of its effect.

Resiliency: how fast the book refills

Resiliency is how quickly prices and depth revert after a trade or shock. In a resilient market, temporary price impacts decay quickly as new limit orders refill the book. In a fragile market, a trade can have a lasting effect.

If you study the causal impact of events (earnings, news, policy announcements) on prices, resiliency shapes the time window over which you should measure the "treatment effect." Measure too early, and you mix temporary microstructure impact with fundamental effects; measure too late, and the impact may have partially reversed.

Immediacy: the speed of execution

Immediacy is the ability to trade quickly when you decide to trade. It is related to tightness and depth but not identical. For example, a market might show reasonable depth but be prone to frequent halts or outages, which reduce immediacy.

For causal inference, immediacy constrains feasible treatment assignments. A strategy that "always trades immediately on a signal" may not be realistic around events when immediacy vanishes (e.g., circuit breakers). Backtests that assume invariant immediacy risk overstating causal effects.

Microstructural Noise and the "True" Price

Daily or weekly returns often behave smoothly enough that we can treat changes in price as changes in underlying value. At higher frequencies, this illusion breaks down. The observed sequence of transaction prices is contaminated by *microstructural noise*.

Sources of microstructural noise

Key sources include:

- **Bid–ask bounce**: trades alternately hit the bid and ask, causing prices to jump up and down by roughly the spread even when fundamental value is unchanged.
- **Discreteness**: prices move in tick increments, not continuously, introducing rounding effects.
- **Asynchronous trading**: different instruments trade at different times, leading to stale quotes and misaligned ticks across assets.
- **Order-processing effects**: delays in updating quotes, batching of orders, and matching-engine details.

If you compute very short-horizon returns (seconds or milliseconds), these noise components can dominate the signal. A "treatment effect" estimated at such horizons may mostly measure how your orders interact with the book rather than any fundamental effect.

Latent efficient price vs. observed prices

It is useful to imagine a hidden, *efficient price* that reflects the market's current best estimate of fundamental value. The midprice is often a better proxy for this latent price than the last traded price, but even the mid can be noisy when depth is thin or quotes are slow to update.

For causal inference, this distinction suggests:

- When measuring short-horizon outcomes, prefer mid-quote changes over last-trade prices where possible.
- Use sampling schemes (e.g., sampling every few seconds or using "tick test" rules) that reduce the influence of bid–ask bounce.
- Recognize that as you push to higher frequency, the outcome you are modeling becomes less a reflection of fundamental value and more a reflection of microstructure mechanics.

Transaction Costs and Slippage as Part of the Causal Environment

In practice, the outcome that matters to traders is not just the change in midprice or last price, but the realized profit and loss *after* transaction costs and slippage. These are not incidental frictions; they are central to the causal environment in which your strategy operates.

Components of transaction costs

Typical components include:

- **Explicit fees**: commissions, exchange fees, taxes.
- **Spread cost**: paying the ask when buying and receiving the bid when selling.
- **Price impact**: adverse movement in the price caused by your own trades.
- **Timing risk**: the risk that prices move unfavorably while your order is being executed.

From a causal perspective, these costs depend on both the state of the market (liquidity, volatility) and your treatment (trade size, urgency, order type). For example, a signal that recommends trading larger sizes may appear profitable in a frictionless backtest but lose money after accounting for the additional price impact it induces.

Slippage and outcome definition

Slippage is the difference between a reference price (often the decision price or a benchmark like VWAP) and the actual execution price. If your causal estimand is defined as "effect on post-trade returns," you must decide:

- which price anchors the start of the return (signal time, order submission, or actual execution?),
- whether the outcome includes or excludes slippage relative to that benchmark.

Different choices correspond to different economic questions. For example:

- If you are evaluating the *predictive power* of a signal given perfect execution, you may anchor at the midprice at decision time and ignore slippage.

- If you are evaluating a *trading strategy*, you should anchor at actual execution prices and include all costs and slippage, because that is what investors experience.

Mixing these notions can lead to misleading causal claims. A signal might seem to cause favorable price moves on a midprice basis but be untradeable once realistic slippage is included.

Endogenous Timing: Who Chooses When to Trade?

Standard causal frameworks often assume that treatment is assigned exogenously or as a function of observable variables. In markets, timing is often *endogenous*: traders decide when to trade based on private information, risk constraints, or algorithmic rules.

Selection on timing

Suppose you observe that when your algorithm trades at certain times, subsequent prices tend to move in its favor. A naive interpretation is that "the algorithm causes the move." But:

- If the algorithm tends to trade when the order book is temporarily unbalanced (e.g., high bid depth), then subsequent price moves partly reflect the reversion of that microstructural imbalance.
- If the algorithm trades after detecting public signals (like volume surges or quote changes) that other market participants also observe, then subsequent price moves may be driven by everyone's reaction to those signals, not by your particular trades.

In both cases, the decision to trade is correlated with unobserved market states that themselves affect future prices, creating a selection problem.

Event studies and overlapping reactions

Even for macro or firm events (earnings, news), endogenous timing appears. Different traders may react at different speeds, and your own trades may be clustered in time with other informed activity. This leads to *overlapping treatments* and blurred definition of "before" and "after."

For causal analysis, this suggests:

- Be explicit about your time window for measuring effects and justify it in light of how fast the order book typically incorporates information.
- Consider designs that exploit exogenous variation in timing (e.g., scheduled announcements, random delays) rather than purely endogenous trade timestamps.

Interference and Spillovers: One Trade Affects Many Outcomes

Most standard causal models assume "no interference": the treatment applied to one unit does not affect the outcome of other units. In markets, this assumption is rarely valid.

Within-instrument interference

Your own trade in an instrument affects subsequent prices in that same instrument:

- A buy order pushes up the price, improving the apparent outcome of your long position but worsening it for any simultaneous short positions.
- Your trade may trigger other traders' algorithms (e.g., momentum or order-flow-following strategies), amplifying the price move.

If you measure "treatment effect" as the price change after your trade, you are partly measuring the mechanical effect of your trade on the price. This is *price impact*, not necessarily an informational effect.

Cross-instrument spillovers

Trades and events in one instrument can affect others:

- Index futures lead underlying stocks; large moves in the future cause correlated moves in constituents.
- Trades in one bond or credit default swap can spill over to similar issuers.

If your treatment involves trading a basket of assets, the outcome for one asset may be influenced by treatments applied to others. This cross-interference complicates attempts to attribute causal effects to specific signals in individual names.

Implications for causal design

In the presence of interference and spillovers:

- Unit-level causal effects (per asset, per trade) may be ill-defined unless you control or model the network of interactions.
- Cluster-level or aggregate effects (e.g., at the portfolio or day level) may be more stable targets for causal inference.
- Experimental designs in markets (such as randomizing execution tactics across similar orders) must acknowledge that one arm of the experiment can influence conditions faced by the other.

Ignoring interference risks attributing to your treatment effects that actually arise from the reactions of other traders or from mechanical market-impact dynamics.

Microstructure-Informed Design Choices

Given these complications, how can you design your causal studies to be robust to microstructure distortions? A few practical principles help.

Choose sampling frequency with care

If your causal question is fundamentally about medium-term behavior (days or weeks), avoid using ultra-high-frequency returns as outcomes. Sampling too frequently:

- magnifies microstructural noise relative to fundamental signal,

- increases sensitivity to idiosyncratic execution details,
- makes interference and order-book dynamics dominate your estimates.

Instead, align your sampling to horizons where spreads, tick size, and bid–ask bounce are small relative to typical price moves at that horizon.

Use quote-based prices where appropriate

When assessing short-horizon effects, consider using mid-quote prices instead of last-trade prices, and filter out trades that occur at off-market venues or with special conditions. This helps:

- reduce bid–ask bounce,
- avoid misinterpreting isolated prints (e.g., late-reported block trades) as contemporaneous reactions to your treatment.

Model or bound transaction costs

Even if your primary causal estimand is defined in terms of frictionless returns, it is wise to:

- estimate realistic trading costs based on spreads, depth, and volatility,
- test how sensitive your causal conclusions are to plausible cost assumptions,
- explicitly separate "signal value" (effect on frictionless prices) from "implementability" (net effect after costs and impact).

Respect execution timing in labels

When constructing labels such as "next-period return after a signal," ensure that:

- the label window begins after the time at which you could plausibly execute trades based on the signal,

- you do not include in the outcome period price moves that your own hypothetical trades would have mechanically caused (unless your question explicitly includes impact).

This often means imposing a small delay between the signal time and the start of the outcome window, especially in very short-horizon studies.

Market microstructure and liquidity transform the tidy world of returns and instruments into a noisy, interactive environment where order books, transaction costs, and timing all matter. For causal inference in trading:

- The limit order book defines what "price" and "liquidity" mean at fine time scales.
- Microstructural noise can overwhelm true effects at high frequencies.
- Transaction costs and slippage are integral parts of the causal environment, not afterthoughts.
- Endogenous timing and interference violate simple causal assumptions and demand careful design.

In later chapters, when we discuss identification strategies and experimental designs, we will repeatedly appeal back to these microstructure concepts. They are the bridge between abstract causal estimands and the messy reality of live trading.

1.4 Factor Models and Risk Premia Basics

By now we have built a careful foundation for measuring returns, organizing market data, and understanding how trades actually occur in the limit order book. The next step is to separate the part of a strategy's performance that is simply *payment for bearing risk* from the part that might plausibly be attributed to a *causal effect* of the strategy's signals, rules, or interventions.

Factor models are the main workhorse for this separation. They provide a structured way to explain returns in terms of broad sources of risk-"the market," "value," "size," "momentum," and others. Whatever is left over after accounting for these sources is often called *alpha*. In this section, we will interpret alpha as the piece of performance where a causal story about your particular strategy has the best chance of being meaningful.

Why Factor Models Belong in a Causal Book

Consider two strategies:

- Strategy A buys high-beta growth stocks.
- Strategy B buys a diversified mix of stocks selected by a proprietary signal but with average market exposure close to one.

Over a bull market sample, both strategies may show positive average excess returns. Without further analysis, you might be tempted to claim that both have discovered profitable causal effects.

However, if you run a factor regression, you might find that:

- Strategy A's performance is almost entirely explained by high exposure to the market and growth factors; its "alpha" is near zero.
- Strategy B still has a positive intercept after controlling for market and style factors; its returns are not just compensation for taking standard risks.

In causal language, factor models give you a *baseline causal story*: assets earn returns because they bear systematic risks that investors dislike and therefore must be compensated for. To claim that your treatment (signal, rule, execution policy) causes extra returns, you need to show effects *over and above* what this baseline story would predict.

The CAPM: A One-Factor Benchmark

The simplest and historically most influential factor model is the Capital Asset Pricing Model (CAPM). While the full theoretical derivation involves investor preferences and portfolio optimization, we only need its empirical form.

CAPM regression

For an asset or strategy i, the CAPM asserts that its excess return over the risk-free rate on day t can be written as:

$$R_{i,t} - R_{f,t} = \alpha_i + \beta_i \left(R_{m,t} - R_{f,t}\right) + \varepsilon_{i,t},$$

where:

- $R_{i,t}$ is the asset's return at time t,
- $R_{f,t}$ is the risk-free rate (e.g., overnight interest rate),
- $R_{m,t}$ is the return on the market portfolio (often approximated by a broad index),
- β_i is the asset's *market beta*, its sensitivity to market movements,
- α_i is the intercept, often interpreted as abnormal performance or "alpha,"
- $\varepsilon_{i,t}$ is an idiosyncratic error term.

Empirically, we estimate α_i and β_i by regressing realized excess returns on the market's excess return.

Interpreting beta and alpha

In the CAPM context:

- β_i measures how much of the asset's return is explained by overall market moves. A beta of 1.5 means that when the market's excess return increases by 1%, the asset's excess return tends to increase by about 1.5%, on average.

- α_i is the average return that cannot be explained by market exposure. If α_i is statistically indistinguishable from zero, the asset or strategy is said to earn no abnormal return: it is simply being paid for taking market risk.

For causal inference, you can think of β_i as capturing a *known causal mechanism*: take more exposure to the market (bear more systematic risk), receive higher expected return as compensation. α_i is the part that needs another explanation-potentially your trading rule, informational edge, or structural advantage.

Beyond CAPM: Multi-Factor Models

Real-world returns are influenced by more than just market risk. Empirical finance has identified several additional broad factors that seem to earn persistent risk premia. Multi-factor models extend CAPM by adding these as explanatory variables.

Style factors

Common equity style factors include:

- **Size**: small-cap stocks vs. large-cap stocks.
- **Value**: cheap stocks (high book-to-market) vs. expensive stocks.
- **Momentum**: stocks that have performed well recently vs. those that have performed poorly.
- **Quality or profitability**: highly profitable, stable firms vs. low-quality firms.
- **Low volatility**: stocks with low past volatility vs. high-volatility stocks.

Each factor is typically represented by a long-short portfolio or a factor return series. For example, a value factor might be defined as the return of a portfolio that is long cheap stocks and short expensive stocks, constructed to be roughly market neutral.

Macro and sector factors

Beyond style, you may include:

- **Sector or industry factors**: returns of sector indices (e.g., technology, financials, energy).
- **Macro factors**: shocks to interest rates, term spreads, credit spreads, inflation surprises, commodity prices, and so on.

These factors capture systematic influences that affect many assets simultaneously. For example, rising interest rates may depress growth stocks more than value stocks; a credit spread widening may hit high-yield bonds and distressed equities.

Multi-factor regression

In a generic K-factor model, we write:

$$R_{i,t} - R_{f,t} = \alpha_i + \sum_{k=1}^{K} \beta_{i,k} F_{k,t} + \varepsilon_{i,t},$$

where $F_{k,t}$ are factor returns (market, size, value, momentum, etc.), and $\beta_{i,k}$ are factor loadings or exposures.

The interpretation is similar to CAPM:

- $\beta_{i,k}$ tells you how sensitive the asset or strategy is to factor k.
- α_i is the average excess return not explained by any of the included factors.

From a causal standpoint, this decomposition allows you to say: "Part of my strategy's performance is just because it happens to be long value and momentum and short size; the remaining part is where my specific treatment might be having a distinct effect."

Risk Premia: Why Factors Earn Returns

Factor models are not just descriptive; they often come with an economic interpretation. A *risk premium* is the extra expected return investors demand for bearing a certain type of risk.

For the market factor, the story is intuitive: a diversified portfolio of risky assets is more volatile and more correlated with economic downturns than a risk-free asset. Investors require compensation for holding it; that compensation is the equity risk premium.

For style and macro factors, similar stories can be told:

- **Size**: small firms may be more fragile, less liquid, and more sensitive to financing conditions, so investors demand higher returns to hold them.
- **Value**: cheap stocks may be distressed or unpopular; investors require a premium to endure the risk that these firms deteriorate further.
- **Momentum**: stocks with strong recent performance may reflect underreaction to information; those who exploit this pattern bear the risk of sharp reversals.
- **Term and credit spreads**: holding long-duration bonds or risky credit exposes you to interest-rate and default risk; those risks are priced.

Different theories compete to explain exactly why each factor earns a premium (risk vs. behavioral mispricing), but for our purposes, the important point is practical:

If a factor is widely recognized and easy to access, its expected return is better thought of as compensation for exposure, not as alpha.

Therefore, when you assess a strategy's causal effect on returns, you should adjust for these known sources of compensation.

Factor Models as Control Variables in Causal Designs

How do factor models concretely enter a causal study? There are several roles they can play.

As regression controls

If you are estimating the effect of a treatment variable $T_{i,t}$ (for example, a signal indicating whether to be long or short) on subsequent returns, a natural specification is:

$$R_{i,t+1} - R_{f,t+1} = \gamma T_{i,t} + \sum_{k=1}^{K} \beta_k F_{k,t+1} + u_{i,t+1}.$$

Here, the factor returns $F_{k,t+1}$ serve as control variables. The coefficient γ is then interpreted as the effect of treatment on excess return *conditional on* factor realizations.

Intuitively, this says: "Given how the market and style factors moved, did treated observations earn more or less than untreated ones?" This helps separate the specific effect of your treatment from broad market swings.

As stratification variables

Another approach is to group observations by their factor exposures (stratification). For example, you might:

- bucket stocks into groups with similar market beta, size, and value characteristics;
- compare treated vs. untreated returns within each bucket.

This is analogous to matching or blocking in experimental design. Within strata defined by factor exposures, units are more comparable, reducing confounding from systematic risk differences.

As outcome adjustments

Finally, you can adjust the outcome itself. Compute a *factor-adjusted return* for each asset or strategy:

$$\widetilde{R}_{i,t} = R_{i,t} - R_{f,t} - \sum_{k=1}^{K} \widehat{\beta}_{i,k} F_{k,t}.$$

This residual return is, by construction, orthogonal to the specified factors (in-sample). You then study the causal effect of $T_{i,t}$ on $\widetilde{R}_{i,t+1}$ rather than on raw excess returns.

The advantage is interpretability: a positive effect on factor-adjusted returns is more plausibly attributable to your treatment than a positive effect on raw returns, which could simply reflect taking more factor risk.

Unconditional vs. Conditional Factor Models

Standard factor models are often estimated *unconditionally*: one set of factor loadings $\beta_{i,k}$ over a long sample. In reality, exposures and risk premia can vary over time.

Time-varying exposures

A strategy's exposures may change with market conditions, signal strength, or risk management rules. For instance:

- a trend-following strategy may have high market beta in strong trends and low beta in choppy markets;
- a value strategy may gradually shift from deep-value names to moderately cheap names as valuations change.

If you treat $\beta_{i,k}$ as fixed when they are actually time-varying, you may misattribute some ordinary exposure changes to alpha.

From a causal perspective, it can be useful to:

- estimate rolling or state-dependent betas (e.g., via rolling windows or conditioning on volatility regimes),
- allow your factor-control specification to include interactions with state variables (e.g., market volatility, interest-rate level).

Time-varying risk premia

The expected returns of factors themselves can also depend on macro conditions. For example, value may perform well in recoveries but poorly during crises; momentum often crashes in sharp market rebounds.

Ignoring this can lead you to overstate strategy-specific alpha when, in fact, you are just loading up on a factor that happens to be in a good phase. Conversely, you may understate an effect if your strategy is concentrated in environments where certain factors are temporarily out of favor.

In more advanced designs, you can model factor expected returns as functions of macro variables and treat the residual as a more refined benchmark. For this introductory section, the key lesson is simply: factor models are approximations, and their parameters are not immutable constants.

Spurious "Causal" Findings from Ignoring Factors

To see the importance of factor adjustment, imagine a naive study:

> "We find that stocks with high dividend yield have higher subsequent returns. Therefore, initiating a high-dividend-yield strategy causes higher returns."

If high dividend yield is strongly correlated with the value factor, and if value has earned a positive premium over your sample, then this finding may simply be rediscovering the value effect. The "treatment" (high dividend yield) is a proxy for value exposure.

A more careful analysis would:

- measure and control for value factor exposure;
- assess whether high-yield stocks have abnormal returns *after* accounting for their value loading;
- interpret any remaining effect in light of this adjustment.

If the effect disappears after factor adjustment, then the causal story is not "high dividend yields cause higher returns," but rather "investors require higher yields to hold value-like stocks, which are riskier in certain dimensions."

This pattern is widespread. Many promising cross-sectional signals turn out, under closer factor scrutiny, to be repackaged exposure to known risk premia. Factor models serve as a filter for such rediscoveries.

Practical Considerations for Traders

Implementing factor models in a trading context raises some practical issues.

Choice of factor set

There is no uniquely correct set of factors. Academic and commercial providers offer different bundles. The right choice depends on:

- your asset class (equities, bonds, FX, commodities),
- your horizon (intraday, daily, monthly),
- your economic story (are you concerned about macro risks, style tilts, or both?).

As a rule of thumb, include at least the major factors widely used in your asset class. For global equities, this usually means: market, size, value, momentum, and perhaps quality and low volatility, plus relevant sector or country factors.

Estimation window and stability

When estimating factor loadings for a strategy or asset:

- Use a window long enough to obtain stable estimates, but short enough to capture changes in exposure.
- Beware of look-ahead bias: do not use future data to estimate loadings that you treat as known at time t.

For strategy-level evaluation, it is common to estimate betas over the full sample after the fact. For live risk management, betas must be estimated using only data available up to the current date.

Interpretation of alpha

Finally, be cautious in interpreting alpha:

- A statistically significant positive alpha suggests that the strategy earns returns beyond those explained by included factors, but it does not prove a particular causal mechanism.
- Omitted factors can masquerade as alpha. If you omit an important risk factor that your strategy is exposed to, the regression will attribute its premium to alpha.
- Multiple testing and model selection can inflate apparent alpha. If you try many specifications and only report the one with the highest alpha, you are effectively p-hacking.

In this book, we will treat alpha as a useful, but not definitive, signal that there may be a strategy-specific causal effect worth investigating with stronger causal designs.

Factor models and risk premia form the bridge between raw returns and causal interpretation:

- CAPM and multi-factor models decompose returns into systematic components (betas times factor returns) and residual alpha.
- Systematic components are best understood as compensation for bearing broad risks, not as evidence of a special edge.
- In causal studies, factor models serve as controls, stratification variables, or outcome adjustments, helping to isolate treatment-specific effects.
- Ignoring factors can turn ordinary risk exposure into spurious "causal" findings.

Armed with this framework, we can now move on to the final section of the chapter, which examines how backtesting practices themselves can create artificial "alpha" if data leakage, survivorship, and other pitfalls are not carefully controlled.

1.5 Backtesting Pitfalls and Data Leakage

Up to this point, we have been building the "physics" of markets: how returns are defined, how data are structured and adjusted, how trades occur in the order book, and how broad risk premia are separated from genuine alpha. This final section of the chapter turns to the "laboratory" where most trading ideas are born and tested: the backtest.

Backtesting is, in effect, a long sequence of causal claims. Every time you say "if I had applied rule S to market data between 2005 and 2020, my wealth would have grown to W," you are implicitly asserting a counterfactual: changing your behavior would have changed your outcomes. For that claim to be credible, the backtest must mimic reality along two key dimensions:

- **Information**: at each decision time, the strategy only sees what would truly have been known then.

- **Population**: the universe of tradable instruments matches what actually existed and was investable at the time.

Violations of these principles generate biased, non-causal conclusions. In this section, we highlight the main failure modes—survivorship, look-ahead, and data snooping—and then translate them into concrete engineering checklists.

Three Families of Backtest Bias

It is helpful to group the most common pitfalls into three overlapping families.

Survivorship bias

Survivorship bias arises when your historical dataset includes only instruments that survived to some later date, excluding those that delisted, merged away, or went bankrupt. For example:

- Using today's index constituents (e.g., current S&P 500 members) and backfilling their histories to 1990.
- Relying on a vendor's "active securities" table without also including delisted or dead instruments.

This is dangerous because many failed or delisted assets performed poorly before disappearing. A strategy that would have bought those assets in real time might look much better in a survivorship-biased backtest where the worst outcomes are simply absent from the sample.

From a causal perspective, survivorship bias changes the target population: you are no longer estimating the effect of your treatment on all tradable securities, but only on those that happened to survive. If survival is correlated with your treatment, or with unobserved confounders, causal interpretation collapses.

Look-ahead bias

Look-ahead bias occurs when a backtest uses information that was not yet available at the decision time. Examples include:

- Using final, restated earnings data to form signals on historical dates before those restatements were published.
- Computing a signal as of the close using prices that include trades occurring after the time you assume decisions were made.
- Assigning sector or index membership using classifications that incorporate future changes (e.g., treating a stock as "technology" years before it was reclassified).

Look-ahead bias is particularly insidious because it often arises from innocent data-processing steps: joining to a current security master, using adjusted price series without tracking when adjustments were applied, or defining a universe based on full-sample metrics.

Causally, look-ahead means your treatment decision at time t is responding to future outcomes. The direction of cause and effect is reversed.

Data snooping and p-hacking

Data snooping refers to using the same dataset repeatedly to search for profitable patterns, trying many rules and parameters until something "works." P-hacking is the statistical version: trying many hypotheses, specifications, or samples and only reporting the ones with impressive-looking performance or p-values.

Events that fall into this family:

- Running hundreds of parameter combinations for a trend rule and selecting the best in-sample performer as "the strategy."
- Trying many alternative definitions of a signal—different look-back windows, z-score thresholds, filters—without accounting for the number of tries.
- Optimizing entry and exit rules, stop levels, and position sizing on the same data used to evaluate the final strategy.

Even if your data are otherwise clean and point-in-time, data snooping inflates apparent alpha. Some strategies will look great by sheer luck; if you search long enough, you will eventually find them. Unless you account for this search, the resulting "effects" are not robust causal relationships but artifacts of overfitting.

Where Bias Enters the Backtest Pipeline

To make these issues concrete, it helps to map them onto the typical stages of a backtest:

1. Data ingestion and cleaning.
2. Feature (signal) construction.
3. Universe selection.
4. Signal-to-trade mapping (portfolio construction).
5. Execution and transaction cost modeling.
6. Performance measurement and evaluation.

Before turning to safeguards, we summarize where the three families of bias most often appear:

- **Survivorship bias**: universe selection, security master joins, index-based filtering.
- **Look-ahead bias**: feature construction, execution timing, corporate-action and fundamentals alignment, use of restated data.
- **Data snooping/p-hacking**: strategy discovery, parameter tuning, multiple testing in performance evaluation.

The diagram later in this section will put these on a single page for reference.

Survivorship Bias in Practice

Survivorship bias can be subtle because many professional data products deliberately filter out "uninteresting" instruments:

- They may only maintain full history for current constituents of flagship indices.

- They may drop tickers with long periods of illiquidity or penny-stock behavior.
- They may regard delisted securities as archival and not include them in main feeds.

To guard against this:

- **Start from a complete, historical security master.** It should list all instruments ever traded in your universe, along with listing and delisting dates.
- **Build universes by date.** On each historical date, select all instruments that met your real-time inclusion criteria *then*, regardless of subsequent fate.
- **Include death.** When an asset delists, record its final return (which may be sharply negative if it went to zero) and then remove it from future dates. Do not silently drop it from the historical record.

A good test is mental: if your backtest never holds any stock that later goes bankrupt or disappears, something is wrong. Real trading strategies must grapple with the full distribution of outcomes, including failures.

Look-Ahead Bias and Point-in-Time Data

Look-ahead bias almost always reflects a failure to respect time in your data joins and feature construction.

Fundamental and classification data

Fundamental data (earnings, book values, analyst estimates) and classifications (sector, index membership) are often stored in vendor databases with a single "current value" per date. If you join such data to historical prices, you implicitly assume that the current value applied throughout history.

To avoid this:

- Use **point-in-time** feeds that record both the effective date of each value and the announcement date (when it became public).
- At each backtest decision date t, only use fundamental values with announcement dates $\leq t$.
- For sector and index membership, use historical classification as of t, not current classification.

Price data and execution timing

Even with prices, look-ahead can creep in. For example:

- Using a daily close price to compute a signal at the "close" but then trading at that same close price—implying you knew the closing print before placing orders.
- Using volume or high/low data from the full day to decide whether today's signal passes a liquidity filter, but assuming trades also occur earlier that same day.

Here, the cure is to **define decision and execution times** clearly:

- If decisions are made at the close of day t, then trades must execute at or after that close (usually the open of day $t+1$ in a simple daily backtest).
- Any feature that uses end-of-day information from t must be applied to trades on $t + 1$, not to trades on the same day.

Think like a trader living in the past: at 15:59, you do not know the official closing price or volume; you only know the prices and volumes observed so far.

Data Snooping, P-Hacking, and Overfitting

Even with perfectly clean data, you can "discover" many spurious strategies if you search long enough.

Why overfitting is inevitable

Financial returns are noisy. Over a sample of, say, 5,000 daily observations, if you test 1,000 independent strategies at the 5% significance level, you expect around 50 to look good by chance alone. If you select the best performer and ignore the 999 that failed, your backtest vastly overstates true performance.

Telltale signs

Symptoms of data snooping include:

- A strategy defined by dozens of hand-tuned thresholds and filters, each justified after the fact by "improving" backtest performance.
- Performance that is extremely sensitive to minor changes in parameter settings.
- Bright-line "magic" parameter values (e.g., a 17-day moving average works, but 16 or 18 days do not) without a convincing economic rationale.

Basic defenses

To limit data snooping:

- **Use out-of-sample and forward tests.** Split your sample into training (for idea generation and parameter tuning) and testing (for honest evaluation). Better yet, roll the split forward to simulate real-time discovery and deployment.
- **Keep a research log.** Record each idea you try, successful or not. If you have run 200 variants before finding one that works, treat its t-statistic with skepticism.
- **Prefer simple, robust rules.** Strategies that are stable across reasonable parameter ranges and subperiods are more likely to reflect genuine structure rather than noise.

We will revisit formal ways to account for multiple testing later in the book. For now, the key is to cultivate a skeptical attitude: a backtest is a starting point, not proof.

A Unifying View: The Backtest Pipeline Diagram

It is easy to lose track of where each bias can enter. The following diagram summarizes the typical backtest pipeline and highlights major entry points for survivorship bias, look-ahead bias, and leakage, along with high-level safeguards.

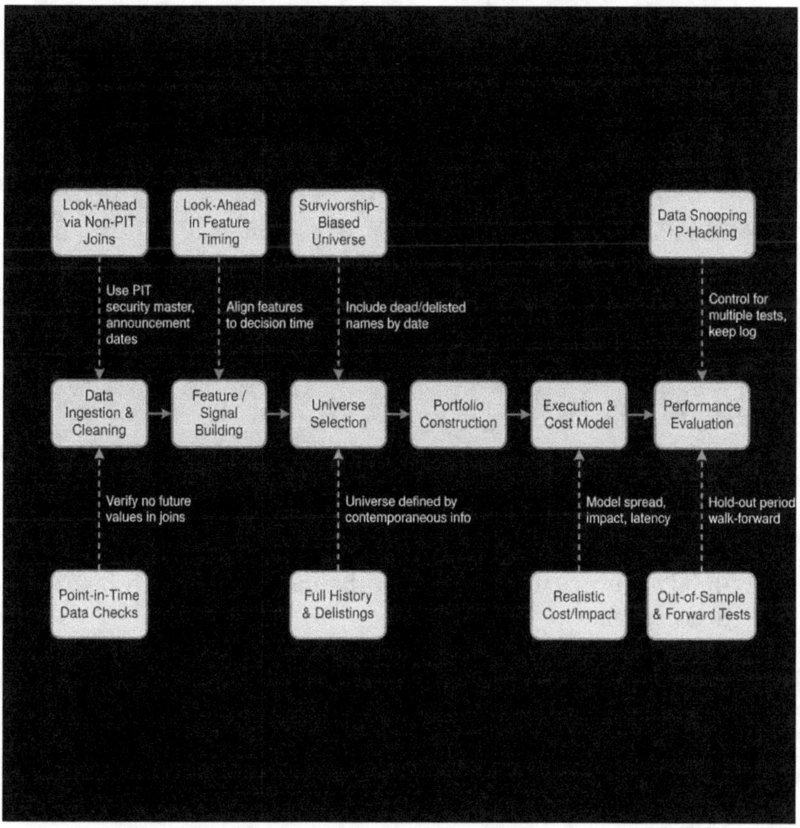

This block-diagram view reinforces that backtest quality is not a single switch but a set of practices applied at every stage.

Engineering Checklists for Causal Backtests

We now turn these ideas into concrete, checklist-style guidelines.

1. Data ingestion and cleaning

Goals: ensure point-in-time integrity and full coverage.

- Use point-in-time price, corporate-action, and fundamental feeds where possible.
- Track announcement dates, effective dates, and ex-dates in your schemas.
- Maintain a full historical security master with listing and delisting dates.
- Log and review any data "fixes" (e.g., removing outliers, filling gaps), as these may introduce implicit look-ahead if not handled carefully.

2. Feature and signal construction

Goals: prevent look-ahead in signals.

- Explicitly define decision times (e.g., at daily close, at 10:00 a.m. intraday).
- Build features using only data with timestamps strictly before the decision time.
- For daily bars, if signals use close prices, apply them to trades on the next bar, not the same bar.
- For fundamentals, use values with announcement dates at or before the decision time; lag them appropriately if publication is delayed.

3. Universe selection

Goals: avoid survivorship and forward-looking filters.

- Construct the tradable universe independently for each date using only contemporaneous information (e.g., trailing volume, price thresholds, exchange listings).
- Do not base universe inclusion on future information (e.g., total return over the next month, eventual index membership).
- Include securities until their actual delisting date, and ensure their final returns reflect any terminal losses.

4. Portfolio construction

Goals: align weights with realistic constraints and factor exposures.

- Respect capacity and liquidity: size positions based on historical volume and depth, not on unrealistic leverage.
- Monitor and record factor exposures (market, size, value, etc.) over time; check that apparent alpha is not just factor tilting.
- Avoid using future realizations (like volatility computed including the next day) to set current position sizes.

5. Execution and transaction costs

Goals: embed microstructure realities into the causal environment.

- Model spreads and fees explicitly; at minimum, subtract half the spread when switching between long and short, and add realistic commission assumptions.
- Include simple, defensible models of market impact for larger trades (e.g., impact proportional to trade size relative to volume).
- Impose latency and execution delays that match your intended trading frequency; do not assume instantaneous fills at midprice.

6. Evaluation and validation

Goals: guard against data snooping and overstated significance.

- Reserve a portion of the data as a genuine hold-out set, not used in strategy design or parameter tuning.

- Use walk-forward or rolling-window tests: repeatedly refit or retune on past data, then evaluate on subsequent, unseen periods.
- Track the number of distinct strategies and parameter combinations that were tried; interpret results in that context.
- Break down performance by subperiod, regime, and market condition. Robust causal effects should not vanish or reverse in slightly different samples.

Backtests as Causal Arguments

In a sense, every backtest is a draft causal story: "Given only the information and instruments available at the time, if we had applied these rules, we would have earned these returns." The role of the checks above is to make that story internally consistent.

When survivorship bias is present, your story silently changes the population. When look-ahead bias is present, your story misrepresents the timing of information and actions. When data snooping dominates, your story confuses noise for signal.

The goal is not perfection—no backtest is perfect—but *structural honesty*: you understand and control the ways in which your simulation differs from reality, and you avoid differences that directly undermine causal interpretation.

In the rest of this book, as we move deeper into identification strategies, experiments, and quasi-experiments, we will continue to return to this theme. Clean causal thinking requires clean empirical foundations. A backtest that respects time, population, and uncertainty is not just a research tool; it is a disciplined way of asking and answering "what if" questions in financial markets.

Chapter 2

Mathematical & Statistical Pillars

This chapter is your quantitative exoskeleton: we strip probability, statistics, and linear algebra down to the tools you'll actually wield when asking causal questions in markets. Instead of abstract theorems in a vacuum, every idea is tied to trading decisions-when a regression can be trusted, when a backtest is lying, and how modern ML fits into rigorous effect estimation. By the end, you'll see that most "mysterious" causal machinery is built from a surprisingly small set of mathematical moves you can learn to perform confidently.

2.1 Probability Foundations

Probability is the language we use to talk precisely about uncertainty. In markets, almost everything that matters is uncertain: tomorrow's return, next quarter's earnings surprise, whether a limit order will be filled, or whether a central bank will hike rates. When we later talk about causal effects—what happens to returns if we change a policy, add a signal, or rebalance differently—we will express our assumptions and conclusions in probabilistic terms.

This section introduces probability in a way that is useful for traders and investors, not as an abstract branch of mathematics. We will:

- Define events and probabilities in a way that naturally fits market questions.
- Introduce conditional probability and Bayes' rule as tools for updating beliefs when new information arrives.
- Clarify independence and conditional independence, and explain why they matter so much for causal reasoning.
- Highlight common fallacies and selection issues that regularly appear in backtests and factor research.

Our goal is that, by the end of this section, you can read and construct probabilistic arguments about markets, and also recognize when a causal claim is really smuggling in a hidden probability assumption.

Events and Probabilities in Markets

We start with the most basic objects: events. An *event* is simply a statement about the world that is either true or false, once uncertainty is resolved.

Examples of events in a trading context include:

- A: "Tomorrow's close-to-close return on the S&P 500 is positive."
- B: "The stock experiences a price gap larger than 3% at the next open."
- C: "Next quarter's earnings surprise for the stock is above analyst consensus."
- D: "Our momentum signal is in the top decile among all stocks today."

A *probability* assigns a number between 0 and 1 to each event, representing your degree of belief that the event will occur, given the information you have and the model you are using.

- $P(A) = 0.6$ means: under your current beliefs or model, you think there is a 60% chance that tomorrow's return is positive.
- $P(B) = 0.02$ means you assign a 2% chance to seeing a large gap at the next open.

It is helpful to keep in mind three key properties:

1. Probabilities are between 0 and 1.
2. An event that is certain has probability 1; an impossible event has probability 0.
3. If two events cannot both happen at the same time (for example, "tomorrow's return is positive" and "tomorrow's return is negative," assuming we ignore the exact zero case), then the probability of "one or the other" is the sum of their individual probabilities.

These rules sound simple, but they already rule out some common errors. For example, if your backtest implicitly assumes that several favorable events "almost always" occur together, you should check that the combined probability is still within the 0–1 range and not unrealistically high.

Conditional Probability: Information Changes Beliefs

In markets, we almost never care about the unconditional probability of an event. Instead, we care about the probability of an event given some information. For example:

- $P(A \mid D)$: probability that tomorrow's return is positive *given* that your signal is in the top decile today.
- $P(C \mid \text{macro surprise is positive})$: probability of an earnings beat given a strong macro release.

This is called a *conditional probability*. Intuitively:

> $P(A \mid B)$ is your probability that A will happen, after you have learned that B has happened (and you treat that information as trustworthy).

In words, conditional probability tells you how your beliefs about A should change when you learn that B is true. If B contains positive news for A, you expect $P(A \mid B) > P(A)$. If B is bad news, you expect $P(A \mid B) < P(A)$.

A practical example:

- A: "The stock's return tomorrow exceeds 1%."
- B: "Today's close is above the 200-day moving average (our momentum filter passes)."

If your signal has predictive power, you hope that $P(A \mid B)$ is higher than $P(A)$, meaning that conditioning on your signal increases the chances of a strong positive return.

Conditional probability also leads to the *law of total probability*, which helps you decompose risks across scenarios. Suppose that the market is either in a bull regime (R = bull) or a bear regime (R = bear), and you have beliefs $P(R = \text{bull}) = 0.7$, $P(R = \text{bear}) = 0.3$. Then the unconditional probability that tomorrow's return is positive can be written as

$$P(\text{positive return}) = P(\text{positive return} \mid \text{bull})P(\text{bull}) + P(\text{positive return} \mid \text{bear})P(\text{bear}).$$

You are simply averaging the conditional probabilities across regimes, weighted by how likely each regime is. This kind of decomposition is at the heart of regime-switching models and scenario analysis.

Bayes' Rule: From Signals to Updated Beliefs

Conditional probability is symmetric in a subtle way. It relates $P(A \mid B)$ and $P(B \mid A)$, but they are not equal in general. Bayes' rule gives the correct relationship between them and is fundamental in causal thinking and in signal evaluation.

In words, Bayes' rule says:

> Posterior probability is proportional to prior probability times likelihood.

To make this concrete, suppose:

- Event R: the market is in a bull regime today.
- Event S: your macro/technical signal currently flashes "bullish."

There are two questions you might ask:

1. How often does your signal flash bullish *if* the market is actually in a bull regime? This is $P(S \mid R)$, the *likelihood* of seeing the signal under a bull regime.
2. Given that you observe a bullish signal, how likely is it that the market is actually in a bull regime? This is $P(R \mid S)$, the *posterior* probability of a bull regime, after taking the signal into account.

Bayes' rule connects these:

$$P(R \mid S) = \frac{P(S \mid R)\, P(R)}{P(S)}.$$

Here:

- $P(R)$ is your *prior* probability of a bull regime before seeing the signal.
- $P(S \mid R)$ is the likelihood: how compatible the observed signal is with a bull regime.
- $P(S)$ is a normalizing constant ensuring probabilities sum to 1 across regimes.

In practice: if your signal is much more likely in bulls than in bears, then observing S should significantly raise your belief that the regime is bullish. Conversely, if the signal happens roughly as often in bears as in bulls, it should not move your belief much.

Bayesian updating is central to:

- Regime detection (bull vs. bear, high- vs. low-volatility states).
- Model comparison (which of several forecasting models fits recent data best?).
- Interpreting event studies (does evidence from the latest earnings season support your causal model of how news affects prices?).

It is also a key tool later when we interpret observed price reactions as evidence *for or against* a causal story.

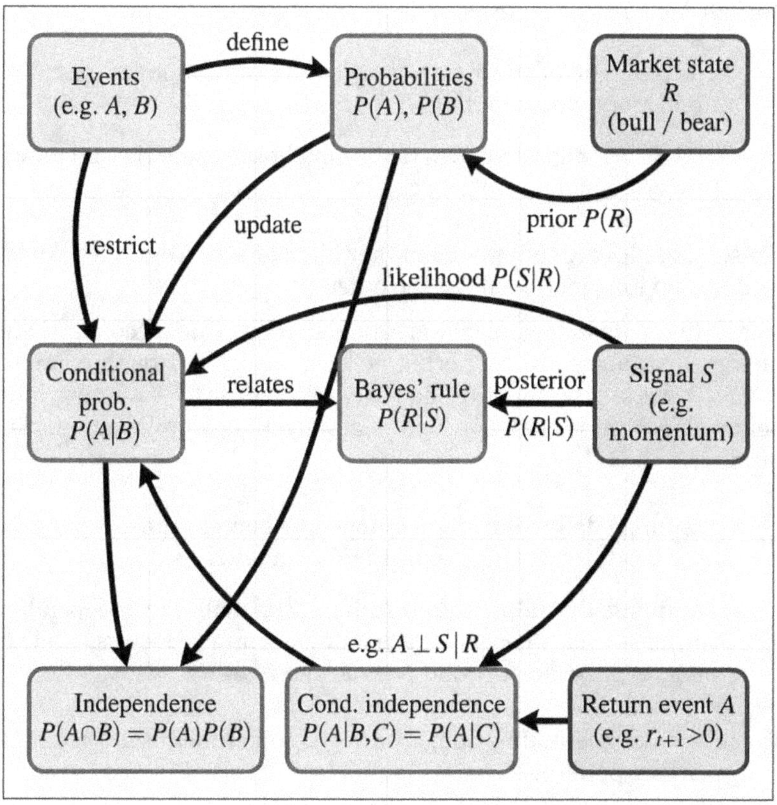

Independence: When Events Do Not Inform Each Other

Two events A and B are *independent* if knowing that one occurred does not change your belief about the other. Formally, this means that

$$P(A \mid B) = P(A).$$

Equivalently, it can be expressed as

$$P(A \cap B) = P(A)\, P(B),$$

which says the joint probability of both A and B is just the product of their individual probabilities.

Market examples of (approximate) independence:

- The outcome of a fair coin toss you use to randomize execution timing, and next month's GDP growth.
- The parity (odd/even) of a randomly chosen trade ID, and tomorrow's closing price of a stock.

These examples are contrived, but they highlight the idea: one variable contains no information about the other.

In practice, true independence is rare in markets. Most economic and financial variables are connected at least weakly (through common macro drivers, risk appetite, liquidity, and so on). Assuming independence where it does not hold is a dangerous simplification. For instance:

- Assuming daily returns are independent across time, when in reality volatility clusters, leads to misestimated risk.
- Assuming that alphas from different signals are independent across stocks, when there are hidden common factors, leads to underestimating portfolio drawdowns.

The independence assumption, however, is sometimes useful as a modeling starting point or as part of a null hypothesis. But good practice requires checking whether the data are compatible with it.

Conditional Independence: Separating Signal From Confounders

Conditional independence is more subtle and more important for causal inference.

Events (or variables) A and B are *conditionally independent given C* if, once you know C, learning about A tells you nothing more about B, and vice versa. Symbolically, people write this as

$$A \perp\!\!\!\perp B \mid C.$$

In words:

> Given C, the variables A and B are independent. Any relationship between them is fully explained by C.

A market example:

- R: market regime (bull or bear).
- S: a momentum signal reading (e.g., positive or negative).
- A: event that tomorrow's return is positive.

It might be that S and A look correlated unconditionally: when your momentum signal is positive, returns tend to be positive. But it could be that both are driven largely by the regime. In a bull regime, signals tend to be positive and returns tend to be positive; in a bear regime, both tend to be negative. Once you condition on the regime R, the signal S may not contain additional information about A. In that case:

$$A \perp\!\!\!\perp S \mid R.$$

For causal inference, conditional independence is the formal way we express assumptions like "after controlling for known risk factors, the variation in our treatment variable is as good as random." For example:

- In a factor model, we might assume that idiosyncratic residuals are independent across stocks after conditioning on common factors.

- In an event study, we might assume that, after conditioning on pre-event characteristics, the timing of the event is independent of future idiosyncratic shocks.

Later, when we talk about identification strategies such as the back-door rule in causal graphs, conditional independence statements will be our main tools. For now, it is enough to recognize that "controlling for" a variable is conceptually about creating conditional independence, not just about throwing covariates into a regression.

Why $P(A \mid B)$ Is Not $P(B \mid A)$

One of the most persistent confusions in applied work is mixing up $P(A \mid B)$ and $P(B \mid A)$. They are usually different, sometimes radically so.

A classic illustration in finance involves earnings announcements:

- E: "The firm has genuinely good news (true positive information about future cash flows)."
- R: "The stock price jumps more than 5% on the earnings announcement."

Two questions:

1. $P(R \mid E)$: Given that there really is good news, what is the probability that we will see a big price jump? This captures how "sensitive" market prices are to fundamental news.
2. $P(E \mid R)$: Given that we observed a big price jump, what is the probability that there was genuinely good news? This is closer to what a trader might care about when screening events ex post.

These are not the same. A market that overreacts will have frequent big jumps even for modest news, making $P(R \mid E)$ large but $P(E \mid R)$ smaller, because many large jumps are driven by noise, positioning, or other non-fundamental shocks.

In causal terms, mistaking $P(R \mid E)$ for $P(E \mid R)$ is like confusing the effect of a cause with the cause of an effect. When you see that trading on a signal is often followed by good returns, you must be careful not to infer that every good return was "caused" by the signal.

Bayes' rule is the correct tool to move between these two probabilities. Practically, this means that when you evaluate signals or strategies, you should always keep track of:

- Base rates: how common is the underlying event (e.g., genuine good news) in your universe?
- False positives and false negatives: how often do you see the market reaction without the underlying cause, or the underlying cause without the reaction?

Ignoring base rates leads directly into the next family of fallacies.

Common Probabilistic Fallacies in Trading and Causal Claims

Several probabilistic pitfalls show up repeatedly in trading research and in causal storytelling. Recognizing them early will save you from overconfident conclusions.

Base-Rate Neglect

Base-rate neglect occurs when you focus on $P(\text{signal} \mid \text{event})$ and forget about $P(\text{event})$ itself.

Example: Suppose a rare type of crisis event occurs in 1% of years. You design a macro indicator that flashes "crisis warning" in 80% of crisis years (high sensitivity) but also in 10% of normal years (false alarms). If the indicator currently flashes, many people instinctively think the probability of a crisis is "high" (maybe around 80%). But Bayes' rule forces you to factor in the base rate (1% of years), so the posterior probability of a crisis is much lower.

Analogous mistakes happen when:

- You see that a factor "works" in most of the subsamples where it was tried, ignoring the number of trials.

- You treat rare but dramatic events (flash crashes, defaults) as if they were much more common than they are, based on vivid recent experience.

Selection Bias and Conditioning on Survival

Backtests often condition on survival. For instance, you may compute historical factor returns only on stocks that are currently in your investable universe, implicitly excluding delisted or bankrupt firms. This is equivalent to conditioning on the event "the stock survived until today."

Formally, you are looking at $P(\text{returns} \mid \text{survival})$ instead of $P(\text{returns})$. If survival is related to past returns or to the factor you study (which it usually is), this conditional distribution will be biased. You will see strategies that look better than they would have in real time.

Similar biases occur when:

- You tune parameters only on strategies that survived an initial screening.
- You analyze only successful funds or managers when inferring the profitability of a style.

In causal terms, conditioning on survival can create spurious relationships, because you are effectively conditioning on a variable that is influenced by both your "treatment" (the strategy) and your outcome (performance).

Confusing Correlation With Causation

Correlation is a symmetric measure: if daily returns and your signal are correlated, then your signal and returns are correlated. Causality is not symmetric: if changing the signal changes returns, that does not imply that changing returns would change the signal in the same way.

From a probabilistic standpoint, correlation is about the joint distribution of two variables. Causation is about how the distribution of one variable would change under hypothetical interventions on the other. Later chapters will formalize this via potential outcomes and do-operators. For now, the key warning is:

A high $P(A \mid B)$ does not, by itself, tell you what would happen to $P(A)$ if you intervened to change B.

When reading empirical results like "stocks with high X tend to have high returns," you should translate this in your head to a conditional probability statement and then ask: what assumptions would be needed for this to also justify a causal statement?

Misinterpreting "Almost Sure" Events

In probability theory, an event with probability 1 is sometimes said to occur "almost surely." This is a technical term: it allows for extremely rare exceptions (events of probability 0) that might still happen in reality.

In finance, this matters because:

- Many models assign probability 0 to extreme moves (e.g., Gaussian returns), but such moves can and do happen.
- An event that is "almost sure" in a model can still fail in the real world, especially over long horizons where tail events accumulate.

For causal inference, treating a probabilistic assumption (such as "no arbitrage" or "no unmeasured confounding") as absolutely certain can lead to overconfident conclusions. A more honest stance is to treat these as high-probability assumptions whose violations you must remain alert to.

From Probability to Causal Language

We have deliberately framed everything in terms of probabilities: events, conditional probabilities, independence, and Bayes' rule. Causal inference in markets will build on this foundation.

In later chapters, when we write things like

- "Returns under treatment" vs. "returns under control,"
- "Ignorability given covariates,"

- "Back-door adjustment set,"

we will be making precise statements about probabilities and conditional independence:

- That certain counterfactual events can be treated as having well-defined probabilities.
- That, conditional on observed variables, potential outcomes are independent of treatment choices.
- That certain sets of variables block all "back-door" paths in a causal graph, which is expressed as a web of conditional independence relationships.

Mastering basic probability now will make those later ideas feel like natural extensions rather than entirely new concepts.

2.2 Random Variables and Distributions

In the previous section we treated uncertainty in terms of events: statements that either happen or do not, with probabilities attached. That language is enough for simple questions such as "what is the chance of a positive return tomorrow?" or "what is the probability of a large gap at the open?"

To analyze trading strategies, risk, and causal effects in more depth, we need a richer language. We rarely care just about whether something happens; we care by *how much*. How large is the return? How big is the drawdown? What is the realized volatility? These are numerical outcomes that are uncertain.

This is where *random variables* and their *distributions* enter. In this section we:

- Define random variables as numerical summaries of uncertain outcomes in markets.
- Introduce expectation, variance, and covariance as core summaries of risk and reward.

- Describe key distributional shapes, especially the contrast between Gaussian and heavy-tailed returns.
- Explain the law of large numbers (LLN) and central limit theorem (CLT) and how they support – and sometimes fail to support – our estimators of means, volatilities, and causal effects.

Throughout, we link each concept to concrete trading and investment questions.

From Events to Random Variables

A *random variable* is a rule that assigns a numerical value to each possible outcome of an experiment or market scenario.

Examples in finance:

- Daily simple return on a stock, defined as $(P_{t+1} - P_t)/P_t$.
- Daily log-return, defined as $\log(P_{t+1}/P_t)$.
- One-day change in the bid-ask spread, measured in basis points.
- Trading volume tomorrow, measured in shares or dollars.
- Realized volatility over the next month, computed from high-frequency returns.

Each of these is a number, but we do not know it in advance. From the perspective of today, it is a random variable.

We distinguish between two broad types:

- **Discrete random variables**, which take values in a countable set (for example, the number of trades in a day, or a credit rating class).
- **Continuous random variables**, which can take any value in an interval or collection of intervals (for example, returns or volatilities, which we typically model as continuous).

The *distribution* of a random variable tells you how its possible values are spread out: which values are likely, which are rare, and how heavily the tails extend.

Distribution Functions: CDFs, PMFs, and PDFs

There are three basic ways to describe a distribution.

Cumulative distribution function (CDF). For any random variable X, its CDF is the function

$$F_X(x) = P(X \leq x).$$

This says, for each threshold x, what is the probability that X is less than or equal to x? For example, if X is daily return:

- $F_X(-0.05)$ is the probability of a loss worse than or equal to -5%.
- $1 - F_X(0)$ is the probability of a positive return.

The CDF is defined for any random variable, discrete or continuous.

Probability mass function (PMF). For a discrete random variable X taking values $x_1, x_2, \ldots$, the PMF gives

$$p_X(x_i) = P(X = x_i).$$

For instance, if X is the number of defaults in a credit portfolio in a year, the PMF gives the probability of 0 defaults, 1 default, and so on.

Probability density function (PDF). For a continuous random variable X, we usually describe its distribution using a PDF $f_X(x)$. This is not itself a probability; instead, probabilities are obtained by integrating the PDF over intervals:

$$P(a \leq X \leq b) = \int_a^b f_X(x)\, dx.$$

When we plot the "histogram" of daily returns and then fit a smooth curve through it, that curve is an estimate of the PDF.

For example, if X is a daily log-return, then:

- The area under the PDF between -0.02 and 0.02 is the probability that the daily return lies within $\pm 2\%$.
- The area in the extreme left tail, say below -0.05, is the probability of a loss worse than 5%.

In practice, we rarely know the true distribution exactly, but we estimate it from historical data and then approximate it with familiar families (Gaussian, Student-*t*, mixtures, and so on).

Expectation: Average Level of a Random Variable

The *expectation* (or expected value, or mean) of a random variable X is the probability-weighted average of its possible values.

For a discrete X with values x_i and probabilities p_i:

$$\mathbb{E}[X] = \sum_i x_i p_i.$$

For a continuous X with PDF f_X:

$$\mathbb{E}[X] = \int_{-\infty}^{\infty} x f_X(x)\, dx,$$

whenever this integral converges.

In finance, expectations are ubiquitous:

- Expected return of a strategy per day, month, or year.
- Expected transaction cost per trade.
- Expected drawdown over a given horizon.

Expectation has some simple but powerful properties:

- Linearity: $\mathbb{E}[aX + bY] = a\,\mathbb{E}[X] + b\,\mathbb{E}[Y]$ for any constants a, b.
- For a portfolio return defined as $R_p = w_1 R_1 + \cdots + w_n R_n$, the expected portfolio return is the weighted sum of individual expected returns, regardless of dependence between assets.

Linearity underlies many portfolio and factor decompositions. For instance, the expected return of a factor-mimicking portfolio is the same linear combination of factor expected returns.

Variance and Covariance: Measuring Risk and Co-Movement

Expectation alone is not enough. Two strategies can have the same expected return but very different risk profiles. We need a measure of how much a random variable fluctuates around its mean.

The *variance* of X is

$$\mathrm{Var}(X) = \mathbb{E}\big[(X - \mathbb{E}[X])^2\big].$$

It is the expected squared deviation from the mean. The square root of the variance is the standard deviation, often used as a volatility measure.

Interpretations in finance:

- Daily return variance captures day-to-day volatility.
- Monthly or annualized variance (scaled appropriately) captures longer-horizon risk.
- Variance of P&L for a strategy indicates how noisy its performance is around its average.

It is useful to remember that high variance means frequent or occasional large deviations from the mean, in either direction. It is a symmetric concept: variance does not distinguish upside from downside volatility. Later, when we study downside risk measures (Value-at-Risk, expected shortfall), we will essentially zoom into one side of the distribution.

Covariance and correlation.

For two random variables X and Y, the covariance is

$$\mathrm{Cov}(X, Y) = \mathbb{E}\big[(X - \mathbb{E}[X])(Y - \mathbb{E}[Y])\big].$$

Intuitively:

- $\text{Cov}(X, Y) > 0$ means X tends to be above its mean when Y is above its mean (and below when Y is below): positive co-movement.
- $\text{Cov}(X, Y) < 0$ means they tend to move in opposite directions.
- $\text{Cov}(X, Y) \approx 0$ suggests weak linear co-movement.

The *correlation* is a normalized version of covariance:

$$\rho_{XY} = \frac{\text{Cov}(X, Y)}{\sqrt{\text{Var}(X)\,\text{Var}(Y)}}.$$

It always lies between -1 and 1.

In portfolio theory, covariance and correlation between asset returns are central to diversification: low or negative correlations can dramatically reduce overall variance for a given expected return. In causal inference, correlations are often the first sign of potential relationships, but we must be careful not to confuse them with causal effects.

Key Distributional Shapes in Finance

Beyond mean and variance, the overall shape of the distribution matters for risk management and inference. Two features are particularly important for financial returns:

- **Skewness** (asymmetry): Are large positive or large negative moves more common?
- **Tail thickness** (kurtosis or "fat tails"): How common are extreme events compared with a Gaussian baseline?

Gaussian (normal) distribution.

The Gaussian distribution is defined by its mean and variance. It is symmetric, bell-shaped, and light-tailed. In a Gaussian world:

- About 68% of probability mass lies within one standard deviation of the mean.

- About 95% lies within two standard deviations.
- Very large deviations (four or five standard deviations) are extremely rare.

Gaussian assumptions make calculations tractable and underlie many classical results (including the CLT). However, financial returns often exhibit:

- More frequent large moves than a Gaussian would predict.
- Slight negative skew (crashes more common than booms).

Heavy-tailed distributions.

A heavy-tailed distribution assigns more probability to extreme outcomes than a Gaussian with the same variance. The Student-t distribution is the standard example used to model returns. It looks Gaussian in the center but has thicker tails.

Implications of heavy tails for trading and risk:

- Higher probability of large drawdowns than Gaussian models suggest.
- Standard deviation underestimates risk when used alone.
- Estimators that rely heavily on second moments (like sample variance) become more unstable.

To visualize this contrast, we can overlay a Gaussian density and a Student-t density fitted to typical daily return data.

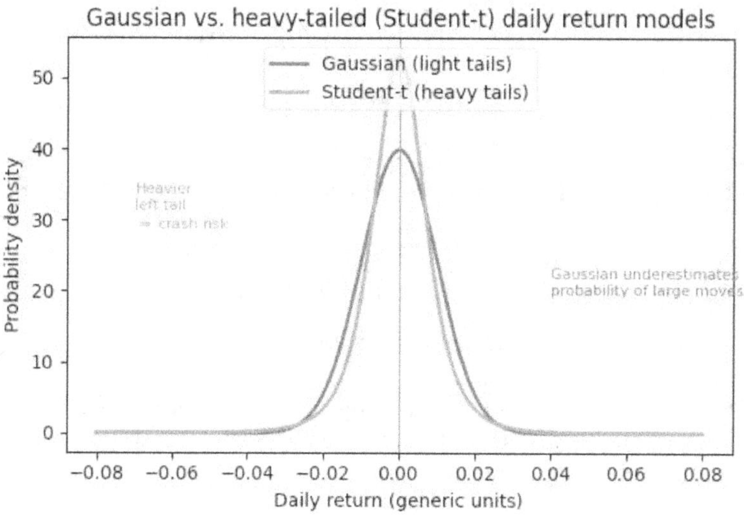

Figure 2.1: Comparison of Gaussian and heavy-tailed (Student-t) models for daily returns. The heavy tails imply a higher probability of large moves and deeper drawdowns than the Gaussian benchmark.

This figure illustrates why tail behavior matters: even if two models agree around typical daily changes, they can disagree sharply about the likelihood of rare but portfolio-dominating events.

Law of Large Numbers: When Averages Stabilize

Estimation in finance almost always relies on historical data: we compute sample means, sample variances, and regression coefficients. A fundamental question is: why should we trust these sample quantities as approximations of their population counterparts?

The *law of large numbers* (LLN) answers this for the mean. Informally:

> If you take the average of many independent observations from the same distribution with a finite mean, the sample average will tend to be close to the true mean.

Suppose you observe daily returns $R_1, R_2, \ldots, R_T$ from a stationary process with true expected return $\mu = \mathbb{E}[R_t]$. The sample mean

$$\bar{R}_T = \frac{1}{T} \sum_{t=1}^{T} R_t$$

is what you typically estimate from historical data. The LLN says that as T grows:

- $\bar{R}_T$ gets closer (with high probability) to μ.
- The probability that $\bar{R}_T$ is far from μ goes to zero.

This justifies statements like "the 10-year average return of this strategy is a reasonable estimate of its expected return." But several caveats are important in financial settings:

- Observations must be "similar enough" over time: strong regime shifts or structural breaks can make early data unrepresentative of the current environment.
- Returns should not have infinite variance or extremely heavy tails; otherwise convergence can be slow or unreliable.
- Serial dependence (autocorrelation) slows down the effective rate at which information accumulates.

In causal inference, the LLN underlies the idea that, with enough observations, average outcomes under treatment and control converge to their expected values, provided our assumptions (such as randomization or ignorability) hold.

Central Limit Theorem: Approximate Normality of Averages

The *central limit theorem* (CLT) goes beyond the LLN. It does not just say that sample averages approach the true mean; it tells us about the *distribution* of the estimation error.

Informally:

> Under broad conditions, the standardized sum (or average) of many independent, identically distributed random variables with finite variance is approximately Gaussian, even if the individual variables themselves are not Gaussian.

In the context of daily returns R_t:

- The distribution of $\bar{R}_T$ is centered near μ.
- As T grows, the scaled error $\sqrt{T}(\bar{R}_T - \mu)$ looks increasingly like a normal distribution with mean 0 and variance σ^2, where σ^2 is the variance of R_t.

This approximate normality is what justifies:

- *Confidence intervals* for expected returns: for large T, $\bar{R}_T \pm 1.96 \cdot \mathrm{SE}(\bar{R}_T)$ gives an approximate 95% interval.
- *t-statistics* and p-values for testing whether a strategy's mean return is different from zero.
- Similar inference for regression coefficients in linear models, which can be written as functions of sample averages.

However, the CLT is not a license to blindly apply Gaussian approximations in any situation. Its limitations are particularly relevant in finance:

- If returns are heavy-tailed, convergence to normality can be slow. For realistic sample sizes, the sampling distribution of $\bar{R}_T$ can have fatter tails than the Gaussian approximation.
- Strong serial correlation (for example, in high-frequency returns or in volatility processes) invalidates simple independence-based CLTs and requires more sophisticated versions.
- In extreme cases (very heavy tails, infinite variance), classical CLTs fail entirely, and sums may converge to non-Gaussian "stable" distributions.

For causal estimators such as difference-in-differences or doubly robust estimators, asymptotic normality (a CLT-like result) is what makes their standard errors, confidence intervals, and hypothesis tests meaningful. Recognizing when heavy tails, heteroskedasticity, or dependence patterns undermine the CLT helps you treat those inferences with the appropriate caution.

Why Heavy Tails Matter for Estimators

Combining the ideas above, we can now see why the tails of the distribution are not just about occasional portfolio pain, but also about the behavior of our estimators.

Consider estimating the mean daily return:

- Under a light-tailed (Gaussian-like) model with variance σ^2, the sampling variability of $\bar{R}_T$ shrinks roughly like $\sigma/\sqrt{T}$, and extreme estimation errors are very rare.
- Under a heavy-tailed model with the same variance but larger kurtosis, extreme daily returns are more common. This increases the frequency of large shocks in the time series, making the path of $\bar{R}_T$ more jagged and slowing down the effective convergence to the true mean.

Practical consequences:

- You may need much longer histories to achieve a desired level of precision in your estimates.
- Backtest performance statistics (Sharpe ratios, t-stats) can be more volatile over time than Gaussian formulas predict.
- Simple Gaussian-based risk metrics (such as 3-sigma VaR) will systematically underestimate tail risks, leading to overconfident leverage and capital allocation.

For causal inference, similar issues arise:

- Estimates of average treatment effects (for example, average impact of a policy change on returns) can be dominated by a few extreme outcomes if the outcome variable is heavy-tailed.
- Standard errors derived under Gaussian assumptions may be too small, and p-values too optimistic.
- Robust estimators and robust standard errors that downweight extremes become especially valuable.

Understanding the distribution of your data *beyond* mean and variance is thus crucial both for good risk management and for credible statistical inference.

Connecting to Causal Inference

Random variables and their distributions provide the backbone for all the causal concepts we will use later:

- Potential outcomes (returns if treated vs. returns if not treated) are random variables with their own distributions.
- Treatment assignment indicators (for example, whether a stock was included in an index reconstitution) are random variables that may or may not be independent of potential outcomes, given covariates.
- Causal effects are often defined as expectations or differences in expectations (average treatment effects, conditional average treatment effects).

The LLN and CLT justify why, with large samples and under appropriate assumptions, we can estimate these expectations and their differences with controlled error. Heavy tails, skewness, and dependence patterns tell us when these justifications become fragile.

By viewing returns, signals, and outcomes through the lens of random variables and distributions, you acquire a set of tools that are both descriptive (what does the data look like?) and inferential (how precisely can I estimate causal effects?). The remaining sections of this chapter will build directly on these tools, turning them into estimators, hypothesis tests, and regression models that we will later embed inside causal identification strategies.

2.3 Estimation and Hypothesis Testing

The previous sections gave us the language of probability and distributions. We can now talk about random variables such as returns, signal values, and realized volatility, and we understand expectations, variance, and the role of heavy tails and limit theorems.

We now turn these ideas into practical tools for learning from data. In trading and causal work, we constantly ask questions like:

- What is the expected return of this strategy?
- How large is the "treatment effect" of an event, such as index inclusion, on a stock's return?
- Is a detected edge statistically distinguishable from noise, or is it likely a data-mined artifact?

Answering such questions requires more than computing historical averages. We need a framework for:

- Constructing *estimators* of unknown parameters or effects.
- Understanding how these estimators behave across repeated samples (their *sampling distributions*).
- Summarizing uncertainty via *standard errors* and *confidence intervals*.
- Making formal *hypothesis tests*, including adjustments for multiple trials and dependence in the data.

This section lays out that framework. Later causal estimators—difference-in-differences, matching, instrumental variables, and doubly robust methods—will plug directly into it.

2.4 Point Estimation: Turning Data into Numbers

A *point estimator* is a rule that takes observed data and produces a single numerical guess for an unknown quantity. The unknown object might be:

- A population parameter, such as the true mean daily return of a strategy.
- A volatility parameter in a stochastic volatility model.
- An average treatment effect (ATE), such as the average change in returns around an event.

If θ denotes the true but unknown value, and we observe data $X_1, \ldots, X_T$, an estimator is a function $\hat{\theta} = \hat{\theta}(X_1, \ldots, X_T)$.

Examples in trading and finance.

- The sample mean return $\bar{R} = \frac{1}{T}\sum_{t=1}^{T} R_t$ as an estimator of $\mathbb{E}[R_t]$.
- The sample variance $s^2 = \frac{1}{T-1}\sum_{t=1}^{T}(R_t - \bar{R})^2$ as an estimator of $\mathrm{Var}(R_t)$.
- The difference in average returns between treated and control stocks in an event study as an estimator of an ATE.

Desirable properties.

When evaluating estimators, we typically consider:

- **Bias**: the difference between an estimator's average value and the true parameter. If $\mathbb{E}[\hat{\theta}] = \theta$, the estimator is *unbiased.*
- **Variance**: how much the estimator fluctuates across samples.
- **Mean squared error (MSE)**: $\mathbb{E}[(\hat{\theta} - \theta)^2]$, which combines bias and variance.

- **Consistency**: whether $\hat{\theta}$ converges to θ as sample size grows, typically guaranteed by the law of large numbers under suitable conditions.

In practice, a small bias can be acceptable if it buys a large reduction in variance. For example, some volatility estimators trade a small bias for much more stability in the presence of jumps.

Construction principles.

Two general approaches, which you will see again in causal settings, are:

- **Method of moments**: Choose $\hat{\theta}$ so that model-implied moments match sample moments. For example, in a simple mean-variance model, the sample mean and variance are the method-of-moments estimators of the true mean and variance.
- **Maximum likelihood**: Given a parametric model for the distribution of the data, choose $\hat{\theta}$ to maximize the probability (likelihood) of observing the data. For example, assuming i.i.d. Gaussian returns, the maximum likelihood estimators of mean and variance coincide with the familiar sample mean and sample variance.

In causal inference, many estimators can be seen as method-of-moments or likelihood-based, even when we do not explicitly describe them that way.

2.5 Sampling Distributions and Standard Errors

A single estimate $\hat{\theta}$ from your backtest is not the full story. If you had rerun the backtest on a different sample of data from the same process, you would likely have obtained a different estimate. The pattern of these hypothetical values is the *sampling distribution* of the estimator.

Why sampling distributions matter.

- They describe the uncertainty in your estimates due to finite sample size.
- They allow you to compute *standard errors*, which measure the typical size of estimation error.
- They underpin confidence intervals and hypothesis tests.

For example, if $\hat{\mu}$ is the sample mean return and its sampling distribution is approximately normal with variance $\sigma^2_{\hat{\mu}}$, then:

- The standard error is $\mathrm{SE}(\hat{\mu}) = \sqrt{\sigma^2_{\hat{\mu}}}$.
- About 95% of the time, $\hat{\mu}$ will lie within two standard errors of the true mean.

Asymptotic approximations.

In practice, we rarely know the sampling distribution in closed form. Instead, we rely on large-sample (asymptotic) results such as the central limit theorem (CLT). Under mild conditions, many estimators satisfy:

- $\hat{\theta}$ is approximately normal for large T.
- The variance of $\hat{\theta}$ shrinks roughly like $1/T$.

This is typically written informally as:

$$\hat{\theta} \approx \mathcal{N}\big(\theta,\ \mathrm{Var}(\hat{\theta})\big).$$

The key is that we can estimate $\mathrm{Var}(\hat{\theta})$ from the data, giving us an estimated standard error. For instance, for the sample mean of i.i.d. returns:

- $\mathrm{Var}(\bar{R}) = \sigma^2/T$, where σ^2 is the true return variance.
- We estimate σ^2 by the sample variance s^2, so $\widehat{\mathrm{SE}}(\bar{R}) = s/\sqrt{T}$.

In more complex estimators (regression coefficients, treatment effects), formulas for standard errors become more involved, but the underlying logic is the same: approximate sampling normality + an estimate of the variance.

Finite-sample vs. asymptotic behavior.

Two important cautions, especially relevant in markets:

- Asymptotic normality may be a poor approximation in small samples, in highly persistent time series, or with heavy-tailed returns.
- Structural breaks or nonstationarity mean that the data are not all drawn from the same distribution, undermining the usual sampling logic.

Later, we will see bootstrap methods and robust standard errors as tools to mitigate some of these issues.

2.6 Confidence Intervals: Quantifying Estimation Uncertainty

A *confidence interval* for a parameter θ is a range of values that, under repeated sampling, would contain the true θ with a specified long-run frequency (typically 95%).

Suppose $\hat{\theta}$ is approximately normal with standard error $\widehat{\mathrm{SE}}(\hat{\theta})$. Then a simple 95% confidence interval is:

$$\hat{\theta} \pm 1.96 \times \widehat{\mathrm{SE}}(\hat{\theta}),$$

where 1.96 is the 97.5th percentile of the standard normal distribution.

Interpretation in trading.

If $\hat{\mu}$ is the estimated mean daily return of a strategy and its 95% confidence interval is $[-0.01\%, 0.05\%]$:

- You cannot say that there is a 95% probability that the true mean lies inside this particular interval for your one backtest.

- You *can* say that if you repeated your experiment many times under the same conditions, 95% of such intervals constructed this way would contain the true mean.

Informally, it is still useful to treat the interval as a measure of estimation uncertainty. Very wide intervals suggest that you do not know the parameter very precisely, even if the point estimate looks attractive.

In causal settings, confidence intervals around estimated treatment effects are especially important. They tell you not only whether an effect is statistically different from zero, but also the range of plausible economic magnitudes (effect sizes).

2.7 Hypothesis Testing: From Evidence to Decisions

While confidence intervals answer "how uncertain is my estimate?," *hypothesis tests* answer questions like "is there evidence against a particular benchmark or null hypothesis?"

Null and alternative hypotheses.

We start by specifying:

- A *null hypothesis* H_0, such as "the strategy's true mean excess return is zero" or "the treatment has no effect on returns."
- An *alternative hypothesis* H_1, such as "the true mean is positive" or "the treatment affects returns."

Test statistics and p-values.

We then:

- Construct a *test statistic* T that measures how far the data deviate from what H_0 predicts. Often T is a t-statistic: estimated effect divided by its standard error.
- Determine the sampling distribution of T under H_0.

- Compute the *p-value*: the probability, under H_0, of observing a test statistic as extreme as, or more extreme than, the T observed in the data.

If the p-value is small (typically below a threshold $\alpha = 0.05$), we say the result is "statistically significant" and reject the null.

Types of errors.

Hypothesis testing inevitably involves two error types:

- Type I error: rejecting a true null hypothesis (false positive).
- Type II error: failing to reject a false null (false negative).

The significance level α is the maximum acceptable probability of a Type I error under repeated use of the test. A lower α makes false positives less likely but increases the risk of false negatives.

In trading, a Type I error means you believe an edge exists when it does not, which can be very costly in real capital. A Type II error means you might discard a real but weak edge. The trade-off depends on your risk appetite and the cost of deploying capital.

Economic vs. statistical significance.

A common misuse of tests is to equate "statistically significant" with "economically important." For instance, with a very long backtest, even a tiny effect size can produce a large t-statistic and a tiny p-value. Before acting on such results, you must ask:

- Is the estimated effect large enough to matter after transaction costs, slippage, and capacity limits?
- Does the direction and magnitude of the effect make sense economically or causally?

Later causal work will emphasize effect sizes and confidence intervals over binary significance labels.

2.8 Multiple Testing and Data Mining

In real research, you rarely test a single hypothesis. You may:

- Try dozens of factor definitions and parameter settings.
- Screen hundreds of candidate signals or event definitions.
- Analyze many subgroups, time periods, and markets.

If you conduct many tests and focus on the ones that "work," you inflate the chance of false discoveries. This is the *multiple-testing* or *data-mining* problem.

The scale of the problem.

Suppose each null hypothesis you test is actually true, and you use $\alpha = 0.05$. If you run 100 independent tests, you expect about 5 to be significant *by pure chance*. If you then publish or trade only those 5, you have fooled yourself.

Family-wise error rate and Bonferroni.

One conservative approach is to control the *family-wise error rate* (FWER): the probability of making at least one Type I error across a family of tests. The simplest correction is the Bonferroni method:

- If you plan to run m tests and want an overall α, test each individual hypothesis at level α/m.
- Equivalently, multiply each p-value by m and compare to α.

Bonferroni is easy and robust but can be very conservative when m is large, increasing Type II errors and potentially filtering out truly useful strategies.

False discovery rate and Benjamini-Hochberg.

An alternative is to control the *false discovery rate* (FDR): the expected proportion of false positives among the rejected hypotheses. The Benjamini-Hochberg (BH) procedure sorts p-values and selects a threshold based on their ranks.

Intuitively, FDR control accepts that some fraction of discoveries will be false but keeps that fraction under control. This is often more appropriate in high-throughput environments (signal libraries, machine learning models) where some level of noise trading is acceptable as long as the overall portfolio edge is positive.

Implications for causal trading claims.

When you present an effect as causal (for example, "index inclusion causes a persistent 50 bps return increase"), readers should know:

- How many similar hypotheses were considered?
- Were any multiple-testing corrections applied?
- Does the effect survive out-of-sample tests, cross-validation, or changes in specification?

Transparent reporting of the testing protocol is an essential part of credible causal claims.

2.9 Robust Standard Errors in Dependent and Heteroskedastic Data

Standard formulas for standard errors typically assume that:

- Errors are independent across observations.
- Errors have constant variance (homoskedasticity).

Financial data violate these assumptions in predictable ways:

- Returns and residuals exhibit volatility clustering (heteroskedasticity).
- Time-series data often show serial correlation.
- Panel data (stocks over time) exhibit cross-sectional correlation due to common shocks (market, sector, style).

Using naive standard errors in these settings leads to underestimated uncertainty and overstated significance. To address this, we use *robust* standard errors.

Heteroskedasticity-consistent (HC) standard errors.

In cross-sectional regressions or simple panels, HC estimators (often called "White" or "sandwich" estimators) adjust the variance matrix of regression coefficients to account for arbitrary heteroskedasticity. They remain valid even when the error variance differs across observations.

For example, in a cross-sectional regression of returns on characteristics, different stocks may have different idiosyncratic volatilities. HC standard errors protect you against incorrectly assuming constant variance.

Heteroskedasticity and autocorrelation consistent (HAC) standard errors.

In time-series regressions, residuals are often both heteroskedastic and serially correlated. HAC estimators (such as Newey-West) adjust standard errors to remain valid under both features.

Use cases include:

- Predictive regressions of returns on lagged variables (valuation ratios, macro indicators).
- Time-series factor regressions where residuals may be autocorrelated.

HAC corrections are critical when assessing whether apparent predictability survives realistic dependence structures.

Cluster-robust standard errors.

In panel data (stocks over time), errors may be correlated within groups:

- Across time for a given stock (firm-level clustering).
- Across stocks in a given day (time clustering).
- Within sectors or regions.

Cluster-robust standard errors allow arbitrary correlation within clusters while assuming independence across clusters. For example, in an event study of index inclusions across many stocks over many days, you might cluster by stock to allow for persistence in residuals for each firm.

Block bootstrap.

Bootstrap methods resample data to approximate sampling distributions without relying heavily on parametric assumptions. For time series, we often use *block bootstraps*, which resample blocks of consecutive observations to preserve dependence patterns within blocks.

Block bootstraps can:

- Provide alternative standard error estimates when analytical formulas are unreliable.
- Help assess the stability of estimates in the presence of strong serial correlation and structural breaks.

These robust tools are not exotic add-ons; they are necessary if you want your inference to match the realities of market data.

2.10 From Classical Inference to Causal Estimation

This section has deliberately focused on "classical" inference: estimators, sampling distributions, confidence intervals, hypothesis tests, multiple-testing corrections, and robust standard errors. In isolation, these tools only address associations in the data.

In the causal part of the book, we will:

- Define causal estimands (such as average treatment effects) as expectations or contrasts of potential outcome distributions.
- Construct estimators for these causal parameters using matching, weighting, regression adjustment, and instrumental variables.

- Use the machinery developed here to attach standard errors, confidence intervals, and hypothesis tests to those causal estimates.

The crucial difference will be in the assumptions: instead of merely assuming independent, identically distributed observations, we will assume specific forms of conditional independence between treatments, covariates, and potential outcomes (ignorability, exclusion restrictions, etc.). Once those assumptions are in place, the probabilistic and inferential tools from this chapter turn into a full-fledged engine for credible causal claims in financial markets.

2.11 Linear Algebra and Optimization Essentials

Up to this point, we have treated our data mostly as lists of numbers: returns over time, characteristics across assets, and so on. In practice, however, trading and causal models are built on *vectors* and *matrices*:

- A vector can represent a portfolio of weights, a set of factor loadings, or an observation of many features for one asset.
- A matrix can represent a time–by–asset return panel, a factor loading matrix, or the design matrix in a regression.

Optimization is what turns these objects into decisions: optimal portfolio weights under risk constraints, regression coefficients that best fit the data, or synthetic control weights that approximate a treated unit with a combination of controls.

This section reviews the core linear algebra and optimization ideas needed for the rest of the book:

- Geometry of vectors: norms, inner products, and projections.
- Matrices as linear maps: rank, eigenvalues, and basic decompositions.
- Optimization basics: unconstrained and constrained problems, convexity.

- Karush–Kuhn–Tucker (KKT) conditions and their interpretation in finance.

We keep the discussion concrete by tying each concept to regressions, factor models, and portfolio design.

Vectors as Portfolios and Data Points

A vector is just an ordered list of numbers. In a financial context, it is often helpful to attach meaning to each component:

- A *portfolio weight vector* $w = (w_1, \dots, w_n)$: w_i is the fraction of capital in asset i.
- A *return vector* $r = (r_1, \dots, r_n)$: r_i is the return on asset i in a given period.
- A *feature vector* $x = (x_1, \dots, x_p)$: x_j is the value of characteristic j (size, value, momentum, etc.) for a given asset at a point in time.

We often picture vectors as arrows from the origin in some geometric space. This picture is more than a metaphor: many key concepts have direct geometric interpretations.

Norms and distance.

The most common way to measure the "size" of a vector is the Euclidean norm:

$$\|x\| = \sqrt{x_1^2 + \cdots + x_p^2}.$$

Geometrically, this is the length of the arrow representing x. In finance:

- $\|w\|$ measures, roughly, how concentrated a portfolio is. For example, an equal-weight portfolio has smaller norm than a concentrated portfolio with the same total capital.
- Differences between vectors, such as $x_i - x_j$, measure dissimilarity between assets or states; $\|x_i - x_j\|$ is the Euclidean distance between them.

Other norms (like the sum of absolute values) matter for regularization (for example, lasso penalties), but the Euclidean norm suffices to explain the geometric ideas.

Inner products and angles.

The inner product (or dot product) of two vectors x and y is

$$x^\top y = x_1 y_1 + \cdots + x_p y_p.$$

It has two useful interpretations:

- As *weighted combination*: if w is a portfolio and r is a return vector for a given period, then $w^\top r$ is the portfolio return.
- As *cosine of an angle*: $x^\top y = \|x\| \|y\| \cos\theta$, where θ is the angle between the vectors. If $x^\top y$ is positive, the angle is acute (they point in roughly the same direction); if negative, they point in roughly opposite directions.

Two vectors with inner product zero are *orthogonal*; geometrically, they meet at a right angle. Orthogonality will be the key to understanding regression residuals and factor decompositions.

Projections and the Geometry of Regression

In linear regression, we model a response variable y (for example, excess returns) as a linear combination of predictors (factors, signals) plus an error:

$$y \approx X\beta + \varepsilon.$$

Here:

- y is a vector of length T (returns over T periods or units).
- X is a $T \times p$ matrix of predictors (each column is a factor, each row is an observation).
- β is a vector of coefficients we want to estimate.

Ordinary least squares (OLS) chooses $\hat{\beta}$ to minimize the sum of squared residuals $\|\varepsilon\|^2 = \|y - X\beta\|^2$. This optimization has a precise geometric meaning: it projects y onto the *column space* of X.

The column space of X is the set of all linear combinations of its columns:

$$\mathcal{C}(X) = \{X\beta : \beta \in \mathbb{R}^p\}.$$

Geometrically, it is a subspace (a flat plane or higher-dimensional generalization) inside $\mathbb{R}^T$.

The OLS fitted values $\hat{y} = X\hat{\beta}$ are the point in $\mathcal{C}(X)$ closest to y in Euclidean distance. The residual vector is

$$\hat{\varepsilon} = y - \hat{y},$$

and it is orthogonal to all columns of X.

In symbols, the *normal equations* $X^\top(y - X\hat{\beta}) = 0$ say exactly this: the residual is orthogonal to each predictor. This is the fundamental geometry of regression.

To visualize:

- Imagine y as an arrow in a high-dimensional space.
- The predictors define a subspace (a flat "plane").
- OLS drops a perpendicular from y onto this plane; the foot of this perpendicular is $\hat{y}$, and the small perpendicular segment is the residual.

This geometric viewpoint will be central when we discuss factor models (projecting returns on factors) and synthetic control (projecting treated units onto the span of donor units with constraints).

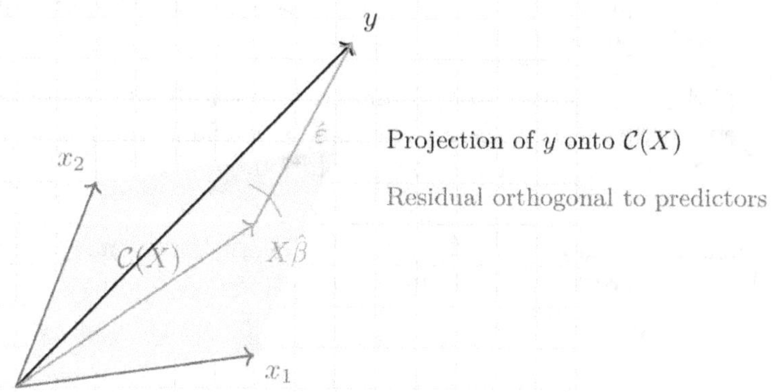

Matrices as Linear Maps: Rank and Invertibility

A matrix A can be viewed as a linear transformation that takes vectors in one space and maps them to another: $x \mapsto Ax$.

In finance:

- A *return matrix* R (time by assets) maps a vector of portfolio weights w to a vector of portfolio returns over time: Rw.
- A *factor loading matrix* B maps factor returns f to asset returns: Bf.
- A *regression design matrix* X maps coefficients β to fitted values $X\beta$.

Two key properties of matrices are:

Rank.

The *rank* of a matrix A is the dimension of its column space: the maximum number of linearly independent columns. Intuitively, it is the number of independent directions that A's columns span.

- If X has full column rank (rank equal to number of columns p), then no predictor is an exact linear combination of others, and the OLS solution is unique.
- If there is perfect multicollinearity (for example, one factor equals the sum of others), the rank is deficient, and the normal equations do not have a unique solution.

Understanding rank helps diagnose collinearity problems in factor models and regression-based causal estimators.

Invertibility.

A square matrix A is *invertible* if there is a matrix A^{-1} such that $A^{-1}A = AA^{-1} = I$, the identity. Invertibility corresponds to being full rank and having a one-to-one mapping between inputs and outputs.

In OLS, when X has full column rank and $T \geq p$, the coefficient vector can be written as

$$\hat{\beta} = (X^\top X)^{-1} X^\top y.$$

Here $X^\top X$ is a $p \times p$ matrix. Its invertibility encodes the idea that the predictors carry enough independent information to identify β.

When $X^\top X$ is nearly singular (ill-conditioned), small changes in data can produce large swings in $\hat{\beta}$. This is one motivation for regularization (for example, ridge regression adds a multiple of the identity to $X^\top X$ to stabilize the inverse).

Eigenvalues, Eigenvectors, and Decompositions

Eigenvalues and eigenvectors capture how a matrix stretches or compresses space in specific directions.

An eigenvector v of a matrix A with eigenvalue λ satisfies

$$Av = \lambda v.$$

This means that A acts on v by simply scaling it; the direction of v does not change, only its length.

In finance, eigen-analysis is central to:

- **Principal component analysis (PCA)**: Decomposing a covariance matrix of returns into uncorrelated components, each associated with an eigenvalue (variance explained) and eigenvector (factor portfolio).
- **Risk decomposition**: Understanding which directions in portfolio space correspond to the largest sources of risk (largest eigenvalues).

If Σ is the covariance matrix of returns, then its eigenvalues $\lambda_1 \geq \cdots \geq \lambda_n$ and eigenvectors $v_1, \ldots, v_n$ can be used to:

- Build factor portfolios v_i capturing common modes of variation.
- Approximate Σ with a low-rank matrix using the first few principal components, useful for risk models and dimension reduction.

Singular value decomposition (SVD).

The SVD generalizes eigen-decomposition to non-square matrices. Any $T \times p$ matrix X can be written as:

$$X = U\Sigma V^\top,$$

where:

- U is $T \times T$ and orthogonal (its columns are orthonormal vectors).
- V is $p \times p$ and orthogonal.
- Σ is $T \times p$ and diagonal (or block-diagonal) with nonnegative singular values on the diagonal.

SVD underlies:

- Rank-revealing decompositions: small singular values indicate near-collinearity.
- Numerical stability in solving least squares: many algorithms use SVD rather than directly forming $(X^\top X)^{-1}$.

- Dimension reduction in high-dimensional factor or feature spaces.

Although we will not need the full technical details, it is useful to know that under the hood, many regression and synthetic control algorithms rely on these decompositions.

Basics of Optimization: Objectives and Constraints

Optimization is about choosing decision variables to minimize or maximize an *objective function*, subject to constraints.

A generic optimization problem looks like:

$$\text{minimize } f(x) \quad \text{subject to } x \in \mathcal{X},$$

where:

- x is a vector of decision variables (for example, portfolio weights, regression coefficients, or policy parameters).
- $f(x)$ is the objective (for example, variance of returns, negative expected utility, sum of squared residuals).
- $\mathcal{X}$ is the feasible set defined by constraints (long-only, leverage limits, budget constraints, no shorting, etc.).

Unconstrained optimization.
If there are no constraints and f is differentiable, we look for points where the gradient is zero:

$$\nabla f(x^\star) = 0.$$

For example, in OLS, the objective is $f(\beta) = \|y - X\beta\|^2$. Setting its gradient to zero yields the normal equations.

Constrained optimization.

In most financial applications, constraints matter:

- A portfolio must satisfy $\sum_i w_i = 1$ (fully invested).
- There may be bounds $w_i \geq 0$ (no shorting) or $|w_i| \leq w_{\max}$ (position limits).
- Risk controls might require $w^\top \Sigma w \leq \sigma^2_{\max}$ (variance constraint).

These constraints shape the feasible set $\mathcal{X}$. The optimal solution is then found where the gradient of f is balanced by the gradients of the constraint functions. The formal expression of this balance is given by the Karush–Kuhn–Tucker conditions, which we discuss later.

Convexity: When Local Optima Are Global

Convexity is a property of functions and sets that makes optimization much easier and safer.

Convex sets.

A set C is *convex* if for any two points $x, y \in C$, the line segment connecting them lies entirely in C. Formally, for any $\lambda \in [0, 1]$,

$$\lambda x + (1 - \lambda)y \in C.$$

Most natural portfolio constraint sets are convex:

- The set of all long-only portfolios with weights summing to 1.
- The set defined by linear inequality constraints, such as sector or factor exposure bounds.

Convex sets are desirable because they have no "holes" or disconnected pieces where optimization algorithms could get trapped.

Convex functions.

A function f is *convex* if its epigraph (the set of points lying on or above its graph) is a convex set, or equivalently, if for all x, y and $\lambda \in [0, 1]$:

$$f(\lambda x + (1 - \lambda)y) \leq \lambda f(x) + (1 - \lambda)f(y).$$

Intuitively, a convex function curves upwards; any line segment between two points on its graph lies above the graph itself.

Examples relevant to finance:

- Quadratic forms like $f(w) = w^\top \Sigma w$ are convex if Σ is positive semidefinite. This is the usual mean–variance risk term.
- The squared loss $f(\beta) = \|y - X\beta\|^2$ is convex in β.
- ℓ_1-norm penalties (sum of absolute values) used in lasso are convex.

Why convexity matters.

If f is convex and the feasible set $\mathcal{X}$ is convex, then *any local minimum is a global minimum*. This has two key implications:

- You do not need to worry about getting stuck in local minima.
- Gradient-based algorithms with mild conditions will find the global optimum reliably.

Most of the optimization problems in this book are designed to be convex (or at least nearly so) for precisely these reasons. When we later discuss nonconvex problems (for example, some machine learning models or complex policy searches), we will proceed more cautiously.

Karush–Kuhn–Tucker Conditions: Optimality with Constraints

The Karush–Kuhn–Tucker (KKT) conditions generalize the idea of "gradient equals zero" from unconstrained optimization to problems with inequality and equality constraints.

Consider minimizing $f(x)$ subject to:

- Equality constraints $g_j(x) = 0$ (for example, sum of weights equals 1).

- Inequality constraints $h_k(x) \leq 0$ (for example, leverage or exposure limits).

Under suitable regularity conditions, if $x^\star$ is an optimal solution, there exist *Lagrange multipliers* λ_j and μ_k such that:

1. **Stationarity:** the gradient of the Lagrangian vanishes:

$$\nabla f(x^\star) + \sum_j \lambda_j \nabla g_j(x^\star) + \sum_k \mu_k \nabla h_k(x^\star) = 0.$$

2. **Primal feasibility:** the constraints are satisfied:

$$g_j(x^\star) = 0, \quad h_k(x^\star) \leq 0.$$

3. **Dual feasibility:** the multipliers on inequality constraints are nonnegative:

$$\mu_k \geq 0.$$

4. **Complementary slackness:** for each inequality constraint,

$$\mu_k \cdot h_k(x^\star) = 0.$$

Complementary slackness is particularly intuitive: if a constraint is *not* binding at the solution (strictly negative $h_k(x^\star) < 0$), then its multiplier μ_k must be zero (it does not affect the optimum); if a constraint is *binding* (exactly zero), its multiplier can be positive, reflecting the shadow price of tightening the constraint further.

Interpreting KKT in portfolio optimization.

Consider a simple mean–variance portfolio problem:

- Minimize $f(w) = w^\top \Sigma w$ (risk) subject to:
- Budget: $g(w) = \mathbf{1}^\top w - 1 = 0$.
- No shorting: $w_i \geq 0$, i.e., $h_i(w) = -w_i \leq 0$.

At the optimum $w^\star$:

- Stationarity says that the gradient of variance, $2\Sigma w^{\star}$, is a linear combination of the gradients of the constraints. Intuitively, the marginal change in risk from adjusting weights is balanced by marginal changes in violating constraints.
- Complementary slackness tells you that if asset i has a strictly positive weight $w_i^{\star} > 0$, then the corresponding multiplier for h_i is zero; the no-short constraint is slack and does not "bite." If $w_i^{\star} = 0$, then the multiplier can be positive, reflecting that loosening this constraint (allowing a small short) could reduce risk.

These multipliers can be read as *shadow prices*:

- How much does the optimal objective (risk, tracking error, etc.) improve if we relax a constraint slightly?
- Which constraints are truly binding and shaping the optimal solution?

In causal policy design (for example, optimizing a trading policy under risk and turnover constraints), KKT conditions help interpret why certain variables or exposures take particular values at optimum.

Links to Regression, Factor Models, and Synthetic Control

The linear algebra and optimization concepts discussed above recur in many places:

Regression as projection and optimization.

- The OLS estimator minimizes a convex quadratic loss in β.
- Geometrically, it projects y onto the column space of X.
- $\hat{\beta}$ can be written using matrix inverses or via decompositions (QR, SVD), which avoid directly inverting $X^{\top}X$ when it is ill-conditioned.

In causal inference, regression adjustment (controlling for covariates) is just this projection, applied to potential outcomes and treatment variables.

Factor models and PCA.

- A linear factor model writes asset returns as $Bf + \varepsilon$, where B is a loading matrix, f factors, and ε idiosyncratic noise.
- Estimating B and f often involves eigen-decomposition or SVD of return covariance or correlation matrices.
- Principal components provide low-dimensional approximations to high-dimensional return spaces, essential for risk control and for constructing balanced causal comparisons.

Synthetic control.

In synthetic control methods, a treated unit is approximated by a weighted combination of donor units:

$$y_{\text{treated, pre}} \approx W y_{\text{donors, pre}},$$

where W is a vector of weights on donors.

Choosing W typically involves solving a constrained optimization:

- Minimize a distance (norm) between the treated pre-treatment trajectory and the synthetic combination.
- Subject to weights being nonnegative and summing to 1 (convex combination).

This is a convex optimization problem in W, often implemented using QP (quadratic programming) or related techniques. The KKT conditions describe which donors receive positive weight and which constraints are binding.

Causal policy optimization.

Later in the book, we will consider optimizing trading policies based on estimated causal effects. For example:

- Maximize expected causal alpha subject to risk and turnover constraints.
- Adjust allocations across signals based on heterogeneous treatment effect estimates.

These problems naturally fit into the convex optimization framework:

- The objective is a function of decision variables (weights, thresholds) and estimated causal parameters.
- Constraints encode practical limits (risk, leverage, liquidity).
- Convexity and KKT conditions provide both computational guarantees and economic interpretations.

Linear algebra and optimization provide the backbone for the models and estimators used throughout this book:

- Vectors and inner products give a geometric language for portfolios, signals, and regressions.
- Matrices as linear maps, along with rank and decompositions, explain when parameters are identifiable and how to compute them stably.
- Convex optimization and KKT conditions formalize how we choose portfolios, regression coefficients, and policy parameters under realistic constraints.

With these tools, we can now treat many causal problems in markets as structured optimization tasks, where the objective involves causal estimands and the constraints encode risk management and implementability. The final section of this chapter will assemble these pieces into full modeling workflows, combining linear models, regularization, and resampling as practical components inside causal estimators.

2.12 Linear Models, Resampling, and Supervised Learning

We now have the core mathematical pillars in place: probability, distributions, estimation, and linear algebra/optimization. In this section we assemble them into the modeling workhorses you will use repeatedly in both predictive trading and causal inference:

- Linear models, interpreted through regression geometry and estimation theory.
- Regularization methods that stabilize estimates in high-dimensional or collinear settings.
- Resampling techniques, especially time-series aware cross-validation, for honest performance assessment.
- Flexible supervised learning algorithms that serve as powerful "nuisance" models inside causal estimators.

The unifying message is that these tools are not only for forecasting; they are also essential components for constructing, adjusting, and validating causal effect estimates in realistic financial data.

Linear Models as the Baseline Workhorse

A *linear model* expresses an outcome y as a linear combination of predictors (features) plus an error term:

$$y = X\beta + \varepsilon.$$

Here y may be excess returns, realized volatility, or a treatment indicator; the columns of X are signals, factors, or covariates.

OLS recap and assumptions.

Ordinary least squares (OLS) chooses $\hat{\beta}$ to minimize the sum of squared residuals, $\|y - X\beta\|^2$. Geometrically, as we saw earlier, this is the orthogonal projection of y onto the column space of X.

For OLS to have its familiar interpretation, several conditions are important:

- Linearity: the conditional expectation of y given X is approximately linear in X.
- Exogeneity: errors have zero mean given X, $\mathbb{E}[\varepsilon \mid X] = 0$.
- No perfect multicollinearity: X has full column rank.
- Well-behaved errors: for standard inference, finite variance and controlled dependence (handled via robust SEs).

In purely predictive tasks, we mainly care whether the linear approximation is accurate enough for out-of-sample performance. In causal tasks, we additionally care that the exogeneity assumption is plausible under our design (randomization, controls, instruments, etc.).

Financial uses of linear models.

- **Factor models:** regress asset returns on factor returns to estimate betas and idiosyncratic risk.
- **Signal stacking:** regress future returns on many signals to estimate their marginal contributions.
- **Outcome regression in causal inference:** regress returns on treatment and covariates to estimate conditional average treatment effects or to build outcome models inside doubly robust estimators.

Because of their simplicity and interpretability, linear models are often the first step in any serious analysis and form the baseline against which more complex methods are judged.

Regularization: Controlling Overfitting and Collinearity

In realistic trading research, you often have:

- Many more predictors (signals, lags, interactions) than truly relevant ones.
- High collinearity among signals (for example, similar value measures, overlapping momentum horizons).
- Limited effective sample size due to autocorrelation and regime changes.

Naive OLS in this setting can produce:

- Large, unstable coefficient estimates.
- Poor out-of-sample performance due to overfitting.
- Inflated standard errors and noisy causal estimates.

Regularization adds a penalty term to the objective, shrinking or selecting coefficients to improve stability and prediction.

Ridge regression.

Ridge regression minimizes

$$\|y - X\beta\|^2 + \lambda\|\beta\|_2^2,$$

where $\lambda \geq 0$ is a tuning parameter. The ℓ_2-penalty shrinks coefficients toward zero but rarely sets them exactly to zero.

Implications:

- Stabilizes estimates in the presence of multicollinearity.
- Effectively adds a multiple of the identity to $X^\top X$, improving the condition number and making inversion safer.
- Distributes weight more evenly across correlated predictors.

In finance, ridge is natural when you expect many small, correlated signals to each contribute modestly rather than a few being exactly zero.

Lasso.

Lasso (least absolute shrinkage and selection operator) minimizes

$$\|y - X\beta\|^2 + \lambda\|\beta\|_1,$$

where $\|\beta\|_1$ is the sum of absolute values of coefficients. The ℓ_1-penalty encourages *sparsity*: many coefficients become exactly zero.

Implications:

- Performs variable selection and shrinkage simultaneously.
- Useful for screening large signal libraries down to a manageable, potentially causal set of drivers.
- Can be unstable when predictors are highly correlated: similar signals may arbitrarily swap in or out.

In causal workflows, lasso-type methods can be used as a first-stage tool (for example, to select instruments or covariates) before final effect estimation under stronger assumptions.

Elastic net.

Elastic net combines the two:

$$\|y - X\beta\|^2 + \lambda_1\|\beta\|_1 + \lambda_2\|\beta\|_2^2.$$

It encourages sparsity while also stabilizing correlated groups of predictors. This is often a sensible default in finance, where you want both feature selection and robustness to highly correlated signals.

Regularization as implicit prior and constraint.

From a Bayesian perspective, penalties correspond to priors:

- Ridge $\leftrightarrow$ Gaussian prior on β.
- Lasso $\leftrightarrow$ Laplace (double exponential) prior.

From an optimization point of view, they act like soft constraints on coefficient magnitudes. In synthetic control and policy optimization, similar penalties can be used to avoid extreme or highly leveraged weights that would be fragile out of sample.

Resampling and Cross-Validation

Estimation and regularization are only half the story. You must also evaluate models honestly and choose hyperparameters (like λ) in a way that reflects real predictive or causal performance.

Resampling techniques approximate out-of-sample performance and sampling variability by repeatedly reusing the data in structured ways. The most common is cross-validation (CV).

IID k-fold cross-validation.

In IID settings (independent observations):

- Randomly split the data into k roughly equal folds.
- For each fold in turn: fit the model on the other $k-1$ folds (training set) and evaluate loss (or predictive accuracy) on the held-out fold (test set).
- Average performance across folds to estimate out-of-sample error.

This procedure is widely used to choose tuning parameters for regularization (e.g., select λ that minimizes CV error).

Why standard k-fold fails for time series.

Financial time series are not IID:

- They exhibit serial dependence and regime changes.
- Using future data to predict the past (even indirectly) creates look-ahead bias.

Randomly shuffling observations into folds breaks the temporal structure and typically leaks information from the future into the training set. This leads to overly optimistic performance estimates and hyperparameters that exploit artifacts of the full sample.

Time-series cross-validation schemes.

Time-aware CV respects the ordering of data. Common schemes include:

- **Rolling-window CV:** For each cutoff time t, train on a fixed-length window of past data (say the previous 3 years) and test on the next period or block. Then roll forward and repeat.

- **Expanding-window CV:** Start with an initial training period, test on the next block, then expand the training set to include that block and repeat.

- **Blocked CV:** Divide the time series into contiguous blocks, use several consecutive blocks for training and subsequent blocks for testing, making sure no test block precedes its training blocks.

These schemes approximate the real-time process of model updating and evaluation. They help detect strategies or hyperparameters that are too sensitive to a particular regime or that rely on leakage.

Bootstrap for uncertainty estimation.

Beyond CV, bootstrap methods allow you to approximate the sampling distribution of an estimator:

- For IID data: resample observations with replacement and recompute the estimator many times.

- For time series: use block bootstrap (resample contiguous blocks) to preserve dependence.

From these replicates, you can:

- Estimate standard errors and confidence intervals for performance metrics (Sharpe ratios, alphas).

- Assess the stability of causal effect estimates under resampled histories or panels.

Bootstrap-based inference is especially helpful when analytical standard errors are unreliable or hard to derive.

Supervised Learning Algorithms as Flexible Nuisance Models

Supervised learning aims to predict an outcome y from features X. Many algorithms go far beyond linearity: decision trees, random forests, gradient boosting, neural networks, and others.

In pure prediction, you choose whichever method and hyperparameters minimize out-of-sample error subject to interpretability and implementation constraints. In causal inference, we often care less about the internal mechanics and more about the ability to flexibly estimate certain *nuisance functions*:

- Propensity scores: $e(x) = P(T = 1 \mid X = x)$, the probability of treatment given covariates.
- Outcome regressions: $m_t(x) = \mathbb{E}[Y \mid T = t, X = x]$ for $t = 0, 1$.
- Conditional treatment effects: $\tau(x) = \mathbb{E}[Y(1) - Y(0) \mid X = x]$.

Here T might be a policy change, signal activation, or index event; Y might be a return or volatility outcome.

Decision trees and ensembles.

A decision tree recursively partitions feature space into regions and assigns a constant prediction in each:

- Trees capture nonlinear interactions and discontinuities.
- However, single trees are unstable and often overfit.

Ensembles of trees address this:

- **Random forests:** average predictions over many trees built on bootstrap samples and random feature subsets. They reduce variance and capture complex structure.
- **Gradient boosting machines (GBMs):** sequentially fit trees to residuals, creating a strong learner by combining many weak learners.

In finance, tree-based models are attractive for capturing threshold effects (e.g., signal only matters when volatility is high) and nonlinear interactions among signals or macro variables.

Regularization and tuning in ML models.

Just as linear models require regularization, ML models require careful tuning:

- Tree depth, number of trees, learning rate, and minimum leaf size are all regularization levers.
- Overly complex models can memorize historical quirks (overfitting), especially in short or noisy financial histories.
- Time-series cross-validation is essential for tuning these models in a way that mimics live trading.

Role in causal inference: nuisance vs. target.

In modern causal methods (for example, doubly robust estimation, targeted maximum likelihood, causal forests), ML models typically serve as flexible estimators of $e(x)$ and $m_t(x)$:

- The *target* parameter is a low-dimensional causal estimand (ATE, conditional ATE, policy value).
- The potentially high-dimensional functions $e(x)$ and $m_t(x)$ are *nuisance* components: we want them estimated well enough to debias the target, but we do not interpret them directly as causal.

This separation allows us to use very flexible algorithms for nuisance estimation without overfitting the causal effect itself, provided we use orthogonalization and sample-splitting / cross-fitting (topics covered later).

Predictive vs. Causal Objectives

It is easy to conflate predictive success with causal insight. The methods in this section can support both goals, but the objective and evaluation criteria differ.

Predictive modeling.

When your aim is to forecast returns or volatility:

- You care about out-of-sample predictive accuracy, risk-adjusted performance, and implementation costs.
- Any variable that helps prediction is welcome, regardless of whether it is causal (for example, seasonal patterns, microstructure effects, technical anomalies).
- Time-series CV and realistic backtests are the main validation tools.

Causal modeling.

When your aim is to understand the effect of a treatment or policy:

- You care about unbiasedness and valid uncertainty quantification for specific estimands (ATE, heterogeneous effects).
- Predictive performance of nuisance models matters only insofar as it contributes to consistent and efficient causal estimates.
- You must think carefully about identification assumptions (ignorability, exclusion restrictions, stable unit treatment value) and design (what data would we have seen under different policies?).

The same toolbox—linear models, regularization, resampling, supervised learning—supports both aims. The key difference is how you use and interpret them:

- In prediction, the model *is* the object of interest.
- In causal inference, the model is a means to an end: estimating or adjusting for conditional expectations and treatment probabilities to isolate causal effects.

Putting It Together: A Typical Workflow

To make the connections concrete, consider a simplified workflow for evaluating a new trading policy that increases exposure when a particular signal crosses a threshold.

1. **Feature construction:** Build a panel of assets over time with the signal, returns, and control variables (size, value, momentum, risk measures).

2. **Treatment definition:** Define a binary treatment T_{it} indicating when the policy would be "on" versus "off" for asset i at time t (e.g., signal above threshold).

3. **Nuisance modeling:**

   - Use a flexible ML model (e.g., gradient boosting) with time-series CV to estimate the propensity score $e(x) = P(T = 1 \mid X)$.
   - Use another model (possibly linear with regularization, or a random forest) to estimate outcome regressions $m_1(x)$ and $m_0(x)$ for treated and control potential outcomes.

4. **Causal estimation:** Plug these estimated nuisance functions into a doubly robust or orthogonalized estimator of the ATE or conditional ATE (details later). Linear algebra and optimization underlie the computation of these estimators.

5. **Uncertainty quantification:** Use asymptotic theory or bootstrap to obtain standard errors and confidence intervals for the estimated effect, possibly with block or cluster structure to respect time and cross-sectional dependence.

6. **Robustness and model diagnostics:**

   - Vary regularization strength and model classes to check stability of the estimated effect.
   - Use time-series cross-validation and placebo tests (randomized or lag-shifted treatments) to assess whether the effect could be an artifact of data mining.

Every step in this workflow uses the concepts developed in this chapter:

- Probability and conditional independence justify the identification strategy.
- Random variables and distributions underpin expectations and sampling variability.
- Estimation and hypothesis testing provide point estimates and uncertainty.
- Linear algebra and optimization compute the necessary projections and solve penalized problems.
- Linear models, resampling, and supervised learners implement practical nuisance and outcome modeling.

With these pillars in place, the rest of the book will focus on explicitly causal designs and estimators—how to set up identification problems in financial markets, and how to use the machinery you now have to move from correlation to credible causal inference.

Chapter 3

From Correlation to Causation: Frameworks & Identification

Most trading signals are built on patterns: when X goes up, Y tends to follow. But profitable intervention requires more than pattern-spotting-it demands understanding what would happen if you actually changed X. This chapter turns loose correlations into disciplined causal claims. You'll learn how to formalize treatments and outcomes, draw causal graphs for real market mechanisms, and apply identification rules that separate genuine edge from confounded noise, selection traps, and equilibrium feedback. By the end, you'll be able to look at a "great" backtest and ask the only question that matters: is this predictive artifact, or a causal lever you can reliably pull?

3.1 Correlation vs Causation in Markets

Most quantitative traders start their careers worshipping correlations. The workflow is familiar: take a large data set of returns and candidate signals, scan for high correlations with future returns or risk, and declare victory when you find a pattern that looks strong and statistically significant. The temptation is to equate *"high correlation with tomorrow's return"* with *"tradable edge."*

This section explains why that shortcut is unreliable. Strong correlations in financial data are cheap to find and surprisingly fragile. What is scarce is a *causal* relationship that survives transaction costs, competition, and regime shifts.

We will focus on three mechanisms that routinely manufacture illusory edge:

- **Confounding:** a hidden driver moves both your signal and your target, creating the appearance that the signal has power when it does not add any incremental causal effect.
- **Simultaneity and equilibrium:** prices, order flow, and liquidity are jointly determined; strong correlations often reflect a market equilibrium rather than a one-way cause.
- **Non-stationarity and regime shifts:** even if a relationship had some causal content in one period, structural changes in policy, microstructure, or competition can erase it.

By the end, we will reframe the trader's question from "Does X correlate with future returns?" to "If we *intervene* on X—by changing a policy, execution rule, or allocation—does the distribution of outcomes change in a predictable way?" That interventionist mindset is where causal inference begins.

Why Correlation Is So Easy to Find in Markets

Financial markets generate enormous streams of data: tick-by-tick prices, quotes, volumes, order book states, macro announcements, sentiment scores, and much more. With millions of observations and hundreds or thousands of candidate signals, some of them will line up with future returns just by chance or because they respond to the same underlying forces.

Three features of market data make spurious or non-tradable correlations especially common:

1. **Shared exposure to a small set of powerful drivers.** Many instruments and signals load on a few dominant risk factors: equity market beta, interest rates, volatility, liquidity, and risk sentiment. Anything that moves with these factors will look related to anything else that moves with them, even if there is no direct influence.

2. **Fast feedback and joint determination.** Order flow changes prices, prices change order flow, and both respond to news and constraints. Cause and effect often run in both directions within the same time interval.

3. **Frequent structural changes.** Regulations, technology, and participant mixes evolve. A pattern that held for several years can vanish abruptly after a policy shift, a microstructure change, or crowding by other traders.

These features mean that a high correlation—no matter how statistically significant—does not by itself tell you what would happen if you *act* on a signal. To trade responsibly, you must ask: what is driving this correlation, and how would it respond if our policy changed?

The Trader's Question: From Prediction to Intervention

It helps to separate two kinds of questions:

- **Predictive question:** "Given what I observe now (signals, state variables), what is the conditional distribution of future returns?" This is the domain of forecasting and machine learning.

- **Causal question:** "If I change my decision variable—turn on a new strategy, increase leverage, route orders differently—how does the distribution of outcomes change, holding everything else about the environment fixed?" This is the domain of policies and interventions.

A correlation between a signal and future returns answers, at best, part of the predictive question: it says returns tend to be higher when the signal is high. But trading decisions are interventions. Switching an execution algorithm, rebalancing a portfolio, or scaling position sizes changes your own footprint in the market and can alter the environment you face.

Causal inference is the language we use to reason about these *counterfactual* questions: what would have happened under policy B if we had not followed policy A? To motivate the need for this language, we now dig into the three mechanisms that make purely correlational reasoning unreliable.

Confounding: Hidden Drivers that Fake Edge

A **confounder** is a variable that affects both your signal and your outcome. Because it influences both, it can induce a correlation between them even if the signal has no direct causal impact.

A simple example: factor exposure disguised as skill

Suppose you discover that your "risk appetite index"—constructed from survey responses and sentiment proxies—has a strong positive correlation with next-month equity index returns. In-sample, when the index is high, equities tend to go up; when it is low, they tend to fall. It is tempting to trade more aggressively when the index is high.

Now imagine that your index is, in reality, a noisy transformation of a small set of standard risk factors:

- Interest rate expectations
- Credit spreads
- Implied volatility

Those same factors also drive the equity market's expected return. In other words, there is a *common cause*: macro risk sentiment moves your index and market returns together. If you already have exposure to those macro factors—say through existing positions or risk constraints—tilting on the index may add no incremental causal effect. You are simply repackaging the same risk.

The signal "works" statistically because it is an alternate measurement of an underlying driver. But it does not follow that *acting* on this proxy, beyond what you already do, improves your P&L. The edge is an illusion created by confounding.

Omitted variables in cross-sectional signals

The same logic applies cross-sectionally. Consider a stock-level signal that appears to forecast future returns: for instance, firms with high recent employee growth show higher subsequent returns in a backtest. Before declaring a causal channel ("hiring leads to improved performance"), you must ask:

- Are high-growth firms also more likely to be small-cap, high-volatility, or growth-style names?
- Are you effectively rediscovering existing size, value, or momentum factors?

If those underlying characteristics are the true drivers of expected returns, then "employee growth" is confounded by them. Once you control for those factors, the incremental correlation might disappear. Without unpacking and addressing confounding, you cannot tell whether the signal has a distinct causal effect or merely rides along with known risks.

Simultaneity and Equilibrium: Who Causes Whom?

In many economic and financial settings, variables are determined simultaneously as part of an equilibrium. Prices, volumes, and spreads do not unfold in a simple one-way causal chain; they settle at levels where supply and demand balance, given constraints and information.

The spread-volatility example

A classic example is the strong positive correlation between bid-ask spreads and short-term volatility. You might be tempted to say: "High volatility *causes* spreads to widen," and then reason that if you could somehow reduce volatility (say through your own trading), you would narrow spreads and save costs.

But in microstructure models and in reality, the relationship runs both ways:

- Higher volatility makes it riskier to quote tight spreads; market makers respond by widening them.
- Wider spreads and lower depth discourage some trading and can amplify price moves when liquidity is thin, feeding back into volatility.

Both volatility and spreads are jointly determined by underlying news, inventory constraints, risk-bearing capacity, and trading technologies. Their correlation reflects an *equilibrium relationship*, not necessarily a simple causal lever you can control.

If you mistake equilibrium correlation for a unilateral mechanism, you may overestimate your ability to change outcomes. For instance, routing orders to a venue with historically lower spreads during high volatility may not preserve those tight spreads once your volume arrives and the equilibrium adjusts.

Price-volume correlations

Another example is the positive correlation between volume and absolute returns. Large moves tend to occur on high volume days. Does volume "cause" returns, or do returns "cause" volume? In reality:

- News and information shocks trigger both large price moves and heavy trading.
- Traders respond to price changes (e.g., stop-outs, margin calls), which in turn create more volume.

The result is simultaneity: volume and returns are both effects of underlying shocks and also influence each other. A strong statistical link does not tell you what would happen if you chose to trade more or less volume yourself; the market's response depends on the whole system adjusting.

Non-Stationarity: When the World Changes Under Your Feet

Even if a correlation once reflected a genuine causal channel, there is no guarantee it will persist. Financial relationships are notoriously **non-stationary**: their statistical properties change over time as technology, regulation, and strategies evolve.

Regime shifts and structural breaks

Consider a simple "macro surprise" strategy: you find that, over several years, positive payroll surprises in a particular country are followed by currency appreciation over the next few hours. The correlation is strong and economically meaningful; you build a strategy around it.

Then a policy shift occurs: the central bank announces a new framework that makes employment less central to rate decisions, or communication practices change so that much of the information is presignaled. After this regime change, the same payroll surprises generate much smaller or even reversed currency reactions. Your once-profitable pattern evaporates.

The in-sample correlation faithfully described one regime. It said nothing about the relationship's robustness to policy changes, competition, or structural innovation. Without thinking in causal terms—what is the underlying mechanism, and will it survive this new environment?—you have no basis for extrapolating.

Crowding and decaying anomalies

Many cross-sectional "anomalies" show similar decay. Suppose a strategy buying stocks with high short-term reversal delivers impressive returns from 2000 to 2010. As awareness spreads and capital crowds into related signals, market makers adjust and other traders arbitrage away the opportunity. The historical correlation between yesterday's reversal and tomorrow's return is not a law of nature; it is a reflection of a specific competitive and microstructure environment.

Non-stationarity does not just add noise; it invalidates naive interpretations of past correlations as timeless causal truths. A causal perspective forces you to ask: which features of this relationship are tied to specific institutions, frictions, or behaviors that may change?

Putting the Pitfalls Together

Confounding, simultaneity, and non-stationarity often interact. For instance:

- A backtest may identify a signal that is, in fact, a proxy for a confounding risk factor (confounding).
- The strength of this proxy may fluctuate with market microstructure or regulatory conditions (non-stationarity).
- Meanwhile, the act of trading on the signal changes order flow and potentially alters the price formation process (simultaneity).

If you treat the historical correlation as an immutable lever—"if the signal is high, we earn 10 basis points on average"—you are ignoring all three mechanisms. A more disciplined approach is to ask:

1. What could be driving both the signal and the outcome (potential confounders)?
2. Are the variables in question jointly determined in equilibrium, and if so, how?
3. Under what institutional, regulatory, or competitive conditions did this relationship hold, and are those conditions still in place?

Only after working through these questions does it make sense to treat a pattern as a candidate causal effect.

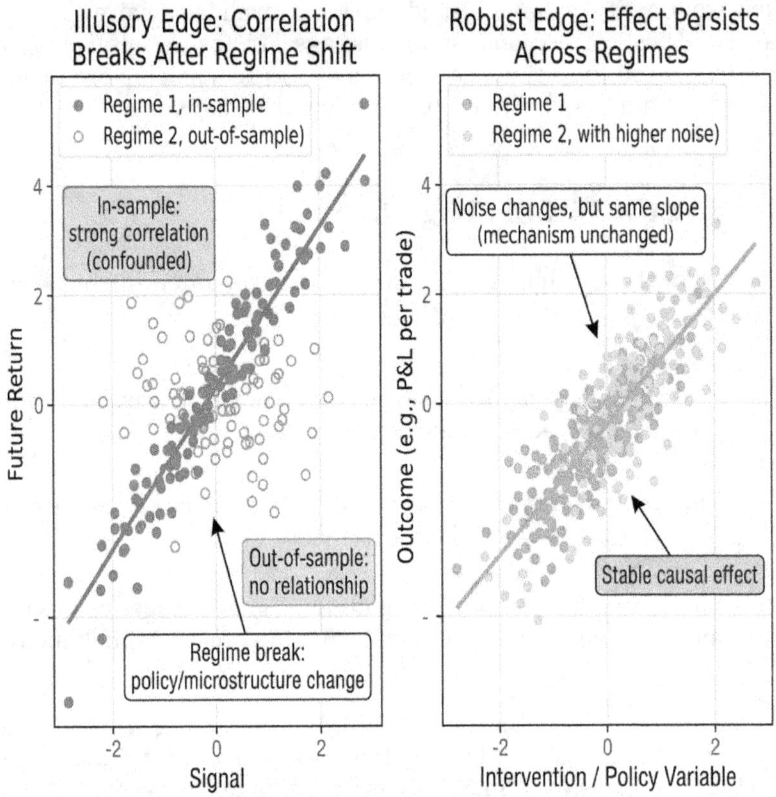

This figure summarizes the contrast we care about:

- On the left, a strong in-sample correlation—perhaps driven by confounding and regime-specific conditions—vanishes once the environment changes.
- On the right, a stable causal effect—generated by a consistent mechanism—survives across regimes, even as noise levels vary.

Your objective as a trader is to locate relationships of the second kind and avoid being seduced by the first.

Reframing the Trader's Question

Viewed through this lens, the central question for a trader is not:

> "Does this signal have a statistically significant correlation with future returns?"

but rather:

> "If we change our policy—allocation, execution rule, risk limit—in response to this signal, how will our outcome distribution change, and why?"

Answering that second question forces you to confront:

- What is the *mechanism* linking the decision to the outcome?
- Which other variables co-move with both (potential confounders)?
- How might the market *respond* to our changed behavior (equilibrium effects)?
- Under what conditions (regime, microstructure, competition) is this mechanism likely to hold?

These are inherently causal questions. The rest of the chapter, and the book, will introduce formal frameworks—potential outcomes and causal graphs—and identification rules that turn these questions into well-defined quantities you can estimate, stress test, and use in risk-aware decision making. Correlations remain useful tools, but only when interpreted as pieces of a larger causal story, not as evidence of edge on their own.

3.2 Decision Loss over Prediction Risk

In the previous section we emphasized that correlations, even when statistically impressive, often do not tell you what will happen if you *act* on a signal. This naturally leads to a deeper question: how should we evaluate our models and signals if correlation and pure predictive accuracy are not enough?

Most data science tools are built to answer a forecasting question: *how close are my predictions to the realized values?* The usual metrics—mean squared error, R^2, classification accuracy—treat all prediction errors as essentially equal, regardless of where they occur and what decisions they trigger.

Traders and portfolio managers face a different problem. What matters is not how accurate the forecast is in the abstract, but how it interacts with your *decision rule*:

- When does the model tell you to enter or exit?
- How large a position does it recommend?
- How much risk, leverage, or liquidity does it put at stake?

This section shifts the focus from **prediction risk**—the uncertainty in the forecast itself—to **decision loss**—the performance you sacrifice because you followed one policy instead of another. We will:

- Contrast forecast-oriented metrics with decision-oriented evaluation.
- Introduce the idea of *counterfactual policy value*: "What would my performance have been if I had followed this other rule?"
- Explain *regret* as the loss relative to a better (causal) policy.
- Connect these ideas to risk-aware performance, including drawdowns, turnover, and liquidity usage.

Throughout, the key message is that causal questions in trading are inherently about *policies*, not just predictions.

Why Forecast Accuracy Is Not Enough

Imagine two return forecasting models, A and B, that you might plug into the same simple trading rule:

"Go long if the forecasted excess return is positive, flat otherwise."

You backtest both models over the same period and compute standard forecasting metrics. Model A has lower mean squared error and higher R^2 than Model B. By standard data-science criteria, A is "better."

However, when you simulate trading with the rule above, you discover something surprising:

- Model A delivers a modest Sharpe ratio and suffers several deep drawdowns.
- Model B, despite being a noisier forecaster overall, produces a higher Sharpe ratio and shallower drawdowns.

How can the "worse" forecaster deliver better trading performance?

Forecasts matter most near the decision boundary

The answer lies in where the forecast errors occur. The trading rule cares mainly about whether the expected return is above or below zero, and perhaps by how much around that region. Errors far away from the decision boundary often do not change the action:

- If the true return is very positive and the model slightly underestimates it, you still go long and profit.
- If the true return is very negative and the model slightly overestimates it (but keeps it clearly negative), you still stay flat and avoid losses.

What hurts you are the errors that flip your action:

- The model predicts a small positive return, but the realized return is moderately negative: you enter a trade you should have skipped.
- The model predicts a small negative return, but the realized return is moderately positive: you miss a good opportunity.

A model can have excellent overall accuracy yet systematically make bad calls near the boundary where you decide whether to take risk. Another model might be noisier overall but get *those* critical moments right more often. From a trading perspective, the second model is superior: it has lower *decision loss* even with higher prediction risk.

Capital-weighted errors versus observation-weighted errors

Forecast metrics typically weight all observations equally. But in trading you do not put equal capital behind every prediction. You might:

- Size positions larger when model confidence is high.
- Trade more aggressively during certain market states.
- Be constrained by liquidity so that some forecasts cannot be fully exploited.

An error when you are lightly invested might be inconsequential; the same magnitude error when you are fully levered can be catastrophic. Decision loss must, therefore, account for where capital and risk are actually deployed, not just how close forecasts are point-by-point.

From Models to Policies

To formalize this shift, it is helpful to distinguish between:

- A **predictive model**: a function that maps information (signals, state variables, history) to a forecast of some quantity (e.g., next-period return).
- A **policy**: a rule that maps information (including potential model outputs) to an *action* (e.g., position size, whether to trade, which venue to use).

The same predictive model can support many different policies:

- A conservative policy that trades only when the forecast is very strong.
- An aggressive policy that scales linearly with the forecast.
- A risk-limited policy that caps positions when volatility or drawdowns are high.

Conversely, different models can feed into the same policy structure. When we talk about *decision loss*, we are evaluating the *policy*, not just the model. The key question is:

> "Given the world as it was, what would have happened if I had followed policy Π instead of the one I actually used?"

This question is inherently counterfactual: we cannot observe both realities simultaneously. We only see what happened under the policy that was actually implemented. Causal inference provides language and tools to approximate these counterfactuals from historical data.

Counterfactual Policy Value

The **value** of a trading policy is the performance it would produce if you used it over a certain period in a given environment. You can define "performance" in different ways, depending on your objective:

- Average P&L per day or per trade.
- Risk-adjusted metrics, such as Sharpe ratio or information ratio.
- Utility-based measures that penalize downside more than upside.

In notation-free language, the *counterfactual policy value* of a candidate policy is:

> "The average performance I would have realized over the historical period if, whenever a decision point arose, I had followed the actions prescribed by this policy, instead of the actions I actually took."

Why is this a causal concept?

- It compares *alternative worlds*: the world where you followed your actual decisions and the world where you followed the new policy.
- It holds the environment "as observed" in the historical data–prices, liquidity, macro events–fixed, while changing only your decisions.

Estimating policy value from data is not trivial, especially when your past actions have influenced the market (a topic developed later in the book). But conceptually, it is the right target. We do not care only that a model could, in principle, forecast returns; we care about the performance of the *trading policy* built from that model.

Example: evaluating two stop-loss rules

Suppose you want to compare two stop-loss policies for an intraday strategy:

- Policy A: always use a tight stop at 0.5% adverse move.
- Policy B: use a looser stop at 1.0% when volatility is low, and a tighter one when volatility is high.

Looking at conditional return distributions alone will not answer which policy is better. You must ask:

> "Over the last two years of intraday data, if I had used Policy A at each decision point, what would my P&L, drawdown, and risk metrics have been? And if I had instead used Policy B, with the same entry signals and market paths, what would those metrics have been?"

Each of these is a counterfactual policy value. The difference between them is a measure of the causal impact of changing your stop-loss rule, given the environment captured in your data.

Regret: How Much Did the Policy Cost Me?

Once we focus on policy value, it becomes natural to talk about **regret**. Regret is the performance you left on the table by using one policy instead of a better one.

There are different notions of "better":

- The best policy you can specify in a certain class (e.g., all policies that map a small set of signals to position sizes using simple thresholds).
- The best policy you could have implemented given your constraints (capital, risk limits, technologies).
- A hypothetical "oracle" policy that knows the true data-generating process.

Conceptually, regret is:

> "The difference between the value of the policy I actually used and the value of a benchmark, better policy, over the same period and environment."

In practice, we might estimate:

- Regret of a policy relative to the best policy found in a validation procedure.
- Regret relative to a simpler benchmark, such as a buy-and-hold or volatility-scaled index.

Regret is a *decision-centric* metric. It does not ask whether your forecasts were accurate; it asks how far your decisions were from the best you could reasonably have done. A model with slightly worse forecasts but much lower regret is preferable: it translates information into actions more effectively.

Risk-Aware Performance: Beyond Average Returns

Trading policies are chosen under risk constraints. A policy with a slightly higher expected return but significantly higher tail risk may be undesirable or even infeasible. Decision loss must therefore be measured with respect to *risk-aware* performance criteria, not just average P&L.

Several risk-related dimensions matter:

Drawdowns

Two policies with similar average returns can have very different drawdown profiles. One may have:

- Frequent but shallow drawdowns that are easy to tolerate and fund.
- The ability to reduce risk quickly during stress.

The other may have:

- Rare but very deep drawdowns that threaten capital and investor confidence.
- Strong reliance on conditions that can break in crises.

In terms of decision loss, a policy that leads to unacceptable drawdowns imposes a large cost, even if its average return looks good. From a causal perspective, you are interested in the *distribution* of outcomes under the policy, not just its center.

Turnover and transaction costs

Policies differ in how intensively they trade:

- High-frequency or highly reactive policies may generate many small trades, exposing you to transaction costs and market impact.
- More stable policies might trade less often, saving costs but potentially missing short-lived opportunities.

Decision loss must be net of these frictions. A policy that seems profitable gross of costs can be dominated, in causal terms, by a simpler or slower policy once you incorporate the causal impact of your own trading on execution prices.

Liquidity usage and capacity

A policy might perform well at small scale but break down as capital grows:

- Larger orders move prices more, degrading entry and exit conditions.
- Liquidity constraints might force partial fills or delayed execution.

From a causal standpoint, capacity is about how the outcome distribution changes as the policy's intensity (e.g., notional traded) increases. Evaluating decision loss requires you to think not just about historical backtest performance at tiny size, but about the *scaling path*—what would happen if we doubled or tripled capital under this same rule?

Bringing It All Together

Putting these elements together, we can summarize the shift from prediction risk to decision loss as follows:

- **Start from decisions, not forecasts.** Define the policy: what actions are taken when, as a function of observable information. Forecasts are inputs, not ends in themselves.

- **Define policy value in causal, counterfactual terms.** Ask: "Holding the market environment fixed as in the historical data, what would my performance have been if I had followed this policy?"

- **Measure regret relative to better policies or benchmarks.** Evaluate how much performance—return, utility, or risk-adjusted metrics—you lose by following one policy versus another plausible or optimal one.

- **Incorporate risk and frictions explicitly.** Assess not just average returns but drawdowns, volatility, turnover, liquidity usage, and capacity effects. Policies are acceptable only if their whole outcome distribution is compatible with your constraints.

This perspective is fundamentally causal: we are not merely describing associations in the data; we are reasoning about the consequences of *changing* our decision rule. In later sections, when we introduce potential outcomes and causal graphs, we will formalize these ideas:

- Policies will become "treatments" or "interventions" in the causal vocabulary.

- Policy value will map to expected outcomes under those treatments.

- Regret will be tied to differences between these expected outcomes under alternative policies.

For now, the crucial takeaway is that evaluating trading systems requires more than chasing better R^2 or lower forecast error. What matters is the causal impact of your decisions on your P&L and risk profile. A modestly accurate model that is tightly aligned with your decision boundary and risk constraints can be far more valuable than a highly accurate model that misguides you at the moments when capital is truly at risk.

3.3 Potential Outcomes and Causal Graphs

So far we have moved from asking, "Does this signal correlate with returns?" to asking, "What happens to my P&L and risk if I *change* my trading policy?" That shift is the essence of causal thinking in markets.

To make this precise and operational, we need a language that can:

- Describe alternative decisions you could have taken.
- Describe the outcomes that would have resulted under each decision.
- Encode what you believe about how different variables in the market influence one another.

In modern causal inference, two complementary frameworks serve this role:

- The **potential outcomes framework** (often called the Neyman-Rubin framework), which focuses on "what would happen if I did X versus Y?" in terms of hypothetical outcomes.
- **Structural causal models with directed acyclic graphs (DAGs)**, which focus on "what causes what?" and represent assumptions as nodes and arrows in a graph.

In this section we translate both frameworks into trading language and show how they fit together. Potential outcomes give us clean definitions of causal effects and policy values; DAGs make our assumptions explicit and tell us when and how those effects can be estimated from data.

Treatments and Outcomes in Trading Terms

Causal inference starts by distinguishing between:

- A **treatment**: something you can, at least in principle, intervene on or choose.
- An **outcome**: a variable whose distribution you care about and that may respond to the treatment.

In trading and portfolio management, typical *treatments* include:

- Turning a strategy *on* or *off*.
- Changing the leverage or risk limit of a fund.
- Adopting a new execution algorithm or routing rule.
- Reallocating capital across factor sleeves (e.g., from value to momentum).
- Modifying a stop-loss or take-profit rule.

Typical *outcomes* include:

- Daily or monthly P&L.
- Execution quality metrics: slippage, implementation shortfall, fill rates.
- Risk metrics: volatility, drawdown, tail losses.
- Operational metrics: turnover, average trade size, holding periods.

Once you define a treatment and an outcome, a causal question becomes concrete. For example:

> "If we switch from execution algorithm A to algorithm B for our large-cap orders, what is the expected reduction in average slippage over the next quarter?"

or

> "If we double the capital allocated to the value factor sleeve while keeping other sleeves constant, how does our portfolio's annualized volatility change?"

The potential outcomes framework gives us a systematic way to define quantities like "expected reduction" or "change" in these questions.

Potential Outcomes: Hypothetical Worlds for Traders

The basic idea of potential outcomes is conceptually simple, even if the notation in the literature can look abstract.

Pick a unit of analysis: this might be an *order*, a *trading day*, a *stock-month*, or an *account*. For each unit, think of the different actions (treatments) you could take and the outcome that would result under each action.

A simple binary treatment example

Suppose you are evaluating whether to use a new execution algorithm, Algo B, instead of your current one, Algo A, for a given order type (say, large parent orders in liquid equities).

For each order i, imagine two hypothetical outcomes:

- $Y_i(A)$: the slippage you would realize if you execute order i using Algo A.
- $Y_i(B)$: the slippage you would realize if you execute order i using Algo B.

Here, "slippage" might be measured in basis points relative to a benchmark price. These are **potential outcomes**: they describe what would happen under each possible treatment.

Of course, in reality, you only ever see one of them:

- If you routed order i with Algo A, you observe $Y_i(A)$ and never see $Y_i(B)$.

- If you used Algo B, you observe $Y_i(B)$ and never see $Y_i(A)$.

This is the core difficulty of causal inference: the **counterfactual**—what would have happened under the treatment you did not choose—is unobserved. Potential outcomes give us names for those missing quantities.

Average treatment effect as incremental impact

From a trading perspective, the natural question is not the individual order's effect (which is inherently unknowable), but the *average* effect across many orders of a similar kind. For example:

> "On average, how much does Algo B reduce slippage compared with Algo A for this order flow?"

In potential-outcomes language, this is the **average treatment effect** (ATE):

> Average reduction in slippage = average of $Y(B) - Y(A)$ across all comparable orders.

You can think of $Y(B) - Y(A)$ as the incremental impact of switching algorithms for a given order. Averaging this quantity over many orders yields the causal effect you care about for policy decisions.

Similar logic applies when treatments are not binary. For instance:

- Different levels of leverage (e.g., 1x, 1.5x, 2x gross exposure).
- Different capital allocations to a factor sleeve (e.g., 10%, 20%, 30%).
- Different parameter settings for a stop-loss rule.

Each treatment level corresponds to a potential outcome for that unit; causal effects are differences between those outcomes.

SUTVA: When Potential Outcomes Behave Well

The potential outcomes framework usually relies on a foundational assumption often called SUTVA, the **Stable Unit Treatment Value Assumption**. In plain language, SUTVA contains two key ideas:

- **Well-defined treatments:** The label "treatment A" means the same thing every time you use it. There is not a hidden mix of different implementations all called "Algo B."
- **No interference between units:** The outcome for unit i depends only on the treatment applied to i, not on treatments applied to other units.

In trading, both aspects can be strained:

- "Momentum strategy" or "Algo B" can hide many implementation variants: different venue mixes, child order scheduling, or risk constraints. If these differ substantially, the treatment is not well-defined.
- Your trades influence prices and liquidity for other orders. The slippage on order i can depend on how you routed order j, or on whether other funds changed their leverage. This violates "no interference."

We will later devote full sections to dealing with interference and heterogeneous treatments. For now, it is important simply to recognize that potential outcomes provide the conceptual backbone: for each decision you might make, there is a hypothetical distribution of outcomes; causal effects are differences between those hypothetical distributions.

Structural Causal Models and DAGs: Drawing Your Assumptions

Potential outcomes tell you what you *want* to know (e.g., the average effect of switching algorithms). They do not, on their own, tell you how to estimate those effects from messy, observational financial data. For that, we need a way to reason about the relationships between variables: which ones cause which, which are common drivers, and which are consequences.

Structural causal models (SCMs) and their graphical representation as **directed acyclic graphs** (DAGs) give us such a language.

Nodes and arrows

A DAG consists of:

- **Nodes**, representing variables of interest (e.g., volatility, choice of algorithm, slippage, P&L, market regime).
- **Directed edges** (arrows) that represent direct causal influences (e.g., "volatility $\rightarrow$ slippage" means volatility directly affects slippage, all else equal).

"Acyclic" means you cannot start at a node and follow directed arrows that eventually lead back to the same node. In other words, the graph has no directed loops.

Formally, each node is associated with a structural equation that says how that variable is generated from its parents (the nodes with arrows pointing into it) plus some unobserved noise. For our purposes, you can think of each arrow as encoding a statement like "changes in X, holding other causes fixed, tend to change Y."

Trading example: execution intervention

Consider a concrete example that joins the earlier discussion of potential outcomes with a graphical view.

You are evaluating a new execution algorithm, Algo B, which is supposed to improve realized P&L by reducing slippage and improving liquidity access. Relevant variables might include:

- T: Treatment, the choice of algorithm (A or B).
- M: Mediator, such as effective liquidity or average slippage.

- Y: Outcome, e.g., realized P&L per order or per day.
- V: Market volatility.
- R: Market regime (e.g., normal vs stressed conditions).

You might believe the following causal stories:

- The choice of algorithm T affects the mediator M (liquidity/slippage): different routing logic leads to different fill patterns.
- The mediator M affects the outcome Y: better liquidity and lower slippage improve P&L.
- Volatility V and regime R affect both M and Y: in stressed markets, liquidity dries up and P&L becomes more volatile, regardless of algorithm.
- Volatility V and regime R also influence which algorithm you choose: in extreme conditions you may force Algo A or B for risk reasons.

We can capture this story in a DAG.

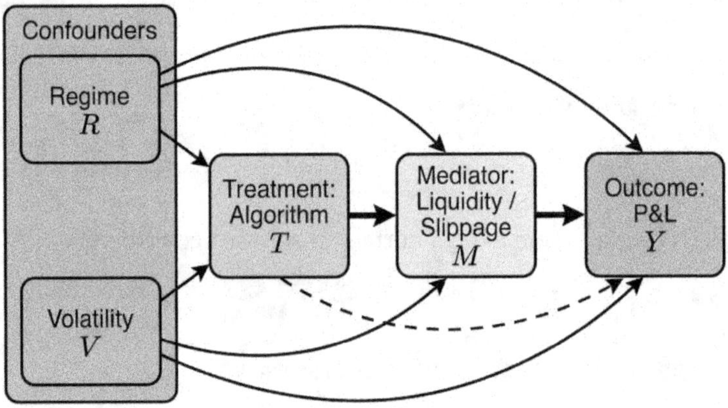

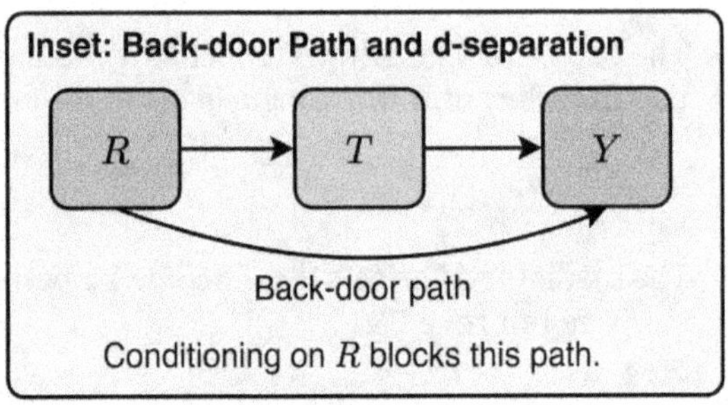

In this diagram:

- T (Algorithm choice) is the **treatment**.
- M (Liquidity/Slippage) is a **mediator** capturing the mechanism.
- Y (P&L) is the **outcome**.
- R (Regime) and V (Volatility) are **confounders**: they affect both the treatment and the outcome (and the mediator).

The bold arrows emphasize the main causal pathway you care about:

$T \to M \to Y$. The dashed arrow from T directly to Y allows for additional effects of algorithm choice on P&L beyond liquidity (for example, information leakage or signaling).

How DAGs Complement Potential Outcomes

DAGs and potential outcomes are two sides of the same coin:

- Potential outcomes define the *causal estimands*: for example, the average difference in P&L if you used Algo B versus Algo A for comparable orders.
- DAGs encode the *assumptions* under which those estimands can be recovered from observational data, and guide which variables you need to control for.

Returning to the execution example:

- Potential outcomes: For each order, $Y(A)$ and $Y(B)$ are the P&L outcomes under Algo A and Algo B. The quantity of interest might be $E[Y(B) - Y(A)]$ in a given regime.
- DAG: The arrows show how algorithm choice T and P&L Y are both influenced by regime R and volatility V. This means that if you simply compare P&L under A vs B without adjustment, you might conflate the effect of the algorithm with the effect of trading in different regimes or volatility states.

In the DAG, paths that go from T to Y but start with an arrow coming *into* T (like $R \to T$) are potential sources of **confounding**. Informally:

- There is a path $T \leftarrow R \to Y$: regime affects both algorithm choice and P&L. If you ignore R, a simple correlation between T and Y mixes up the effect of regime with the effect of algorithm.
- There is a similar path through volatility V.

The graphical machinery (developed more fully in the next section) tells you that, to estimate the causal effect of T on Y, you need to *block* these back-door paths. In practice, that often means conditioning on or adjusting for R and V—for instance, by comparing Algo A and B only within the same regime and volatility buckets, or by including them as covariates in a model.

From a potential-outcomes perspective, conditioning on the right set of variables allows you to argue that, within strata of these covariates, the assignment of T is "as good as random." This makes it plausible that differences in observed outcomes between treatments reflect causal effects rather than confounding.

Assumptions Made Visible

One of the major benefits of DAGs in a trading context is that they force you to surface and debate your assumptions:

- Do you believe market regime affects your choice of algorithm? If yes, include an arrow $R \to T$.
- Do you believe algorithm choice feeds back into volatility at your current size? If not, you might exclude an arrow $T \to V$.
- Do you think P&L directly influences future regime classification in your modeling horizon? Probably not at the level of the overall market regime.

These are qualitative judgments, but highly consequential. Different DAGs lead to different adjustment strategies and different interpretations of the same data. Two quants may look at the same historical record of algorithm choices, volatility, and P&L, but if they posit different causal graphs, they will reach different conclusions about the effect of switching algorithms.

Making the DAG explicit turns vague intuition into concrete structure. It also allows you to check for common pitfalls:

- Are you controlling for variables that are actually *colliders* (common effects) rather than confounders? Doing so can introduce bias.

- Are you missing obvious common causes that should be in the graph?

We will return to these patterns—confounders, mediators, colliders—in the identification section. For now, it is enough to see how DAGs serve as a map from your story about the world to the statistical procedures you will use.

From Conceptual Frameworks to Practical Use

At this point, we have:

- Defined treatments and outcomes in trading language.
- Introduced potential outcomes as a way to describe what would happen under alternative decisions (policies).
- Introduced DAGs as a way to encode causal assumptions and mechanisms visually.

Together, they support the policy-centric view developed earlier:

- A trading **policy** (e.g., "use Algo B in these conditions, Algo A otherwise") is a rule for choosing treatments as a function of observed variables.
- The **value** of a policy is an expectation over potential outcomes: the performance you would get if you followed that policy consistently.
- DAGs tell you under what conditions and with what adjustments you can use observed market data to approximate those policy values and compare them, thereby quantifying decision loss and regret.

In the next section, we develop **identification rules**: practical conditions, expressed in terms of DAGs, that tell you when a causal effect—such as the incremental P&L impact of switching algorithms, altering leverage, or modifying fees—is recoverable from observational data.

We will also show how failure to respect these rules leads directly to misleading backtests, overestimated edges, and poor real-money performance.

For now, you should take away two main points:

- Every serious trading question about "what if we change X?" can be phrased in terms of potential outcomes: alternative hypothetical results under different decisions.
- Every serious attempt to estimate such effects from data rests on unspoken assumptions about what causes what; DAGs provide a disciplined way to write those assumptions down, critique them, and derive appropriate adjustment strategies.

With these conceptual tools in place, we can now confront the central question of causal inference for traders: under what conditions, and by which methods, can we move from correlations observed in market data to credible estimates of the causal impact of our trading decisions?

3.4 Identification Rules and Bias Mechanisms

In the previous sections we shifted from raw correlations to causal questions and introduced two key tools:

- **Potential outcomes**, which define what we mean by the causal effect of a trading decision or policy.
- **Causal graphs (DAGs)**, which encode our assumptions about how variables in markets influence one another.

We can now ask the central practical question: *given the data we actually have, and the way the world works, can we identify the causal effect we care about?* This is the problem of **identification**.

Identification is about whether a causal quantity-such as "the expected change in P&L if we double leverage" or "the effect of offering a fee discount on client flow"-can be expressed in terms of the distributions we can observe in historical data. If the answer is yes, we can design estimators and worry about statistical precision. If the answer is no, no amount of data or machine learning cleverness will recover that causal effect without new assumptions, instruments, or experiments.

This section provides a set of practical rules and patterns for traders:

- The **back-door criterion**: when we can control for confounding by conditioning on an appropriate set of variables.
- The **front-door criterion**: when an observed mediator can rescue identification even with unobserved confounders.
- A high-level view of **do-calculus**: the algebra that justifies more complex identification steps.
- Recognition of common **bias mechanisms** in financial data: confounders, colliders, and selection effects such as survivorship and fill bias.

Throughout, we focus on intuitive explanations and concrete trading examples.

Back-Door Criterion: Blocking Confounding Paths

Recall that in a DAG, a **back-door path** from treatment T to outcome Y is any path that starts with an arrow pointing into T and eventually reaches Y following the directions of the arrows or going against them. These paths represent ways in which T and Y can be statistically associated even if T has no causal effect on Y-typically via confounders.

The back-door criterion gives a precise rule:

> A set of variables Z satisfies the back-door criterion for estimating the causal effect of T on Y if:
>
> - No element of Z is a descendant of T; and
> - Z blocks every back-door path from T to Y in the DAG.

If such a set exists and is observed, then the causal effect of T on Y can be identified by conditioning on Z.

In less formal language: if we can find variables to condition on so that, within each stratum of those variables, the assignment of T is as good as random with respect to Y, then differences in outcomes between T levels inside each stratum can be interpreted causally.

Example: leverage changes and fund returns

Suppose you want to estimate the effect of changing a fund's gross leverage T on its monthly return Y. You suspect the following:

- Managers raise leverage when they see attractive opportunities.
- They also raise leverage when volatility is low and funding is cheap.
- These same conditions affect returns even for a fixed leverage level.

Let:

- T: Fund leverage (e.g., gross exposure).
- Y: Fund return next month.
- O: Opportunity set proxies (e.g., factor spreads, dispersion).
- V: Market volatility and funding conditions.

You might draw a DAG with:

- $O \to T$ and $O \to Y$.
- $V \to T$ and $V \to Y$.
- $T \to Y$ (the causal effect you care about).

There are back-door paths:

$$T \leftarrow O \rightarrow Y, \quad T \leftarrow V \rightarrow Y.$$

If you simply regress Y on T, you will mix up the effect of leverage with the effect of attractive opportunities and benign volatility conditions. Intuitively, "leverage works" partly because you tend to lever up when conditions are good.

The back-door criterion tells you that if you condition on O and V-for instance, by including them as covariates or stratifying on them-then the remaining association between T and Y can be interpreted (under the DAG's assumptions) as causal. Within strata where opportunities and volatility are similar, variations in leverage are closer to "as good as random."

In practice, this forces you to:

- Think hard about what drives both leverage choices and returns.
- Collect and control for those variables when estimating the effect of leverage.

The message is not that back-door adjustment is automatic, but that the DAG gives a checklist: "find and block all back-door paths."

Front-Door Criterion: Using Mediators When Confounders Are Hidden

Sometimes, key confounders are unobserved or poorly measured. For example:

- A client's true risk appetite affects both their response to a fee discount and their subsequent trading behavior, but you do not observe risk appetite directly.
- A trader's private alpha signals affect both her order aggressiveness and realized P&L, but you do not observe the internal signal.

In these cases, back-door adjustment may be impossible: there is no observed variable you can condition on to break the confounding paths. Surprisingly, sometimes you can still identify causal effects if you observe a **mediator**-a variable through which the treatment affects the outcome.

The **front-door criterion** describes one such situation. Roughly, it says:

> If the treatment T affects the mediator M, which in turn affects the outcome Y, and if:
>
> - All back-door paths from T to M are blocked by observed variables.
> - All back-door paths from M to Y are blocked by observed variables once we condition on T.
> - There is no direct unmediated path from T to Y unaccounted for.
>
> then the causal effect of T on Y can be identified by combining the effect of T on M and the effect of M on Y.

Example: fee discounts and client flow

Consider a broker who offers fee discounts and wants to understand their causal impact on client trading volume. Let:

- T: Fee discount offer (yes/no or level).
- M: Change in effective trading costs (e.g., realized commission per share, including discounts and routing changes).
- Y: Client trading volume with the broker over the next quarter.
- A: Client risk appetite and opportunity set (unobserved).

You might believe:

- A (risk appetite) affects both T and Y: high-value clients get more discounts and also trade more.

- T affects M: offering discounts reduces effective costs.
- M affects Y: lower realized costs encourage more trading.

The path $T \leftarrow A \rightarrow Y$ is a confounding back-door path that you cannot block directly, because A is unobserved.

However, suppose you are comfortable that:

- Apart from T, there is no other unobserved cause of M (once you control for observables like asset class and market conditions).
- Conditional on (T, A), any additional unobserved factors affecting M do not also directly affect Y other than through M.

Then the front-door criterion tells you that you can:

- Estimate how the discount T changes effective costs M (this is a causal effect from T to M).
- Estimate how changes in M affect volume Y, while controlling for T.
- Combine these pieces to recover the causal effect of T on Y, even though A remains unobserved.

Conceptually, you are using the observed mediator M as a "lens" through which to see the effect of T, shielding yourself from the unobserved confounder A.

Front-door situations are more specialized than back-door ones and rely on stronger structural assumptions. But when they arise-for example, when you can observe detailed microstructure changes (mediators) that fully carry the effect of an intervention-they can be powerful.

Do-Calculus: A Map for Complex Identification

Back-door and front-door criteria are particular instances of a broader algebra of interventions known as **do-calculus**. In notation, $P(Y \mid$

$do(T = t))$ denotes the distribution of Y when we *intervene* to set $T = t$, as opposed to just conditioning on $T = t$ in observational data.

Do-calculus, in essence, provides a set of transformation rules that allow you to manipulate expressions involving $do(\cdot)$-that is, hypothetical interventions-into equivalent expressions involving only observable conditional probabilities, whenever this is possible under the DAG's assumptions.

For practitioners, you do not need to memorize the formal rules. What matters is the intuition:

- **Cutting incoming arrows**: $do(T = t)$ corresponds to modifying the DAG by removing (or "cutting") all arrows into T and setting it externally.
- **Substituting intervention distributions**: once you conceptually cut the graph, you ask whether the resulting interventional distribution can be expressed in terms of the original observational distribution by clever conditioning and averaging.
- **Systematic search**: do-calculus provides a systematic way to check if such transformations exist, beyond simple back-door or front-door situations.

In complex trading settings-such as market microstructure with feedback, or policy changes that propagate through multiple mediators-formal do-calculus can, in principle, be used to justify identification strategies. In this book, we mainly rely on the intuitive patterns (back-door, front-door, collider avoidance) that are often sufficient in practice, but you should know that there is a deeper, rigorous machinery underneath.

Common Bias Mechanisms in Financial Data

Identification is not just about knowing when we can estimate causal effects; it is equally about recognizing when we *cannot*, or when naive conditioning introduces bias. Three graphical patterns show up repeatedly in trading and investment data:

- **Confounding** (blocked by back-door adjustment).
- **Front-door mediators** (sometimes enabling identification).
- **Colliders and selection bias** (conditioning makes things worse).

To anchor these ideas, we now introduce a compact figure with three DAGs, each tied to a financial example.

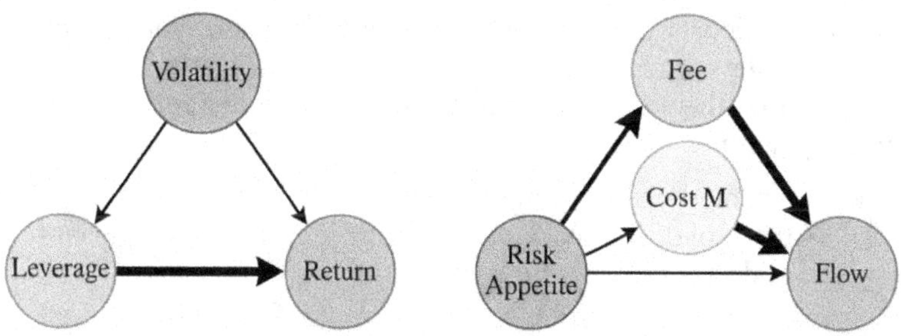

(a) Confounding / Back-Door
Adjust for Volatility to block
$V \to L \to R$ back-door

(b) Front-Door Mediator
Use Cost M to infer Fee $\to$ Flow
effect despite unobserved Appetite

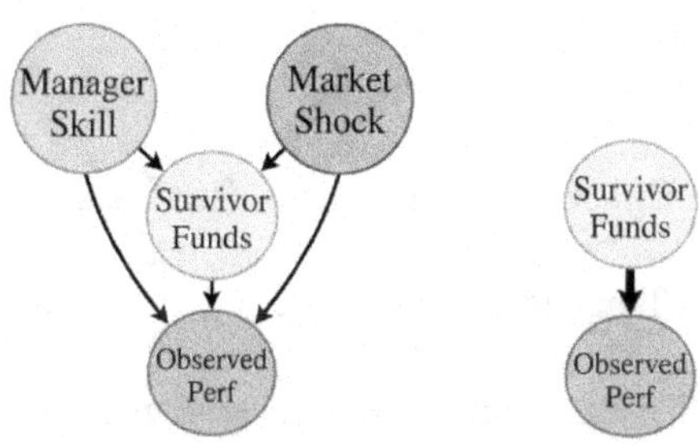

(c) Collider

Use Cost M to infer
Fee $\to$ Flow effect despite
unobserved Appetite

Conditioning on Survivors
opens spurious path
Skill $\leftrightarrow$ Shock

Let us now unpack each panel.

Confounding via common risk factors

Panel (a) shows a classic confounding pattern:

- V: Volatility.
- L: Leverage.
- R: Return.

Volatility affects both leverage choices and returns. If you compare returns when leverage is high versus low without adjusting for volatility, you confound the effect of leverage with the effect of benign or stressed volatility regimes.

Back-door remedy: condition on volatility (and other relevant risk factors). Within volatility buckets, variations in leverage are closer to "as good as random," making the comparison more causal.

Front-door mediation via trade costs

Panel (b) reprises the fee discount example. Here:

- F: Fee level (treatment).
- M: Effective cost per share (mediator).
- Q: Client flow (outcome).
- A: Risk appetite (unobserved confounder).

Risk appetite A affects both fee offers F and flow Q. But if F only affects Q through M, and if you can block back-door paths into M and then from M to Q by controlling for observed variables, the front-door criterion can sometimes be used to identify the causal effect of fee changes on flow.

Colliders and selection bias: survivorship and fills

Panel (c) introduces a different pattern: a **collider**. A collider is a variable that has two (or more) arrows pointing into it. Here:

- $Skill$: Manager skill.
- $Shock$: Market shock severity.
- $Survivor$: Indicator of whether the fund survives a crisis period.
- $Perf$: Observed performance.

Both skill and shocks influence survival: good managers and favorable shocks increase the chance of survival. Skill and shocks also influence performance directly. The key feature is that $Survivor$ sits at the intersection: $Skill \rightarrow Survivor \leftarrow Shock$.

By default, skill and shocks might be independent. But if you *condition* on survival-say, by analyzing only the funds that survived the crisis-you create a spurious association between skill and shocks:

- Among survivors, a manager who experienced a bad shock must, on average, have had higher skill to still be around.
- Conversely, managers who benefited from good shocks can afford to be less skilled and still survive.

This induces negative correlation between skill and shocks in the selected sample, even if they were independent in the population. As a result, naive analyses of "skill versus performance" on survivor-only data can be badly biased. You might understate true skill dispersion or misattribute performance to timing rather than ability.

The same logic appears in order-level data:

- You only observe execution prices for filled orders, not for all order attempts.
- Fill status may depend on both your aggressiveness and contemporaneous market conditions.

Treating "filled orders" as if they were a random sample can induce collider bias: you have conditioned on a variable (fill) that is influenced by both your strategy and the market, opening a spurious association pathway.

The graphical lesson is crucial: *do not control for or stratify on colliders* when trying to estimate causal effects. Unlike confounders, which should be conditioned on, colliders should usually be left unconditioned in causal analyses.

Putting Identification to Work

The identification rules and bias mechanisms in this section translate directly into better trading research practice:

- Before running a regression or backtest, sketch a DAG for your question: what is the treatment, what is the outcome, and what other variables influence both?

- Use the back-door criterion to decide which variables should be in your adjustment set. Do not rely solely on generic "control for everything you can" heuristics; they can introduce collider bias.

- Look for situations where mediators are observed and may allow front-door identification when key confounders are unobserved.

- Be vigilant about selection: survivorship in fund databases, fill bias in order data, and conditioning on "high Sharpe" or "low drawdown" subsamples can all distort causal interpretation.

In later chapters, we will connect these identification ideas to specific estimators-such as inverse-probability weighting, matching, and double-robust methods-and to quasi-experimental designs in financial markets. But even before diving into estimation, the habit of drawing graphs, checking for back-door and front-door opportunities, and avoiding collider traps will significantly improve the reliability of your empirical findings and the robustness of your trading decisions.

3.5 Interference, Mediation, and Granger Limits

The previous sections equipped us with a policy-centric language for causal effects and with graphical tools to reason about identification and bias. We deliberately worked in a simplified world where each unit's outcome depended only on its own treatment, and where we focused on direct links from a decision to a result.

Real markets are messier. Three complications are especially important:

- **Interference**: one trader's actions affect other traders' outcomes through common prices and liquidity.
- **Mediation**: many interventions operate through intermediate variables (like liquidity, depth, or information leakage), not just through a direct jump from "policy" to P&L.
- **Granger limits**: temporal predictability in time series (Granger "causality") does not, by itself, imply a stable or useful causal lever.

Ignoring these issues often leads to overoptimistic backtests and fragile strategies. This section explains each in turn and ties them back to the causal tools developed so far.

Interference: When Your Trades Affect Others

In our earlier discussion of potential outcomes, we invoked SUTVA—the assumption that each unit's outcome depends only on its own treatment, not on the treatments of others. This is rarely true in markets.

Interference occurs when the treatment applied to one unit changes the outcomes of other units. In trading:

- Your order flow moves prices that other traders face.
- A change in exchange fees alters the liquidity provision strategies of many participants.

- A new margin rule changes leverage for all funds simultaneously, affecting volatility and cross-asset correlations.

Units can be orders, instruments, accounts, or traders. In all cases, the key point is that treatments and outcomes are linked through shared state variables—most notably prices and liquidity.

Example: venue routing and cross-trader spillovers

Suppose you adopt a new smart order router that aggressively takes liquidity on a specific venue. You might define:

- Treatment T_i: whether order i is routed with the new router or the old one.
- Outcome Y_i: the implementation shortfall (slippage) for order i.

If your flow were negligible, you could reasonably assume that Y_i depends only on T_i and on market conditions that are unaffected by your individual orders. SUTVA would be roughly valid.

However, if your participation rate is material, your routing choice changes:

- The queue and depth on the targeted venue.
- Subsequent prices seen by your other orders.
- Prices and liquidity seen by *other* traders, whose reactions can feed back into the book.

Now the outcome for order i depends on the treatment assignments for other orders j—both your own and others'. A naive "A/B test" that randomizes T_i across orders but ignores these interactions can be misleading: the environment under the "new router" condition is different *because* the router is deployed.

Market-level interventions

Interference is even more pronounced for policy changes at the market level, such as:

- A change in tick size.

- A new short-selling restriction.
- A modification to margin or capital rules.

These are treatments applied at the market or asset level, not at the individual trader level. The outcome for trader A depends on how traders B, C, and D respond. In such cases, "experiments" or natural experiments must be analyzed with explicit attention to spillovers and network effects—who trades with whom, through which instruments, and over what horizons.

The takeaway is not that causal inference fails in the presence of interference, but that the unit of analysis and the causal estimand must be redefined:

- Instead of "effect on a single trader holding others fixed," you might estimate "effect of the intervention on the *aggregate* distribution of outcomes," or "effect on early adopters versus late adopters," recognizing the interactions.
- Graphically, this means adding explicit nodes for prices and liquidity that connect multiple agents' treatments and outcomes.

Mediation: Pathways from Decisions to Outcomes

Even when interference is limited or can be approximated away, many trading decisions work through **mediators**: intermediate variables on the causal pathway from treatment to outcome.

Why pathways matter

Earlier we saw that adopting a new execution algorithm (treatment) may:

- Change your effective liquidity access and realized slippage (mediators),
- Which then change your P&L and risk profile (outcome).

You might care about the *total* effect of the algorithm on P&L, but you may also want to know:

- How much of the effect comes from reduced explicit costs versus reduced market impact?
- How much is due to timing improvements versus information leakage?

These are questions about **direct** and **indirect** effects:

- The **indirect effect** operates through the mediator(s): "Algo B $\rightarrow$ improved depth $\rightarrow$ better P&L."
- The **direct effect** captures pathways not running through the mediator, such as a change in signaling that affects how other traders respond.

Understanding mediation helps in several ways:

- **Design**: If most of the benefit comes from one pathway (say, reduced signaling), you can focus future improvements there.
- **Risk control**: If the indirect effect is highly sensitive to certain conditions (e.g., liquidity evaporating), you learn where the strategy is fragile.
- **Transferability**: If the mechanism is clearly tied to a specific market structure, you can better judge whether the effect will carry to other venues or regimes.

Example: routing policy and information leakage

Imagine two routing policies for large block trades:

- Policy A: Route aggressively to lit venues.
- Policy B: Use dark pools first, then lit venues if needed.

You measure:

- T: routing policy (A or B).

- M: information leakage proxy, for example, average pre-trade price drift after your first child order.
- Y: trade-level implementation shortfall.

A DAG might have $T \to M \to Y$, with a possible direct arrow $T \to Y$ (for immediate price impact differences). You can ask:

- What fraction of the total effect of switching from A to B on Y is mediated by changes in leakage M?

Formally decomposing effects into mediated and direct components requires additional assumptions and often stronger identification conditions than estimating the total effect. But even a qualitative understanding—backed by graphs and focused diagnostics—can be valuable. For instance:

- If you see that B materially reduces leakage M but has only modest impact on Y in liquid names, you infer that leakage was not the main constraint there.
- In illiquid, information-sensitive names, you may see a larger portion of the effect run through M.

This pathway thinking reinforces the earlier lesson: robust strategies are those whose mechanisms you can describe and stress test, not just those that show a nice $T \to Y$ backtest number.

Why Granger "Causality" Is Not Causality

Time-series analysis in finance often uses **Granger causality** as a diagnostic. The definition is purely predictive:

> A series X is said to Granger-cause Y if past values of X contain information that helps predict future values of Y, beyond the information in past Y (and possibly other covariates).

This notion is useful for forecasting. It is *not* a causal statement in the interventionist sense we have emphasized. There are several reasons.

Common drivers and omitted variables

Granger tests typically operate within a specified forecasting model (such as a vector autoregression). If that model omits important common drivers, then:

- X may appear to Granger-cause Y simply because both respond, with different lags, to some unmodeled process Z (macro news, policy expectations, risk sentiment).

For example:

- Equity index volatility may appear to Granger-cause credit spreads.
- In reality, both may respond to underlying macro uncertainty or funding stress.

In a DAG, this is just confounding in the time dimension. From a policy standpoint, you have no guarantee that intervening on X (if you even can) will move Y as the predictive model suggests.

Equilibrium and simultaneity

Markets often exhibit feedback loops:

- X_t (order flow in one asset) affects prices and liquidity, which in turn influence Y_{t+1} (order flow or returns in another asset).
- Y_t then feeds back into X_{t+1}.

In finite-order models, this joint determination can manifest as bidirectional Granger "causality": X Granger-causes Y and Y Granger-causes X. These patterns capture equilibrium adjustment dynamics, not necessarily clean levers you can pull.

For trading decisions, the question is:

> "If I increase my trading in asset X according to some policy, will asset Y's returns change in the same way the Granger model forecasts when X happens to be high?"

The answer may be no, because the model conflates endogenous responses of other agents with exogenous variations in X. Your intervention changes the equilibrium, not just the path of X holding everything else fixed.

Regime dependence and structural breaks

Granger relationships are notoriously unstable across regimes. A macro variable may predict an asset in one policy framework and fail—or reverse—after a change in:

- Central bank reaction functions.
- Capital flow regulations.
- Market microstructure (e.g., introduction of electronic trading).

From a causal perspective, this is expected: the mechanisms that connect X and Y depend on institutional and behavioral structures. When those change, the predictive link tells you little about how an intervention on X will work going forward.

Predictability versus manipulability

Perhaps the most important conceptual distinction is between **predictability** and **manipulability**:

- A variable can be useful for prediction without being a feasible or safe target for intervention.
- For example, implied volatility might Granger-cause future realized volatility, but you cannot costlessly set implied volatility; you can only trade options, moving prices and attracting other traders' responses.

Causal leverage requires a variable you can influence through realistic actions, with a reasonably stable mapping from those actions to outcomes. Granger causality alone does not guarantee either property.

Bringing It Back to Causal Design

Interference, mediation, and Granger limits all reinforce the core theme of this chapter: causal inference for traders is about *interventions on policies* in an interacting system, not just about finding patterns in data.

Practically, this means:

- When analyzing historical policy changes or natural experiments, think carefully about spillovers. Are you estimating an effect that holds other agents' behavior fixed, or an equilibrium response?
- When evaluating new strategies or execution tools, articulate the mediating pathways and, where possible, measure them. This helps in diagnosing breakdowns and transportability to new markets.
- Use Granger-style predictability tests as tools for *forecasting*, not as proof of causality. Before building risk on a Granger relationship, ask: what is the DAG? What are the confounders? Is there an identifiable mechanism I can stress test?

In later chapters, we will explore experimental and quasi-experimental designs—randomized pilots, instrumented regressions, event studies—that are explicitly tailored to these realities: markets where agents interact through shared prices and liquidity, where mechanisms run through mediators like depth and spreads, and where time-series predictability can be fragile. The tools of causal inference will allow you to move beyond "it Granger-causes" to "it is an actionable, identified causal lever under clearly stated assumptions."

Chapter 4

Estimands, Heterogeneity & Estimation under Observables

Trading decisions rarely fail because we lack models; they fail because we aim at the wrong quantity. This chapter is about choosing the right causal target-average, conditional, or local-and then hitting it reliably when all you have are historical market data and observed covariates. You will learn how to translate abstract estimands into P&L-relevant questions, diagnose where your data can and cannot speak, and deploy modern estimators that squeeze credible causal signals from noisy markets without overfitting to regimes that will never return.

4.1 Average Treatment Effects (ATE/ATT/ATC)

In earlier chapters we distinguished prediction from causation and introduced the potential-outcomes view: every trade or account has at least two possible futures, one under "do not apply the strategy" and one under "apply the strategy." We now make this more precise by defining the main *population-level estimands* used throughout causal inference and by translating them into trading and P&L language.

Think of an *estimand* as the precise causal quantity you wish to know, before you choose any method to estimate it. Different estimands answer different business questions. A common source of confusion in practice is that desks implicitly want one estimand (for example, "what happened to the trades we actually treated?") but they apply methods that identify another (for example, "what would happen if we treated everybody?"). The goal of this section is to make those distinctions explicit.

We focus on three core objects:

- the *Average Treatment Effect* (ATE),
- the *Average Treatment Effect on the Treated* (ATT),
- the *Average Treatment Effect on the Controls* (ATC).

All three live in the same potential-outcomes world, but they average over different sub-populations of trades or accounts. We will link each of them to concrete trading questions and explain when each is appropriate, under two key assumptions that we will use repeatedly:

- **Overlap (positivity):** every type of trade you care about sometimes receives the strategy and sometimes does not;
- **Unconfoundedness:** after conditioning on observed features, the decision to apply the strategy is as good as random.

Potential outcomes for trades and accounts

To fix ideas, suppose we are evaluating a new execution algorithm versus a legacy algorithm. For each order i, we observe:

- a binary *treatment* T_i:
  - $T_i = 1$ if the order was routed using the new algorithm,
  - $T_i = 0$ if it was routed using the legacy algorithm;
- a realized outcome Y_i, such as the implementation shortfall in basis points (negative means worse performance, positive means improvement);
- a vector of observed characteristics X_i, such as order size, instrument, liquidity, volatility, time of day, and client type.

In potential-outcomes language, we imagine that each order i has two latent outcomes:

- $Y_i(1)$: the shortfall that would be realized if the new algorithm is used;
- $Y_i(0)$: the shortfall that would be realized if the legacy algorithm is used.

For each order we observe only one of these: $Y_i = Y_i(1)$ when $T_i = 1$ and $Y_i = Y_i(0)$ when $T_i = 0$. The *individual treatment effect* is $Y_i(1) - Y_i(0)$, but this difference is never directly observed.

In trading, each "unit" i can be:

- a single order or child order,
- a daily account-level P&L,
- a symbol-day combination,
- a portfolio-day for a strategy.

You should always be clear about what your unit is, because the meaning of all average effects depends on this choice.

Average Treatment Effect (ATE): "What if we treated everyone?"

The *Average Treatment Effect* is the simplest population estimand. It asks:

> On average over all eligible units (orders, accounts, symbols), how would outcomes change if we switched everyone from control to treatment?

In symbols, the ATE is the difference between the average potential outcome under treatment and the average potential outcome under control in the target population:

$$\text{ATE} = \mathbb{E}[Y(1)] - \mathbb{E}[Y(0)].$$

In our execution example, ATE answers:

> If *every* eligible order this quarter had been executed via the new algorithm instead of the legacy algorithm, how much would average implementation shortfall have changed?

If your unit is a symbol-day with outcome "daily return of the strategy," ATE becomes:

> If we had run the new signal-driven strategy on *all* eligible symbols and days in the universe, what would have been the average change in returns relative to our benchmark or baseline strategy?

ATE is the appropriate estimand when:

- you are considering a *full rollout* of a strategy across all assets or all accounts;
- you want a single number that summarizes the policy change at the population level;

- your backtest universe is meant to represent the real deployment universe.

In practice, many questions asked in investment committees are ATE questions: "If we move all mid-cap flow to the new algo, what is the average cost difference?"; "If we switch all stat-arb trades to this new entry rule, what is the typical impact on P&L?"

ATT: "What happened to the ones we actually treated?"

Sometimes you do not care about all eligible units, but specifically about those that *actually received* the treatment.

For instance, suppose the new algorithm was rolled out only for a subset of clients who opted in. You might ask:

> For the orders that actually used the new algorithm, how much better or worse did they do than they would have under the legacy algorithm?

This is the *Average Treatment Effect on the Treated* (ATT). Formally, it is the average treatment effect *conditional on being treated*:

$$\text{ATT} = \mathbb{E}[Y(1) - Y(0) \mid T = 1].$$

ATT is particularly relevant in three trading situations:

- **Evaluating a past rollout.** You have already treated a subset (for example, a pilot program) and you want to know how much incremental P&L that subset gained or lost relative to the counterfactual of not having treated them.
- **Reporting realized impact.** For a product or strategy that is only available to certain clients or asset classes, management often wants a statement like: "On accounts currently using Strategy X, average monthly P&L is 15 bps higher than it would have been without the strategy."

- **Risk attribution.** If a strategy underperformed, you might ask: "For the trades we actually put through this model, how much of the loss is attributable to the model itself versus market conditions?" This is inherently an ATT question.

Note that ATT does *not* tell you what would happen if you rolled the strategy out to previously untreated clients or assets. Those units may differ in important ways.

ATC: "What if we treated those we are currently not treating?"

The mirror image of ATT is the *Average Treatment Effect on the Controls* (ATC). It asks:

> For the units that did *not* receive the strategy historically, what would their outcomes look like under treatment versus control?

Formally,

$$\text{ATC} = \mathbb{E}[Y(1) - Y(0) \mid T = 0].$$

ATC becomes central when your main decision problem is *expansion*:

- You currently apply an execution algorithm only to large-cap orders and want to know what would happen if you started using it on small-cap or emerging-market orders.
- You have deployed a signal-driven strategy only for internal capital and are considering offering it to external clients.
- You are deciding whether to move a set of "holdout" accounts into an existing risk model.

In these settings, management's practical question is usually:

> If we turn on the strategy for these currently untreated assets/accounts, how much incremental P&L should we expect?

That is exactly ATC, not ATE and not ATT.

How ATE, ATT, and ATC relate in practice

All three estimands are averages of the same underlying individual effects $Y_i(1) - Y_i(0)$, but they average over different subsets:

- ATE averages over *all* eligible units.
- ATT averages over *treated* units.
- ATC averages over *control* units.

They are generally different because treated and control units tend to differ systematically. For example, suppose the new algorithm is initially used only for large, liquid orders. Those are exactly the trades where the algorithm might perform best. Then the ATT (effect on treated large-liquid orders) will likely be more favorable than the ATC (effect on the smaller, less liquid orders that were not initially treated). The overall ATE is something in between, depending on how many units are in each group.

Understanding which subgroup you are averaging over is critical for interpreting empirical results. If you estimate an ATT using pilot-program data but then implicitly treat it as if it were an ATE when making a full-rollout decision, you are extrapolating beyond the subgroup where you have direct empirical support.

A visual summary of the estimands

Immediately after defining these estimands, it is helpful to fix the picture of which population each one refers to. The following diagram shows this schematically.

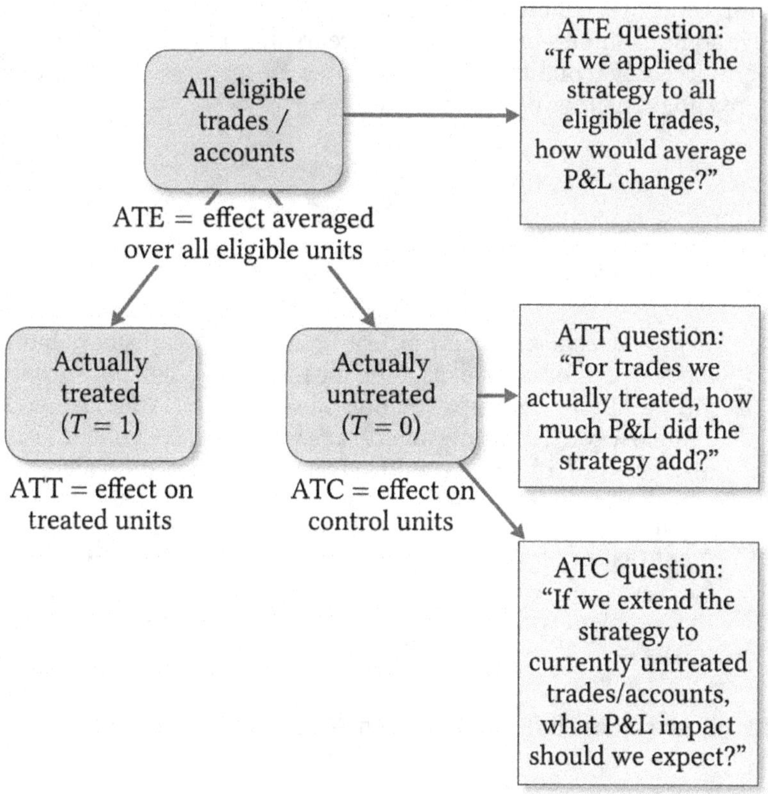

This schematic is intentionally simple: three boxes for populations and three boxes for questions. As you design a study, you should be able to point to exactly which box your estimand lives in.

Overlap (positivity): when estimands are not identifiable

So far we have defined ATE, ATT, and ATC as abstract averages over potential outcomes. To learn them from historical data, we need some structure. One key structural requirement is *overlap* (also called *positivity*).

Informally, overlap means: for every type of unit you care about, you have some examples in the data that are treated and some that are not. More precisely, conditional on covariates X, the probability of treatment should neither be zero nor one:

$$0 < P(T = 1 \mid X = x) < 1$$

for all covariate values x in the population you care about.

In trading terms:

- If you *never* use the new algorithm for micro-cap stocks but *always* use it for large-caps, then for micro-caps you only observe $Y(0)$ and for large-caps you only observe $Y(1)$. You have no in-sample way to learn how micro-caps would behave under the new algo or how large-caps would behave under the legacy algo.
- If you are trying to evaluate a strategy for a particular client segment that never used it historically, you cannot identify the ATT (they were not treated) and you also cannot identify the ATC for that segment without additional assumptions or external instruments.

The consequences differ by estimand:

- For **ATE**, you need overlap across the entire eligible population. If some region of the covariate space (for example, very illiquid names) always receives treatment or always receives control, their contribution to ATE cannot be identified from observational data alone.
- For **ATT**, you only need overlap *for treated units*. Intuitively, for each treated order, you must be able to find comparable untreated orders with similar X to infer what would have happened under control. If certain treated orders have no comparable controls, they cannot contribute to a well-identified ATT.
- For **ATC**, the requirement is symmetric: you need overlap for control units. For each untreated order, you must be able to find similar treated ones.

A frequent pattern in trading data is that a new strategy starts in "easy" segments (for example, large liquid names or sophisticated clients) and only later moves to harder segments. In such cases you may have good overlap for the initial treated segment (making ATT relatively well-identified) but poor overlap for segments that were always left untreated (making ATC and ATE harder to pin down).

When overlap fails badly, any statement about what would happen if you flipped treatment in those non-overlap regions is largely extrapolation or model-based speculation. This is one reason why many empirical studies in finance explicitly restrict their estimand to a subset of the universe where treatment and control are both observed.

Unconfoundedness: when observables are enough

The second key assumption we will use throughout this chapter is *unconfoundedness* (also called *selection on observables* or the *back-door* condition). It states that, conditional on the observed covariates X, the treatment assignment T is as good as random with respect to the potential outcomes:

$$(Y(0), Y(1)) \perp T \mid X.$$

In plain language:

> Once we control for X, there are no additional unobserved factors that jointly affect both the decision to apply the strategy and the potential outcomes.

In trading practice, this means that:

- You have recorded all the relevant risk measures, liquidity measures, client characteristics, market-state indicators, and internal routing rules that drive both treatment decisions and outcomes.
- Conditional on those observables, the remaining variation in who gets treated and who does not can be treated like random variation.

For example, if the desk uses the new execution algorithm whenever the expected participation rate, volatility, and spread cross certain thresholds, and you have these variables in X, then after conditioning on them, whether a given order happens to be treated may be close to random. If, however, the desk also uses some informal, undocumented judgment that you cannot capture in X (for example, trader intuition about hidden liquidity), then unconfoundedness may fail.

Under unconfoundedness and overlap, all three estimands—ATE, ATT, and ATC—are, in principle, identifiable from observational data. You can construct comparison groups that mimic randomized experiments within strata of X. The remainder of this chapter will discuss specific estimators (matching, weighting, doubly robust methods) that exploit these assumptions.

A crucial practical point is that unconfoundedness is *assumption*, not a testable property. You cannot prove from the data alone that you have controlled for all relevant confounders. Good domain knowledge is essential: you must think through how treatment is assigned in your trading system and whether your data truly captures the drivers of that decision.

Choosing the right estimand for your trading question

Before you reach for any estimation tool, you should ask: which estimand matches the business question?

- **Use ATE** when your decision is about a *universal policy change*:
  - "Should we switch all orders in this asset class to the new algorithm?"
  - "Should we adopt this risk-parity overlay for all portfolios in the platform?"
- **Use ATT** when you care about the impact on *those already treated*:
  - "For the accounts currently subscribed to Strategy X, what is the realized causal uplift in P&L?"

  - "For the set of orders routed through Dark Pool A, what is the effect relative to the counterfactual of routing them elsewhere?"

- **Use ATC** when you are considering *expansion to untreated segments*:
  - "If we extend the new execution algorithm to the remaining clients, what P&L impact should we expect?"
  - "If we start applying this signal to small-cap names that were previously excluded, what change in returns should we forecast?"

Clarity about the estimand simplifies everything that follows:

- It tells you which part of the data is most informative (treated vs control).
- It determines what kind of overlap you must check.
- It guides how you interpret the output of matching, weighting, or causal ML methods.

In the next sections we will move from these conceptual targets to concrete estimation strategies under unconfoundedness: first using matching and propensity weighting to construct balanced comparison groups, and then using doubly robust and machine-learning-based approaches to estimate both global effects (ATE/ATT/ATC) and heterogeneous effects across assets, accounts, and market regimes.

4.2 Heterogeneous Effects and CATE

In the previous section we focused on global quantities such as the ATE, ATT, and ATC. Each of those summarises the impact of a strategy with a *single* number: an average effect over all eligible trades, over treated trades, or over untreated trades.

For trading, that is often too coarse. Markets are not homogeneous, and neither are your trades or clients. A strategy that adds value for one segment can destroy value for another. In this section we formalise this idea of *heterogeneous treatment effects* and introduce the *Conditional Average Treatment Effect* (CATE) as the main way to describe and exploit that heterogeneity.

We will:

- explain why heterogeneity is the rule rather than the exception in financial markets;
- define CATE and relate it to ATE/ATT/ATC;
- show how CATE connects directly to segmentation, targeting, and "uplift" style allocation decisions;
- discuss the practical trade-off between granularity and statistical noise.

Throughout, we continue to work under the same assumptions as before: potential outcomes exist for each unit, and, when needed, the overlap and unconfoundedness conditions hold so that we can learn from historical data.

Why a single effect is rarely enough in markets

Consider an execution algorithm that smart-routes orders across venues to reduce slippage. In the previous section, we may have asked:

> On average, over all the orders in our test universe, how many basis points of implementation shortfall does the new algorithm save relative to the old one?

Suppose we find an ATE of +2 bps: on average, the new algorithm improves shortfall by 2 bps. That sounds attractive, but it hides potentially important variation:

- For small, highly liquid orders in mega-cap stocks, the improvement might be +0.5 bps: the legacy algorithm was already good enough.

- For large orders in mid-cap or less liquid names, the improvement might be +5 to +10 bps: the new smart-router really helps.
- For certain very illiquid names or during stressed market conditions, the new algorithm might *worsen* outcomes by a few bps because it chases phantom liquidity or over-fragments fills.

If you only look at the overall ATE, you may happily roll out the algorithm to everyone, including the segments where it hurts you. More importantly, you miss an opportunity to *target* the strategy aggressively to the segments where it creates the most value.

This pattern is not unique to execution:

- A signal-based equity strategy may work well in low-volatility stocks but poorly in high-volatility names.
- A leverage overlay may help diversified institutional portfolios but be disastrous for concentrated, retail-heavy accounts.
- A dynamic hedging rule may be beneficial in calm markets but overly costly in high-turnover, high-vol regimes.

In each case, the causal effect of "turning on" the strategy depends on observable features of the trade, asset, account, or market regime. Our goal in this section is to describe and quantify that dependence.

From global ATE to conditional effects

Let us recall the potential-outcomes notation from before. Each unit i (order, account-day, symbol-day, and so on) has:

- a treatment indicator T_i (e.g., 1 if the strategy is applied, 0 if not),
- an outcome Y_i (e.g., return, P&L, slippage),
- a vector of covariates X_i capturing observable characteristics.

The potential outcomes are $Y_i(1)$ and $Y_i(0)$, and the individual treatment effect is $Y_i(1) - Y_i(0)$, which we never directly observe.

The global ATE is:

$$\text{ATE} = \mathbb{E}[Y(1) - Y(0)].$$

This averages over all units, regardless of X. To capture heterogeneity, we instead ask:

> Among units with a given set of observable characteristics $X = x$, what is the average treatment effect?

This leads to the *Conditional Average Treatment Effect*:

$$\tau(x) = \mathbb{E}[Y(1) - Y(0) \mid X = x].$$

We will refer to $\tau(x)$ as the "CATE at x."

In words, CATE is:

> The expected incremental impact of the strategy for trades/accounts/periods that look like x.

Here "look like x" might mean "large orders in highly liquid US equities during the open," or "small-cap stocks with high volatility and wide spreads," or "retail accounts with low turnover."

Once you allow the effect to depend on X, several useful facts follow immediately:

- The overall ATE is the average of CATEs across the population, weighted by how often each X occurs.
- The ATT and ATC can be seen as averages of CATEs over treated or control units, respectively.
- Different segments (defined by X) can have positive, near-zero, or negative CATEs.

Thus, instead of thinking in terms of one global number, you can think of a "treatment effect surface" over the feature space X.

Examples of CATE in trading contexts

Let us make this more concrete with a few examples.

Example 1: Execution algorithm by order size and liquidity

Suppose X includes order size (in ADV buckets) and a liquidity score for the instrument. You might estimate CATE as a function of (size, liquidity).

You may discover patterns such as:

- For small orders in very liquid instruments, $\tau(x)$ is close to zero: both algos perform similarly.
- For medium and large orders, especially in moderately liquid names, $\tau(x)$ is strongly positive: the new algo reduces shortfall significantly.
- For extremely illiquid instruments, $\tau(x)$ is slightly negative: the new algo's aggressiveness leads to worse prices.

From a risk and allocation standpoint, this tells you:

- You can safely route all eligible medium and large orders through the new algo.
- There is little benefit to re-engineering the flow of small-liquid orders.
- You should consider exemptions or safeguards for the illiquid tail of the universe.

Example 2: Signal strategy by volatility and market regime

Suppose you run a long-short strategy based on a cross-sectional signal, and you treat "using the signal to size positions" as the treatment. Let X include the stock's volatility and an indicator of the volatility regime (e.g., low, normal, high VIX).

CATE may reveal that:

- In low-volatility regimes, the signal generates positive alpha in medium-volatility stocks but weak or negative alpha in extreme-volatility names (these are dominated by idiosyncratic noise).
- In high-volatility regimes, the signal's benefit shrinks or even turns negative for many stocks, as macro-driven moves overwhelm cross-sectional patterns.

Knowing this, you might:

- scale back the strategy in high-volatility regimes or tighten risk constraints,
- restrict deployments to volatility buckets where the CATE is consistently positive,
- treat high-volatility names as a separate segment with stricter thresholds.

CATE as a tool for segmentation and targeting

In marketing and credit risk, CATE-based thinking is often described in terms of "uplift" or "incremental response." The same logic applies naturally in trading.

At a high level, a CATE function $\tau(x)$ lets you:

- **Segment** the universe into groups based on X;
- **Estimate** the expected treatment effect within each group;
- **Rank** groups or individual units by their predicted incremental benefit;
- **Allocate** scarce resources (capital, risk, engineering effort) toward the highest-impact units.

Let us go through these steps in trading language.

Segmentation

Segmentation means defining meaningful groups based on covariates. Examples include:

- liquidity buckets (mega-cap, large-cap, mid-cap, small-cap, micro-cap),
- volatility buckets,
- client types (institutional, HFT, retail),
- order characteristics (size, urgency, participation constraints),
- time-of-day or trading session,
- market regimes (risk-on vs risk-off, high vs low spread environment).

Initially, you might work with relatively coarse segments, such as "large-liquid," "large-illiquid," "small-liquid," and "small-illiquid." Later, more advanced methods can allow segments to be defined flexibly by machine learning.

Within-segment effect estimation

Once you have segments, you can estimate an average treatment effect within each segment-effectively a CATE that is piecewise constant over those groups.

For example, you could estimate:

- the average effect of the new execution algorithm for large-liquid orders,
- the average effect for small-illiquid orders,
- and so on.

If you are working under unconfoundedness and overlap, you might use matching or weighting within each segment, or interact treatments with X in a regression model. In more advanced chapters we will show how causal forests and meta-learners automate much of this segmentation and estimation.

Ranking and targeting: uplift-style allocation

Once you have estimated $\tau(x)$, even approximately, you can order segments or individual units by their predicted incremental benefit:

- Highest $\tau(x)$: "deploy aggressively"-these trades or accounts are where the strategy adds the most value per unit risk or cost.
- Medium $\tau(x)$: "deploy cautiously"-the strategy is mildly beneficial or neutral; you might treat these only when capacity allows or under favorable conditions.
- Negative $\tau(x)$: "avoid or protect"-the strategy is expected to hurt; you might explicitly disable it or add constraints for these segments.

This is the essence of uplift-based allocation: you are not asking, "Where is the raw P&L highest?" but "Where does *turning on the strategy* change P&L the most, relative to not using it?" That is a causal question by design, and CATE is the estimand that answers it.

For instance:

- Rather than routing all orders through the new algorithm, you route only those with positive predicted CATE, thereby avoiding negative segments and improving overall realized P&L.
- Rather than offering a strategy indiscriminately to all clients, you first target those accounts with the highest predicted uplift in risk-adjusted returns.

A useful internal mental model is:

> Every trade or account comes with a "strategy sensitivity score," namely its predicted CATE. My job is to use that score to decide *who* should receive the strategy and *when*.

Monotonicity and response types

Thinking about heterogeneity often leads naturally to classifying units into response types, drawing on ideas from monotonicity and principal stratification.

A simple conceptual classification is:

- **Responders:** units with positive treatment effect, $Y(1) - Y(0) > 0$, so the strategy helps them.
- **Non-responders:** units with near-zero effect, $Y(1) - Y(0) \approx 0$, where the strategy is largely irrelevant.
- **Adverse responders:** units with negative effect, $Y(1) - Y(0) < 0$, where the strategy hurts.

Of course we cannot observe each unit's individual effect directly, but CATE-based models aim to approximate this classification using X:

- For segments with strongly positive CATE, most units are likely responders.
- For segments with near-zero CATE, many units are non-responders.
- For segments with negative CATE, many units are adverse responders.

A monotonicity-type belief might be that as you move along some dimension (say liquidity), the effect of the strategy is non-decreasing or non-increasing. For instance, you might reasonably assume that an execution improvement cannot *worsen* outcomes once liquidity is above a certain threshold, or that a particular signal is never more harmful in low-volatility names than in extremely high-volatility names. Such domain-informed monotonicity assumptions can guide the structure of your CATE model and prevent overfitting to noise.

Granularity versus variance: how fine should your segments be?

A natural temptation, once you start thinking in terms of CATE, is to define very narrow segments: "large US tech stocks, traded in the first 15 minutes of the day, on Tuesdays, under high VIX, in accounts with turnover above X, with order size between Y and Z, and so on."

The problem with extremely fine segmentation is that each cell in your segmentation grid will contain very few observations. When you estimate the effect in such small cells, your estimates become noisy. You risk "discovering" patterns that are really just sampling variability.

This is the central trade-off:

- **More granularity** (more detailed X or finer bins) allows your model to adapt to genuine differences across assets, accounts, and regimes.
- **More granularity** also means fewer observations per cell or region, which increases estimation variance and the risk of overfitting.

In practice, you manage this trade-off by:

- starting with a small set of economically meaningful covariates (e.g., liquidity, volatility, size, client type),
- using relatively coarse buckets to ensure enough data in each group,
- gradually increasing flexibility using regularized or machine-learning-based CATE estimators that "borrow strength" across similar units while still allowing for heterogeneity.

Later in the chapter we will see how causal forests, meta-learners, and other causal ML tools handle this systematically: they search for heterogeneity across many covariates but control variance through regularization, cross-validation, and cross-fitting.

CATE under unconfoundedness and overlap

CATE is an estimand, not an estimator. To connect it to data, we still rely on the same two identification assumptions as for the ATE:

- **Overlap:** for each relevant region of X, you must observe both treated and untreated units. If, for example, the new execution algorithm was never used for micro-caps, you cannot learn $\tau(x)$ for micro-cap x from those data alone.

- **Unconfoundedness:** conditional on X, the assignment of treatment is as good as random. If unobserved trader judgment about "difficult" orders affects both routing decisions and slippage, and is *not* captured in X, then CATE estimates that ignore this will be biased.

When both assumptions are plausible, you can interpret your estimated CATE function causally: it tells you, given current observables X, how much *changing treatment* (applying or not applying the strategy) will change expected outcomes.

If either assumption fails badly in some region of X (for example, no overlap in certain segments, or obvious unmeasured confounders), then CATE in those regions becomes speculative. In practice, traders often:

- restrict their CATE analysis to regions of good overlap,
- treat predictions in extrapolation regions with caution or as scenario analysis rather than hard forecasts,
- complement observational estimates with targeted experiments or pilots to validate effects in new segments.

From concept to implementation

To summarise, CATE gives you a way to express what traders often do informally:

- They know that some strategies "work better in large caps" or "are dangerous in small illiquid names."
- They adjust their behavior based on the market regime: "we dial this down in stressed conditions."
- They tailor offerings to client types: "this is a good product for low-turnover institutions, but not for leveraged retail."

By formalising these intuitions as $\tau(x)$—a conditional average treatment effect dependent on X—you can:

- measure these differences rigorously,
- integrate them into systematic allocation rules,
- and evaluate, via backtests and out-of-sample tests, whether your targeting improves realized P&L.

In the sections that follow, we move from defining CATE conceptually to the practical methods used to estimate it under unconfoundedness. Matching and propensity weighting will show how to construct balanced comparison groups in the space of X, while doubly robust estimators and causal machine learning will provide scalable tools to estimate both global effects (ATE/ATT/ATC) and heterogeneous effects $\tau(x)$ across assets, accounts, and regimes.

4.3 Local Effects with Instruments: LATE

So far in this chapter we have assumed that, after conditioning on observed covariates, treatment assignment is "as good as random." Under that unconfoundedness assumption, we could define and interpret ATE, ATT, ATC, and CATE as causal effects that are, in principle, learnable from observational data.

In trading applications, this assumption is often strained. Desk behavior, trader judgment, and internal risk signals are only partially captured in your recorded covariates. For example:

- A trader may decide whether to use a new execution algorithm based on a subjective sense of "difficulty" that is not in any database.
- A portfolio manager may choose whether to follow a signal based on unrecorded macro views.
- A risk committee may loosen or tighten constraints in ways that depend on political or institutional factors you do not observe.

In such cases, even after conditioning on rich X, there remains unobserved confounding: unmeasured variables affect both the treatment decision and potential outcomes. Under unconfoundedness violations, the matching and weighting tools discussed later in the chapter can no longer be trusted to recover global causal effects.

One way to regain some causal traction is to exploit *instruments*: variables that shift the probability of treatment in a way that is plausibly independent of potential outcomes, except through their influence on treatment. When we do this, the main estimand is usually no longer the global ATE, but a *Local Average Treatment Effect* (LATE): an effect for a specific subpopulation, the *compliers*.

This section explains how LATE arises, who the compliers are in trading examples, and how the key assumptions—monotonicity and exclusion—shape the interpretation of instrumental-variables (IV) estimates.

Instruments in trading: intuitive examples

An *instrument* is a variable Z with two core properties:

- It influences the probability of receiving treatment T (instrument *relevance*).
- It has no direct effect on the outcome Y other than through its effect on T (the *exclusion restriction*).

Additionally, we assume that Z is "as good as random" with respect to the unobserved confounders affecting Y.

In trading, potential instruments often come from:

- **Randomized nudges or defaults.** For example, an order-management system that, for a random subset of orders, defaults to the new algo, while for others it defaults to the legacy algo.
- **Quasi-random routing rules.** For instance, a router that alternates traffic across two venues based on a hash of order ID or timestamp bits, unrelated to expected P&L but affecting which venue is used.

- **Policy discontinuities**. Rules that change deterministically at certain thresholds: e.g., a new risk overlay that applies only when portfolio volatility exceeds a specific level, or an execution policy that changes when order size exceeds a desk-specific cutoff.
- **Operational shocks**. Exchange outages, temporary halts on specific venues, or internal capacity constraints that force rerouting of flow.

In each example, the instrument Z nudges or forces some trades toward treatment and others away from it, for reasons that are plausibly independent of the fine-grained drivers of Y.

Compliance types: compliers, always-takers, and never-takers

A central insight in LATE theory is that different units respond differently to the instrument Z. To interpret an IV estimator, we need to classify units by their *potential treatment status* under different instrument values.

For simplicity, suppose Z is binary ($Z = 1$ means "encouraged toward treatment," $Z = 0$ means "not encouraged") and treatment T is also binary ($T = 1$ if the strategy is used, $T = 0$ otherwise).

For each unit i we can imagine two potential treatment statuses:

- $T_i(1)$: whether unit i would receive treatment if $Z = 1$,
- $T_i(0)$: whether unit i would receive treatment if $Z = 0$.

This yields four conceptual *compliance types*:

- **Compliers**: $T_i(1) = 1, T_i(0) = 0$. These units follow the instrument: they take treatment when encouraged and do not when not encouraged.
- **Always-takers**: $T_i(1) = 1$, $T_i(0) = 1$. They receive treatment regardless of the instrument.

- **Never-takers**: $T_i(1) = 0$, $T_i(0) = 0$. They never receive treatment, regardless of the instrument.
- **Defiers**: $T_i(1) = 0$, $T_i(0) = 1$. They do the opposite of what the instrument suggests: they avoid treatment when encouraged and take it when not encouraged.

In real data, we do not observe $T_i(1)$ and $T_i(0)$ for the same unit; we only see one of them. But this classification is conceptually useful.

In trading contexts:

- Compliers might be orders whose venue or algo choice truly follows the router's default or the random assignment.
- Always-takers are orders that the trader *always* routes through the new algo, regardless of router default, perhaps because of client-specific settings or strong trader preference.
- Never-takers are orders that never use the new strategy, even when defaulted to it (e.g., because of special constraints).
- Defiers would be traders who systematically override the router, doing the opposite of whatever it suggests—this is typically implausible at scale.

LATE: a local effect for compliers

When we use IV methods with a valid instrument and impose an additional monotonicity assumption (no defiers, discussed below), the canonical result is that the IV estimand recovers a *Local Average Treatment Effect (LATE)*:

$$\text{LATE} = \mathbb{E}[Y(1) - Y(0) \mid \text{compliers}].$$

That is, IV does not identify the ATE over all units, nor the ATT or ATC, but the average causal effect for the subpopulation whose treatment status actually changes in response to the instrument.

In trading language:

> LATE is the expected incremental P&L impact of the strategy for those trades or accounts whose use of the strategy is genuinely driven by the instrument (e.g., the randomized router or policy rule).

For example, consider a router that, for a random 50% of orders, defaults to Venue A (treated), and for the other 50%, defaults to Venue B (control). Some traders always override the default and choose Venue A (always-takers); some always choose Venue B (never-takers); but a meaningful fraction of orders just follow the default (compliers). An IV estimate of the causal effect of routing to Venue A versus B on realized spreads or P&L is a LATE for these *complier orders*.

Why you rarely get the global ATE from IV

From the perspective of the previous sections, LATE can seem disappointing: we used to talk about ATE, ATT, ATC, and CATE; now we are told that with instruments we obtain a local effect only for compliers.

However, in settings with strong unobserved confounding, IV/LATE may be the *only* credible causal effect you can estimate. It answers a well-defined and practically relevant question:

> When we change the instrument (e.g., change the default, flip the router rule, cross a policy threshold), how does expected P&L change *for the trades whose treatment status actually changes as a result*?

This is often directly tied to operational decisions. For example:

- If you are considering changing the default execution venue for certain orders, LATE tells you the impact on those orders that follow the default.
- If you are evaluating a risk policy that tightens leverage when a risk score crosses a threshold, LATE tells you the effect on those portfolios whose leverage truly responds to crossing that threshold.

Trades or accounts that never comply with the instrument (always-takers and never-takers) are not directly informative about the effect at the margin of the instrument; IV effectively downweights them.

Key assumptions for LATE: relevance, exclusion, and monotonicity

To interpret an IV estimate as a LATE, three main assumptions are required.

Instrument relevance

The instrument must shift the probability of treatment:

$$\Pr(T = 1 \mid Z = 1) \neq \Pr(T = 1 \mid Z = 0).$$

In trading, this means:

- The router default must actually change the fraction of orders using the new algo.
- The policy threshold must actually change behavior (e.g., leverage or hedging) when crossed.

If Z has almost no influence on T, then there are almost no compliers, and the IV estimator becomes weak and unstable. This is the familiar "weak instruments" problem: estimates are noisy and can be badly biased in finite samples.

Exclusion restriction

The exclusion restriction states that Z affects the outcome Y only through T:

$$Z \text{ affects } Y \text{ only via its effect on } T.$$

In words:

> Conditioning on treatment, the instrument has no additional direct effect on P&L.

This is often the most contentious assumption in trading. Consider some examples:

- If Z is "Venue A is temporarily down," and treatment is "route to Venue B," then Z might affect P&L in multiple ways, not only through venue choice: it may correlate with broader market stress, changes in liquidity, or reaction from other market participants.
- If Z is "risk score above threshold," and treatment is "apply leverage cap," then crossing the threshold might also trigger other desk behaviors (e.g., closer manual monitoring, different communication patterns) that independently affect P&L.

When designing or exploiting instruments, you should therefore ask:

> Can I plausibly argue that the only channel from Z to P&L runs through the treatment variable I am studying?

If the answer is "no," your IV estimates may be picking up multiple effects, and the interpretation as a treatment effect becomes questionable.

Monotonicity (no defiers)

The monotonicity assumption rules out defiers. Formally, it assumes:

$$T_i(1) \geq T_i(0) \quad \text{for all } i,$$

so that moving the instrument from 0 to 1 never causes someone to move from treatment to control. In other words, the instrument weakly encourages treatment for everyone: it never discourages it.

In trading:

- A router default that is always toward the new algo when $Z = 1$ and always toward the old algo when $Z = 0$ satisfies monotonicity if traders never systematically reverse it ("do the opposite of the default").

- A policy rule that makes leverage caps tighter when a score crosses a threshold satisfies monotonicity if managers never systematically respond by *increasing* risk when caps tighten.

Monotonicity is critical because it ensures that the subpopulation whose treatment changes when you manipulate Z (the compliers) has a clear direction: they move from control to treatment as Z goes from 0 to 1. Without monotonicity, the IV estimand would average over a mixture of compliers and defiers, and its interpretation becomes opaque.

In many institutional trading settings, monotonicity is plausible: systems and policies are usually designed so that "encouragement" is consistent (e.g., defaults are stable, thresholds always tighten or always loosen policy in the same direction), and traders are not systematically trying to invert these signals. Still, you should think carefully about whether there might be pockets of behavior that violate this, especially under stress.

Trading-focused examples of LATE

Let us walk through two stylized examples to solidify the intuition.

Example 1: Randomized router default for venue choice

Suppose you experiment with a router that, for each eligible order, randomly assigns a default venue:

- $Z = 1$: default venue is Dark Pool A (treatment).
- $Z = 0$: default venue is Lit Exchange B (control).

Traders can override the default but often just accept it.

Here, $T = 1$ if the order actually routes to A, and $T = 0$ if it routes to B. The outcome Y could be realized spread, fill rate, or implementation shortfall.

If:

- the randomization mechanism is truly random and independent of order quality beyond what is already in X,

- the default significantly changes the probability of routing to A,
- and there is no direct effect of the default itself on Y (beyond the venue choice),

then Z is a valid instrument.

The IV/LATE estimate will tell you:

> For the subset of orders that follow the router default (compliers), what is the average causal impact on Y of being routed to Dark Pool A rather than Lit Exchange B?

This is a local effect. It does not necessarily equal the effect for always-takers (orders that are always sent to A regardless of the default) or never-takers (orders that always go to B). But for operational decisions that change the default routing for the marginal orders, LATE is directly relevant.

Example 2: Risk constraint rollout by desk

Imagine a risk committee that, due to capacity and governance constraints, rolls out a new intraday drawdown limit desk by desk, over time. The order and timing of desks receiving the new rule is driven partly by administrative convenience rather than trading characteristics.

Let:

- Z indicate whether a desk is under the new risk policy in a given month (1) or not yet (0).
- T indicate whether a specific account-day actually operates under tightened risk limits; some accounts or PMs may voluntarily adopt the rule early (always-takers), some may find ways to avoid it despite rollout (never-takers), but many will comply when their desk is officially under the policy.
- Y be daily P&L volatility or a risk-adjusted performance metric.

If:

- the rollout sequence is unrelated to unobserved account-level risk appetite or alpha opportunities,
- the desk-level policy does not affect Y through other channels than the risk limits (for example, it does not change incentives, staffing, or reporting in ways that independently affect P&L),
- and PMs do not systematically lever up when the rule tightens (monotonicity),

then desk-level policy assignment Z can be interpreted as an instrument.

The LATE in this context is:

> The average effect of the tightened risk constraint on Y for accounts whose behavior (treatment status) actually changes when their desk comes under the new policy.

That is, the effect for *complier accounts*, not for those that were always conservative (never-takers) or always aggressive (always-takers).

Comparing LATE to ATE/ATT/ATC and CATE

How does LATE fit into the taxonomy of estimands from the earlier sections?

- ATE, ATT, and ATC describe global effects averaged over all units (or all treated, or all controls).
- CATE $\tau(x)$ refines these effects by conditioning on observed covariates X.
- LATE is a different kind of conditional effect: it is conditional on *complier status*, which is defined by how units respond to the instrument, not by covariates X.

In general:

$$\text{LATE} = \mathbb{E}[Y(1) - Y(0) \mid \text{compliers}]$$

and this need not equal:

- the ATE, unless compliers are representative of the whole population in terms of treatment effects,
- the ATT, unless compliers are exactly the treated population,
- any particular CATE at a covariate value x, unless compliers happen to be concentrated in that region of X.

In trading terms, compliers are often the *margin* of behavior that moves when policies or defaults change. For example, they may be mid-complexity orders that rely on system defaults, rather than the simplest or most idiosyncratic trades. The IV/LATE estimate thus tells you what effect to expect when you change that margin, not necessarily when you force everyone to adopt the strategy.

Misinterpreting LATE as ATE can lead to overconfident extrapolation. For instance, if compliers are mainly medium-sized, liquid orders, but you use LATE to forecast what would happen when routing *all* orders (including very large or very illiquid ones) through a new venue, you may be stepping beyond what the data genuinely support.

Practical guidance for traders using IV/LATE

To use IV methods sensibly in trading and to interpret LATE correctly, keep the following points in mind:

- **Be explicit about the instrument.** Identify the actual mechanism that shifts treatment (router default, policy threshold, outage, random assignment) and check its relevance empirically.
- **Argue for exclusion with domain knowledge.** Think carefully about all possible channels from Z to Y. If there are plausible direct channels other than through T, the IV story becomes fragile.
- **Assess monotonicity.** Consider whether there are meaningful pockets of defiers; if yes, interpret your IV estimates with caution.

- **Describe the compliers.** Use observed data to characterize which trades or accounts are most affected by Z. Even though you cannot see complier status directly, you can often infer the likely profile of compliers (e.g., mid-sized orders, certain clients, certain time windows).
- **Align decisions with LATE's scope.** Use LATE to support decisions that operate through the same margin as the instrument (changing defaults, adjusting thresholds), not necessarily for sweeping changes to all units far from that margin.

In environments where unobserved confounding is severe and experiments are infeasible, IV/LATE may be your best option for extracting credible causal insights from naturally occurring shocks or policy rules. It complements the unconfoundedness-based methods in the rest of this chapter: where rich observables and careful design suffice, you can aim for ATE/ATT/ATC and CATE; where they do not, you may have to settle for local effects—LATE—but with a clearer understanding of *whose* P&L you are truly learning about.

4.4 Matching and Propensity Weighting

Up to this point in the chapter we have focused on *what* we want to estimate: ATE, ATT, ATC, and CATE. We also introduced two central assumptions—overlap and unconfoundedness—that, if plausible, let us identify these estimands from observational data.

We now turn to *how* to estimate them in practice when we believe all relevant confounders are observed. The methods in this section share a common "design-first" philosophy:

> Before looking at outcomes or running regressions, use covariates to construct a pseudo-experiment where treated and control units are comparable. Only then compare outcomes.

In trading language, the idea is to make the set of orders (or accounts, or days) that received the strategy look, in terms of observed features, like the set that did not. If successful, any remaining average outcome difference can credibly be attributed to the strategy itself rather than to differences in liquidity, volatility, client mix, or market state.

We will cover three tightly related tools:

- **Matching:** pair or group similar treated and control units in covariate space;
- **Stratification (subclassification):** bin units into strata by a balancing score and compare within strata;
- **Propensity score weighting:** reweight observations so the weighted covariate distributions of treated and control units align.

We also discuss diagnostics, stabilized weights, and practical issues in high-dimensional market data.

The design-first mindset in trading

In observational trading data, treatment is rarely random. For example:

- You send larger, more urgent orders to a particular algo.
- You apply a new strategy only to certain liquid names or clients.
- You hedge selectively in more volatile regimes.

If you simply compare raw average outcomes between treated and untreated units, you are almost certainly mixing true causal effects with selection effects. For example, trades executed with a high-touch algo may have worse slippage not because the algo is bad, but because those trades are inherently more difficult.

The design-first approach mimics randomization by:

1. using observed covariates X (size, liquidity, volatility, client, time-of-day, regime) to create a balanced sample where treated and control units have similar X distributions;

2. *only then* comparing outcomes Y to estimate ATE/ATT/ATC, often with simple differences in means.

Conceptually, you are building a "matched control universe" for your treated trades or a "reweighted control universe" that looks like treated trades on observables. This is very close to what good traders do informally when they say, "Compare this algo's performance against similar orders on the other venue."

Matching on covariates

Matching methods aim to pair each treated unit with one or more "similar" control units based on X. The simplest variant is nearest-neighbor matching.

Nearest-neighbor matching

Suppose you want to estimate the ATT of a new execution algo (treatment) on implementation shortfall Y:

- Treated units: orders using the new algo ($T = 1$).
- Controls: orders using the legacy algo ($T = 0$).
- Covariates X: order size in ADV buckets, liquidity measures, volatility, spread, time-of-day, client type.

Nearest-neighbor matching proceeds roughly as:

1. Define a distance measure between two units based on X (e.g., Euclidean distance after scaling covariates, or Mahalanobis distance).
2. For each treated order, find one or more control orders that are closest in X.
3. Form matched pairs or matched sets.

4. Estimate the average difference in Y between each treated order and its matched controls; average these differences over all treated orders.

Intuitively, you are asking: "For each order we actually sent to the new algo, what happened to highly similar orders that went through the legacy algo?" This approximates the missing counterfactual $Y(0)$ for each treated order and targets the ATT.

Caliper and quality controls

Nearest-neighbor matching can fail when the nearest control is still far away in covariate space. To avoid bad matches, we often impose a *caliper*: a maximum allowed distance between a treated unit and a matched control.

Orders with no adequate matches (e.g., extremely large, illiquid treated orders with no similar controls) are then dropped from the estimand's effective support. Operationally this means:

- you are explicitly restricting your ATT to the subpopulation where overlap is good;
- you transparently acknowledge that you cannot say much about the causal effect for those extreme trades because you lack comparable controls.

This is healthy: it prevents hidden extrapolation into regions of poor overlap.

Matching in practice

In trading workflows, matching is quite natural:

- You can match orders placed on Venue A to similar orders placed on Venue B, then compare slippage.
- You can match accounts using a new strategy to similar accounts not using it, based on size, turnover, volatility, and holdings profile.

- You can match days when a risk overlay was active to similar days when it was inactive, within the same account or strategy.

After constructing matches, you can estimate simple differences in means or run regressions on the matched sample with T as the key regressor. Importantly, the outcome model is not doing the heavy lifting; the design (matching) has already created a comparable treated-control set.

Stratification and subclassification

Matching operates at the level of individual units. An alternative is to stratify units into bins based on a *balancing score*, then compare outcomes within each bin.

A common choice of balancing score is the *propensity score*, which we discuss shortly, but you can also stratify on simple features or risk scores.

Basic idea

Suppose you create bins (strata) of orders based on, say, order size and liquidity: small-liquid, small-illiquid, medium-liquid, medium-illiquid, large-liquid, large-illiquid. Within each stratum, you:

1. check that there are both treated and control orders (overlap),
2. compare average Y between treated and control orders within the stratum,
3. aggregate stratum-level effects into an overall ATE or ATT, weighting by stratum size or treated mass.

This is essentially a coarse version of CATE: you are estimating a piecewise constant treatment effect function over meaningful segments of the universe.

Stratification on the propensity score

When the number of covariates is large, you can first compress X into a single scalar, the *propensity score* $e(X)$, defined as the probability of treatment given X. You can then stratify units into, say, quintiles of $\hat{e}(X)$ and compare treated versus control outcomes within each quintile.

The key property (under unconfoundedness) is that, conditional on the true propensity score $e(X)$, treated and control units have similar X distributions. This makes $e(X)$ a powerful balancing score: if you get balance in $e(X)$, you get balance in X (approximately).

Propensity scores and inverse probability weighting

Matching and stratification work on the "unit" side: they select or group observations. Propensity score weighting takes a complementary view: rather than selecting units, it assigns *weights* to them so that, in the weighted sample, treated and control covariates look alike.

Propensity score: definition and estimation

The *propensity score* is:

$$e(X) = \Pr(T = 1 \mid X).$$

In practice we estimate $e(X)$ from data via a model of treatment assignment. Examples include:

- logistic regression of T on X (size, liquidity, volatility, client type, time-of-day, regime indicators),
- regularized models (lasso, elastic net) when X is high-dimensional,
- tree-based models or gradient boosting when treatment assignment is complex and non-linear.

Crucially, the propensity model is part of the *design* stage: it aims to capture how the desk actually decided to apply the strategy, not to predict outcomes Y.

Inverse probability weighting (IPW)

Once you have estimated $\hat{e}(X)$, you can form weights that re-balance the sample. For the ATE, a common choice is:

- Treated units: weight $w_i = 1/\hat{e}(X_i)$;
- Control units: weight $w_i = 1/(1 - \hat{e}(X_i))$.

Intuition:

- Orders that had a low probability of being treated (e.g., unusual treated orders) receive larger weights, because they represent a larger "effective" segment of the population under a hypothetical randomized design.
- Orders that had a high probability of being treated (e.g., ones that almost always get the new algo) receive smaller weights.

In the reweighted sample, the distribution of X among treated units and the distribution of X among controls are, ideally, similar. Under unconfoundedness and overlap, comparing weighted average outcomes between the two groups then recovers the ATE.

For ATT and ATC, the weighting formulas change slightly (for example, controls are reweighted to look like treated units for ATT), but the basic idea remains: use propensity-based weights to create balance in X.

Stabilized weights

Raw IPW weights can be highly variable, especially when some units have $\hat{e}(X)$ close to 0 or 1. This is common in trading data: certain segments almost always receive treatment or almost never do.

Such extreme weights inflate variance and make estimates unstable. Two common remedies are:

- **Trimming:** discard units with $\hat{e}(X)$ very close to 0 or 1 (e.g., below 0.02 or above 0.98). This focuses the estimand on regions of good overlap.
- **Stabilized weights:** multiply the raw weight by a marginal treatment probability to keep average weights close to 1. For ATE, stabilized weights often take the form:

$$w_i^{stab} = \frac{T_i \cdot p}{\hat{e}(X_i)} + \frac{(1 - T_i) \cdot (1 - p)}{1 - \hat{e}(X_i)},$$

  where p is the overall treated fraction. You do not need to memorize this formula; the key idea is that stabilized weights temper extremes while preserving balance.

In trading implementations, it is good practice to:

- inspect the distribution of weights,
- cap or trim extreme weights,
- and report how sensitive your estimates are to such trimming.

Diagnostics: checking covariate balance

Matching and weighting are only useful if they achieve the goal of balancing covariates between treated and control groups. Therefore, diagnostics are central to a design-first workflow.

Rather than relying on p-values, a common and intuitive diagnostic is the *standardized difference* (or standardized mean difference) for each covariate X_j:

$$\text{StdDiff}_j = \frac{\bar{X}_{j,treated} - \bar{X}_{j,control}}{s_j},$$

where s_j is a pooled standard deviation. Values near zero indicate that treated and control groups have similar means for that covariate.

A typical workflow is:

1. Compute standardized differences for each covariate in the *raw* sample (before matching/weighting).
2. Apply your matching or weighting procedure.
3. Compute standardized differences again, in the matched or weighted sample.
4. Check that differences have shrunk substantively, ideally below some threshold (commonly 0.1 or 0.2 in absolute value).

Balance plots

A convenient way to visualize this is with a "love plot" or balance plot: for each covariate, show two dots on a horizontal axis of standardized difference—one for raw balance, one for adjusted balance—with a vertical line at zero and perhaps dashed lines at ± 0.1 to mark acceptable imbalances.

This allows you to quickly see:

- which covariates were badly imbalanced before design,
- how much improvement matching/weighting delivers,
- whether any covariates remain concerningly imbalanced.

Right after this paragraph we include such a balance diagnostic plot as a template.

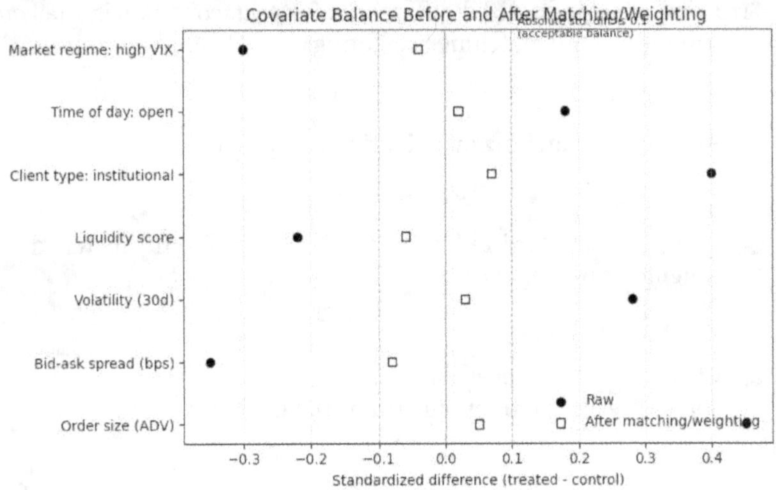

In your own analyses, you should routinely generate such plots and include them in internal documentation for strategy reviews. They make the quality of your design choices transparent.

Overlap and its implications for design

Balance diagnostics often reveal more than just the success of your method—they also reveal *overlap problems*. If certain segments of X have only treated or only control units, no design method can magically fix that. For example:

- If all micro-cap orders use the legacy algo and none use the new algo, you cannot learn the effect for micro-caps from these data.
- If all high-turnover retail accounts use Strategy A and no similar accounts use Strategy B, you cannot compare the strategies credibly in that segment.

In terms of estimands, you are forced to:

- restrict your ATE/ATT/ATC to the subpopulation with overlap,

- or be explicit that estimates for non-overlap regions are extrapolations relying on model assumptions rather than empirical balance.

Trimming on propensity scores, as mentioned earlier, is one way to enforce this in weighting; caliper restrictions play a similar role in matching.

High-dimensional market covariates

Trading datasets often have dozens or hundreds of potentially relevant covariates:

- multiple liquidity and microstructure measures,
- risk factor exposures (industry, style, country),
- client attributes and behavioral features,
- market-state indicators at intraday or higher frequency.

Trying to match exactly on all of them is infeasible; you would find no close matches, and overlap would appear artificially poor. Propensity-based and dimension-reduction strategies help manage this complexity.

Regularized propensity models

Instead of a simple logistic regression, you can fit a regularized model (lasso, ridge, elastic net) for T on X:

- This shrinks or zeroes out coefficients on weak predictors of treatment,
- focuses the design on the most important drivers of treatment assignment,
- and reduces overfitting in high dimensions.

The goal is not perfect prediction of T, but capturing enough of the treatment assignment mechanism to achieve balance on the confounders that matter for Y.

Dimension reduction and summary scores

You can also reduce dimensionality by:

- building a small number of composite risk scores that summarise many correlated variables (e.g., a "liquidity score," "difficulty score," "client sophistication score"),
- using principal components or factor models to condense related variables before matching or weighting on them.

Again, domain knowledge is key: you should think about which aspects of X are most likely to drive both treatment and outcomes, and prioritize those in design.

Pre-specifying confounders

A practical and often underappreciated step is to *pre-specify* a set of confounders before looking at treatment effects. For example:

- For execution studies: size, urgency, liquidity, volatility, spread, venue availability, time-of-day.
- For strategy studies: volatility, beta, turnover, liquidity, sector, market cap.

You then design matching or weighting to balance these pre-specified variables, rather than fishing over hundreds of features ex post. This makes your design more robust and less driven by noise.

Integrating design methods into a backtest pipeline

Finally, consider how to embed matching and propensity weighting into a systematic research workflow.

Separating design from analysis

A core principle is to separate, as much as possible, the design stage from the analysis stage:

1. In the design stage, you use X (and T) but not Y to:
    - specify the propensity model,
    - select matching or weighting approach,
    - tune calipers or trimming thresholds,
    - check covariate balance and overlap.
2. Once you are satisfied with balance, you "freeze" the design.
3. In the analysis stage, you then estimate treatment effects using Y on the matched or weighted sample.

This discipline reduces the risk of overfitting your design to outcome patterns and preserves the conceptual analogy with randomized experiments, where treatment assignment is decided before outcomes are realized.

Avoiding leakage and look-ahead bias

When working with time series or panel data, it is easy to accidentally leak future information into the design:

- Propensity models should use only information available at the time the treatment decision was made.
- Matching should be done on contemporaneous or lagged variables, not future ones.
- If you re-estimate propensity models over time, treat this as you would any other model retraining: use rolling windows or other procedures that respect temporal ordering.

Think of the design process as something that could, in principle, be implemented in real time, given the information set available at that moment.

Choosing between matching, stratification, and weighting

There is no single "best" design method; the choice depends on your data and goals:

- **Matching** is intuitive, easy to explain, and well suited when you have relatively rich overlap and do not face extreme sample size constraints. It naturally targets ATT.
- **Stratification** is simple and effective when a small number of strong confounders drive treatment. It maps closely to how traders think about buckets and segments.
- **Propensity weighting** scales better to high dimensions and complex treatment rules but requires careful attention to overlap, extreme weights, and diagnostics.

In many serious studies, practitioners combine them. For example:

- Estimate a propensity score;
- Trim units with poor overlap;
- Use the remaining sample for nearest-neighbor matching or stratification on propensity score;
- Within the matched/stratified sample, use simple or weighted regression to estimate ATE/ATT/ATC.

These design-based estimators form the backbone for more advanced methods later in the chapter. Doubly robust estimators and causal machine learning will build on the same logic—balance on observables, avoid extrapolation outside overlap, and keep the target estimand clear—while allowing more flexible models for both treatment and outcomes.

4.5 Doubly Robust Estimators and Causal ML

The previous section introduced design-first tools—matching, stratification, and propensity weighting—that use *observed* covariates to mimic randomized experiments under unconfoundedness and overlap. Those approaches are powerful and conceptually transparent, but they face two practical challenges in trading data:

- Markets are complex and high-dimensional; simple parametric models for treatment or outcomes are often misspecified.
- We want to exploit flexible machine learning to capture nonlinearities and interactions, but naive use of ML can introduce new biases, especially when we plug predictions directly into effect formulas.

This section introduces methods that directly address these issues:

- **Doubly robust estimators** such as Augmented Inverse Probability Weighting (AIPW) and Targeted Maximum Likelihood Estimation (TMLE), which combine an outcome model and a propensity model in a way that remains consistent if *either* model is correctly specified.
- **Orthogonalization** and **cross-fitting**, which make effect estimators less sensitive to small errors in nuisance models and reduce overfitting when using flexible ML.
- **Causal ML frameworks**—meta-learners (S-, T-, X-, R-learners) and causal forests—that turn any regression or classification algorithm into tools for estimating ATE and CATE in trading settings.

We remain in the unconfoundedness and overlap world: all confounders are assumed observable and correctly measured; the goal is to *estimate* the causal effects more robustly and flexibly.

From design-only to model-assisted estimation

Design-first approaches focus almost exclusively on balancing covariates. Once you have a balanced sample (e.g., via matching or weighting), a simple difference in means or a low-dimensional regression is often sufficient.

However, when:

- data are noisy and high-dimensional,
- treatment and outcome processes are complex,
- and you care about efficient use of information,

you can often do better by using models of both the treatment process and the outcome process—*as long as you guard against model misspecification and overfitting*.

Doubly robust methods operationalize this idea:

> Combine an outcome model and a propensity model in a way that, if at least one is correct, the resulting effect estimator is consistent. Moreover, small errors in these models only have a second-order impact on the final estimate.

This is particularly attractive in trading, where we may have rich knowledge about treatment assignment (e.g., routing rules) but only approximate outcome models, or vice versa.

Two building blocks: propensity and outcome models

We start from two familiar objects:

- The **propensity score** $e(X) = \Pr(T = 1 \mid X)$, estimated by a treatment model.
- The **outcome regression** $m_t(X) = \mathbb{E}[Y \mid T = t, X]$ for $t \in \{0, 1\}$, estimated by outcome models.

In trading terms:

- $e(X)$ captures how likely a trade or account with features X is to receive the strategy (e.g., be routed to a new algo, use a particular signal, be hedged).
- $m_1(X)$ predicts performance (e.g., shortfall, alpha, P&L) if the strategy is used; $m_0(X)$ predicts performance under baseline behavior.

Traditional IPW estimators use $e(X)$ alone; standard regression estimators use $m_t(X)$ alone. Doubly robust methods use both simultaneously.

Augmented Inverse Probability Weighting (AIPW)

AIPW is a canonical doubly robust estimator of the ATE. It can be thought of as:

> Outcome regression plus a weighted correction term that uses the propensity scores to fix any systematic bias in the regression, and vice versa.

At a high level, the steps are:

1. Estimate $\hat{e}(X)$, $\hat{m}_1(X)$, and $\hat{m}_0(X)$ using your preferred models (logit, trees, boosting, neural nets, etc.).
2. For each unit i, compute a pseudo-outcome that combines:
    - the predicted outcomes $\hat{m}_1(X_i)$ and $\hat{m}_0(X_i)$,
    - the realized outcome Y_i,
    - and the treatment indicator T_i with inverse-propensity weights.
3. Average these pseudo-outcomes across units to estimate the ATE (or adapt formulas for ATT/ATC).

The exact algebra is not essential here. The intuition is:

- The outcome model provides a baseline prediction of what each unit would earn under each treatment arm.
- The IPW-like correction tilts things so that, in expectation, any systematic under- or over-prediction in one model is corrected using information from the other.

Doubly robust property

AIPW is *doubly robust*: if either

- the propensity model $e(X)$ is correctly specified, or
- the outcome regression models $m_t(X)$ are correctly specified,

then the AIPW estimator of ATE is consistent (given unconfoundedness and overlap). It need not be perfect at both.

In trading, this is useful because:

- You may model treatment well (e.g., you know the routing rules precisely), but outcome dynamics are complex. Or
- You may have strong predictive models for returns or shortfall but only approximate information about how traders decide to apply the strategy.

AIPW lets you safely combine these two sources of structure. You can, for instance, use a carefully engineered propensity model plus a flexible ML return model and still preserve correct effect estimation if at least one is sufficiently accurate.

Orthogonalization: making estimators insensitive to small errors

The deeper reason AIPW works well with flexible ML is the idea of *orthogonalization* (also called Neyman orthogonality). In non-technical terms, an orthogonal estimating equation is constructed so that:

> Small estimation errors in the nuisance models (propensity and outcome) have only a second-order effect on the main parameter of interest (the treatment effect).

Geometrically, you can think of projecting the parameter of interest onto a direction that is nearly orthogonal to the space spanned by errors in nuisance models. Small deviations in those models then move you mostly sideways rather than directly in the direction of the parameter.

Practically, this means:

- You can plug in high-capacity ML models (random forests, boosting, deep nets) for $e(X)$ and $m_t(X)$ without needing them to be perfectly specified.
- As long as those models are reasonably accurate and not overfitted, the final effect estimate remains stable and asymptotically normal, enabling standard error estimation.

AIPW is one example of such an orthogonal estimator; TMLE and R-learners, discussed below, use similar principles.

Cross-fitting: guarding against overfitting with ML

When you use ML to estimate nuisance models, a major risk is *overfitting*: the model learns noise in the sample and fits Y or T too closely. If you then compute AIPW-type corrections on the same data, these overfitted predictions can introduce bias into your effect estimates.

Cross-fitting is a simple yet powerful remedy:

1. Split your data into K folds (e.g., 2 or 5 folds), respecting time ordering if needed.
2. For each fold k:
    - Estimate nuisance models $e(X)$, $m_t(X)$ using all data *except* fold k.

- Compute predictions $\hat{e}(X_i)$, $\hat{m}_t(X_i)$ only for units i in fold k using these out-of-fold models.

3. Combine all folds and use the out-of-fold predictions in your AIPW or TMLE formulas.

This guarantees that:

- For each unit, the nuisance model predictions are made using data that did not include that unit's outcome.
- Overfitting the nuisance models cannot directly "cheat" by using a unit's own noise to bias the pseudo-outcome.

In trading applications, you should also ensure that cross-fitting respects temporal structure:

- Use rolling or block cross-fitting where training folds precede test folds in time to avoid look-ahead bias.
- Avoid mixing future information into past estimates when constructing nuisance models.

With orthogonality and cross-fitting in place, doubly robust estimators become a solid foundation for plugging modern ML into causal effect estimation.

Targeted Maximum Likelihood Estimation (TMLE)

Targeted Maximum Likelihood Estimation (TMLE) is another doubly robust framework that more explicitly "targets" the estimand of interest.

The workflow is:

1. Fit an initial outcome model $\hat{m}_t^{(0)}(X)$ using flexible ML (possibly ignoring treatment at this stage).

2. Use the estimated propensity scores $\hat{e}(X)$ to construct a clever "tilting" update to $\hat{m}_t^{(0)}(X)$, focusing specifically on improving fit in parts of the outcome model that most affect the target estimand (e.g., ATE).
3. Compute the effect estimate from this *targeted* outcome model.

The details involve solving a simple, low-dimensional regression or score equation that adjusts $\hat{m}_t^{(0)}(X)$ only in the directions most relevant for the causal estimand. Intuitively:

- The initial ML model captures as much structure as possible.
- The TMLE step nudges that model just enough to make it align with the causal estimating equation defined by the propensity scores.

TMLE shares the double robustness property: if either the initial outcome model or the propensity model is correct, the estimator is consistent. It also achieves good efficiency properties and lends itself to robust inference.

In trading, TMLE is attractive when:

- you already have powerful predictive models for returns or slippage (perhaps built for forecasting or risk management),
- you want to adapt those models minimally to answer specific causal questions about strategy deployment or policy changes.

A causal ML pipeline: putting it together

Before diving into meta-learners and causal forests, it is useful to summarize the generic causal ML pipeline that now emerges:

1. **Specify the estimand:** ATE, ATT, ATC, or CATE for a particular unit and horizon.
2. **Choose nuisance models:** flexible ML models for:

- treatment assignment $e(X)$,
- outcome regression $m_t(X)$.

3. **Estimate nuisance models with cross-fitting:** ensure out-of-fold predictions to avoid overfitting bias.

4. **Apply an orthogonal, doubly robust estimator:** AIPW, TMLE, or R-learner style residualization, using the nuisance predictions.

5. **Estimate uncertainty:** use asymptotic variance formulas or bootstrap methods adapted to the orthogonal estimator.

The following diagram summarizes this workflow and its connections to meta-learners.

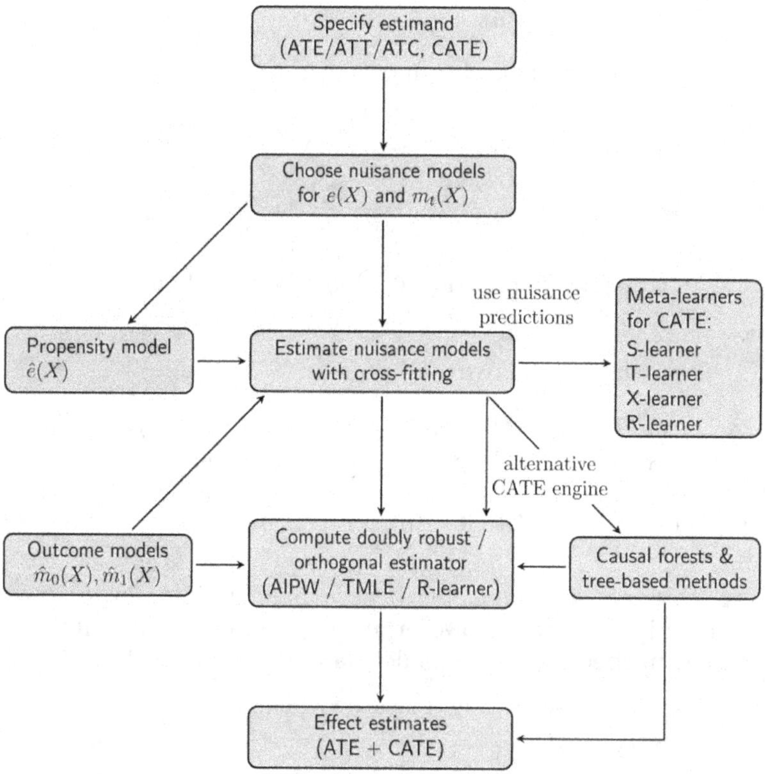

Meta-learners: turning prediction engines into effect estimators

Meta-learners are templates that show how to use off-the-shelf prediction algorithms (for regression or classification) to estimate treatment effects. They are particularly helpful for CATE $\tau(x)$, but they can also provide ATEs as averages of CATEs.

We briefly outline four common meta-learners and their intuition.

S-learner

The S-learner fits a single outcome model:

$$m(X,T) \approx \mathbb{E}[Y \mid X,T].$$

Procedure:

1. Train one model of Y on (X,T) jointly, e.g. a boosted tree: $Y \sim f(X,T)$.
2. For each x, obtain two predictions:
   - $\hat{Y}(1,x)$: predicted outcome if treated ($T=1$),
   - $\hat{Y}(0,x)$: predicted outcome if untreated ($T=0$).
3. Define $\hat{\tau}(x) = \hat{Y}(1,x) - \hat{Y}(0,x)$.

The S-learner is simple and often behaves like a flexible regression with treatment interactions. However, if treatment effects are subtle relative to main effects of X, the model may underemphasize T.

In trading, the S-learner might be used when:

- you expect treatment and control outcomes to share much of the same structure (e.g., both algos respond similarly to many market features),
- you want a single large model that encompasses both regimes.

T-learner

The T-learner fits separate models for treated and control outcomes:

1. Train $m_1(X) \approx \mathbb{E}[Y \mid X, T=1]$ on treated units.
2. Train $m_0(X) \approx \mathbb{E}[Y \mid X, T=0]$ on control units.
3. For each x, define $\hat{\tau}(x) = \hat{m}_1(x) - \hat{m}_0(x)$.

This is intuitive and aligns with earlier outcome-regression ideas. It allows each arm to have its own complex structure, useful when:

- the execution profile of the new algo is fundamentally different from the legacy algo,
- or when strategy-on and strategy-off regimes exhibit very different patterns.

However, if one arm is much smaller or has limited overlap in X, the corresponding model may be weak in those regions, leading to unstable CATE estimates.

X-learner

The X-learner improves on the T-learner when treatment probabilities differ greatly across units. It proceeds in two stages:

1. Fit T-learner models $\hat{m}_1(X)$ and $\hat{m}_0(X)$.
2. Impute individual treatment effects separately in each group:
   - For treated units, define pseudo-effects: $\tilde{\tau}_i^{(1)} = Y_i - \hat{m}_0(X_i)$.
   - For control units, define pseudo-effects: $\tilde{\tau}_i^{(0)} = \hat{m}_1(X_i) - Y_i$.
3. Fit separate models of these pseudo-effects on X in each group, then combine them—often weighting by propensity scores—to obtain $\hat{\tau}(x)$.

Intuitively, the X-learner uses the better-observed arm (treated or control) to inform the imputed counterfactual in the other arm, then directly models the treatment effect. It can be particularly effective when:

- one group (say controls) is abundant and easier to model accurately, while treated units are sparse,
- or vice versa.

In trading, this might align with a setting where the new strategy has been rolled out only sparsely so far, while baseline behavior is well represented in the data.

R-learner

The R-learner is closely connected to orthogonalization and doubly robust ideas. It works roughly as:

1. Estimate the propensity score $\hat{e}(X)$ and the overall outcome regression $\hat{m}(X) = \mathbb{E}[Y \mid X]$.
2. Compute residuals for outcome and treatment:
    - $\tilde{Y}_i = Y_i - \hat{m}(X_i)$,
    - $\tilde{T}_i = T_i - \hat{e}(X_i)$.
3. Regress $\tilde{Y}$ on $\tilde{T}$ with a model that allows the coefficient on $\tilde{T}$ to vary with X; this varying coefficient is $\tau(X)$.

The key orthogonalization step is residualizing both Y and T on X. This removes much of the confounding structure, leaving an equation where the dependence of $\tilde{Y}$ on $\tilde{T}$ is directly informative about the treatment effect, largely insensitive to small errors in the nuisance models.

The R-learner:

- is naturally compatible with cross-fitting and ML for nuisance models,
- behaves like a flexible AIPW/AIPW-for-CATE,
- often performs well in high-dimensional settings.

For trading, R-learners are a strong default when you want both ATE and CATE with robust properties and are willing to build a slightly more complex pipeline.

Causal forests and tree-based CATE estimators

While meta-learners rely on generic ML regressors, *causal forests* and related tree-based methods are built from the ground up to estimate heterogeneous treatment effects.

Conceptually, a causal forest:

- partitions the covariate space X into regions (tree leaves) where treatment effects appear relatively homogeneous,
- estimates local effects within each leaf using balanced splits that aim to create treated-control comparability,
- aggregates many such trees (like a random forest) to stabilize estimates and provide uncertainty measures.

Key advantages in trading contexts:

- **Automatic interaction discovery:** causal forests can discover segments such as "large-cap, high-volatility, morning session" where effects differ, without you pre-specifying all interactions.
- **Built-in honesty and orthogonality:** modern causal forest implementations use sample-splitting (honesty) and orthogonalization tricks to reduce bias and overfitting.
- **Uncertainty quantification:** they provide standard errors or confidence intervals for $\tau(x)$, which is crucial when making capital allocation decisions based on predicted uplift.

For example, you might feed a causal forest:

- X: size in ADV, spread, volatility, liquidity score, client type, time-of-day, market regime indicators,
- T: indicator of using the new execution algo,
- Y: implementation shortfall.

The forest will learn a function $\hat{\tau}(x)$ that tells you, for each type of order, the expected shortfall improvement from using the new algo. You can then:

- rank order buckets of flow by predicted CATE,
- restrict deployment to regions where $\hat{\tau}(x)$ is robustly positive,
- use the estimated effect and its uncertainty to guide rollout decisions and risk limits.

Practical recommendations for traders

Given the toolbox now on the table, how should a trading or quant research team proceed?

1. **Start simple:** For global ATE/ATT questions with moderate dimensionality, begin with:
    - a well-specified propensity model (logit or regularized logit),
    - a reasonable outcome regression (e.g., linear model or tree-based method),
    - an AIPW estimator with basic cross-fitting,
    - and thorough balance diagnostics.
2. **Add CATE when targeting matters:** When you need segment-level decisions (where to deploy, which clients/assets), layer on:
    - a meta-learner (T- or R-learner) or a causal forest,
    - with orthogonalization and cross-fitting of nuisance models.
3. **Respect identification assumptions:** None of these methods can fix missing confounders or lack of overlap. Keep thinking in terms of:
    - "Do we have all the key drivers of both treatment and outcomes in X?"

- "Is there support in the data in the regions where we want to apply the strategy?"

4. **Integrate into backtests carefully:** As with matching and weighting:

    - design and estimate nuisance models using only information available at decision time,
    - avoid data leakage and look-ahead,
    - validate effect estimates out-of-sample and in mock rollouts when possible.

5. **Communicate clearly:** When presenting results, emphasize:

    - which estimand is being estimated (ATE vs ATT vs CATE),
    - how nuisance models were built and validated,
    - how robust the conclusions are to model choices and tuning.

Doubly robust estimators and causal ML do not replace the conceptual work of defining the right estimand or checking overlap and unconfoundedness. Rather, they sit on top of that foundation, allowing you to harness the full power of modern machine learning while keeping causal effect estimates stable, interpretable, and relevant for trading decisions.

Chapter 5

Quasi-Experiments & Causal Time-Series Panels

Markets rarely grant you clean randomized trials, yet they're constantly hit by policy changes, index rebalances, eligibility thresholds, and one-off shocks. This chapter shows you how to treat those frictions and events as quasi-experiments, stitching together time-series and panel methods so you can tell whether a trading edge is truly causal-or just another backtest illusion.

5.1 Difference-in-Differences and Event Studies

In the previous chapter we focused on the basic potential-outcomes logic for causal claims in markets: define a treatment, think carefully about the counterfactual path of outcomes without that treatment, and then look for settings where the treated and untreated paths are comparable. We now turn to two workhorse designs that operationalize this logic in time-stamped financial data: *difference-in-differences* (DiD) and *event studies*.

Both are, at heart, ways to answer a simple question:

> *How would treated assets have evolved over time if they had remained untreated?*

In market applications, "time" is almost always central: regulation arrives on a date; index rebalancing occurs overnight; a new trading venue opens at a known point in calendar time. DiD and event-study designs exploit these timing features to construct plausible counterfactual trends for treated assets, using the behavior of other assets as a yardstick.

Throughout this section, think in terms of a concrete example:

- Treatment: A new liquidity regulation that applies only to banks above a certain size threshold.
- Outcome: Daily CDS spreads or equity returns of bank stocks.
- Units: Individual banks (or portfolios of banks), observed over many days.

We will use this type of setting to motivate each step of the design, estimation, and diagnostic process.

The Core Difference-in-Differences Idea

Suppose a regulation takes effect on day T^*. Some banks (the treated group) are covered by the rule; others (the control group) are not. We observe an outcome Y_{it} (say, log CDS spread) for bank i on day t, for t both before and after T^*.

The simplest DiD setup compares two changes:

1. The change in outcomes for treated banks from pre to post.
2. The change in outcomes for control banks from pre to post.

The difference between these two changes is the "difference-in-differences." Intuitively:

- The treated change reflects both the regulation effect and any underlying market trend (for example, a general decline in spreads).
- The control change reflects only the underlying market trend.
- Subtracting the control change from the treated change removes (differences out) that common trend, leaving an estimate of the regulation's causal effect.

This logic carries directly into a regression with many assets and many days. A standard baseline DiD specification is:

- Unit fixed effects: one intercept per asset i capturing time-invariant differences (size, business model, average risk).
- Time fixed effects: one intercept per day t capturing market-wide movements (macro news, volatility spikes).
- A treatment indicator that turns on for treated units after the intervention date.

The coefficient on the treatment indicator is interpreted as the *average treatment effect on treated units*, after adjusting for unit-specific levels and common time shocks.

Event Studies as Dynamic DiD

The basic DiD framework is inherently "two-period": it asks how much the average level of an outcome changes from "before" to "after." In markets, however, we are rarely satisfied with a single before/after contrast. We usually care about the *dynamic response*:

- Do spreads start moving in anticipation of the regulation?
- Is there a sharp jump exactly on the event date?
- Do effects fade out or build up over weeks and months?

Event-study designs generalize DiD by replacing a single post-treatment indicator with a set of *event-time* indicators. For each day relative to the event—for example, 10 days before, 5 days after, 30 days after—we estimate a separate treatment effect. Each of these coefficients says: "relative to a baseline pre-event period, how far above or below would the outcome have been if we had turned off the regulation?"

You can think of an event study as a high-resolution DiD:

- DiD tells you the average treatment effect across the entire post period.
- Event studies trace out a treatment-effect path over time.

This is particularly powerful in trading contexts where timing matters for implementation—if you expect a delayed market response, you do not want to size your trade as if all the effect is instantaneous.

Panel Structure: Treated and Control Assets over Time

Both DiD and event studies rely on panel data: repeated outcomes for many assets over time. Before we formalize anything, it is useful to have a mental picture of the panel:

- Rows: Assets (treated and control).
- Columns: Time (days or months).
- Entries: Outcomes (returns, spreads, volumes).

The treatment pattern shows up as blocks of ones and zeros in this panel: for a treated asset, the treatment indicator is zero before the event date and one after; for a control asset, it may remain zero throughout.

Right after we introduce this conceptual setup, it is convenient to link the data layout to its main output: the event-time coefficient path. The following diagram highlights how the panel structure and dynamic coefficients fit together.

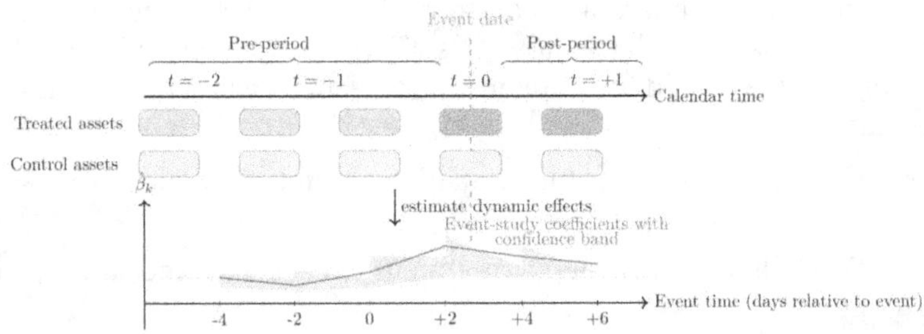

This figure combines three elements:

- A panel of treated and control assets evolving through pre and post periods.
- An event date that splits time into "before" and "after."
- An estimated path of event-time coefficients with confidence bands, summarizing the dynamic causal effect.

We now turn to the assumptions needed for this panel design to have a causal interpretation.

The Parallel-Trend Assumption

The central identifying assumption in DiD and its event-study extension is the *parallel-trend* assumption. Informally:

> In the absence of treatment, treated and control assets would have followed parallel paths over time.

That does not mean their levels must be equal; treated banks may have systematically higher spreads than controls. It means that, absent the intervention, the *change* in outcomes over time would have been the same in both groups, once you adjust for common time shocks.

Why is this plausible in some financial settings?

- If the treatment is triggered by a regulatory rule (for example, "assets above \$X billion"), treated and control banks near the threshold may be very similar except for the rule.
- Market-wide factors (interest rates, volatility, macro news) hit all banks at roughly the same time, and are captured by time fixed effects.
- Persistent differences across banks (size, average risk profile) are absorbed by unit fixed effects.

Parallel trends is *not* guaranteed just because you include fixed effects; it is an additional assumption about how untreated potential outcomes move. Your job is to argue, using institutional detail and data, that it is plausible—and to show where it might fail.

Diagnosing Parallel Trends: Graphs, Placebos, and Tests

Because parallel trends is untestable in the strict sense (we never observe the treated group in a world where the regulation never happened), we lean heavily on diagnostics using *pre-treatment* data.

Graphical checks. Plots are the first line of defense. Common practices include:

- Plot the average outcome for treated and control assets over time, normalized to zero at a reference date.
- Overlay event-study coefficients for pre-treatment periods (for example, $k = -10, \ldots, -1$ days relative to the event).

If parallel trends holds, the treated-control gap should be roughly flat in the pre period, and pre-event coefficients should cluster around zero within statistical noise.

Placebo interventions. Another useful diagnostic is to pretend the event happened earlier than it did, and re-estimate the DiD or event study. If you "assign" a fake treatment date several months before the true regulation and still find a large "effect," that casts serious doubt on parallel trends.

Formal pre-trend tests. Regression-based event studies allow you to formally test whether pre-treatment coefficients are jointly equal to zero. This is often done by:

- Choosing one pre-event period as the omitted baseline.
- Estimating coefficients for earlier pre-event periods.
- Running an F-test for the joint null that all those coefficients equal zero.

These tests should be interpreted with care: failing to reject does not prove parallel trends; passing the test with flying colors is encouraging but not definitive. Nonetheless, clear upward or downward pre-trends are strong evidence against the design.

In applications that might inform trading or risk limits, you should treat parallel-trend diagnostics as a non-negotiable requirement. Without them, DiD estimates are little more than dressed-up correlations.

Staggered Adoption: When Units Are Treated at Different Times

In many regulatory or institutional changes, not all assets are treated at the same date. Banks cross a size threshold in different years, firms are added to an index at different rebalancing dates, or exchanges roll out new fee structures in stages. This is known as *staggered adoption*.

Naively throwing staggered treatment timing into a two-way fixed-effects regression with a single treatment indicator can create subtle problems:

- Already-treated units may act as "controls" for units treated later.
- Heterogeneous treatment effects over time can induce negative or hard-to-interpret implicit weights on different comparisons.

To see the intuition, imagine three firms:

- Firm A: Treated in 2018.
- Firm B: Treated in 2020.
- Firm C: Never treated.

When you estimate a simple two-way fixed-effects DiD, the comparison that identifies the effect for 2019 includes A (already treated), B (not yet treated), and C (never treated). But if A's treatment effect is large and grows over time, treating A as a "control" for B in certain periods produces contaminated comparisons.

Modern DiD methods handle staggered adoption more transparently by:

- Defining *group-time average treatment effects*: for each cohort (for example, "treated in 2018") and each event time k, estimate the effect for that cohort at that relative horizon.
- Using only not-yet-treated and never-treated units as controls for a given treated cohort and time.
- Aggregating these group-time effects with explicit, user-chosen weights (e.g., by market capitalization) rather than opaque regression weights.

From a practical standpoint, the message is:

> When treatment timing is staggered, do not rely blindly on a single two-way fixed-effects coefficient. Use methods that respect event time and cohort structure, and always inspect group-specific dynamics.

For trading applications, staggered adoption is more the rule than the exception. You will frequently care about how effects evolve for early versus late adopters, which directly calls for this group-time perspective.

Abnormal Returns and Event-Study Mechanics

So far we have spoken in terms of general outcomes (like spreads), but much of empirical finance uses *returns*-based event studies. The core steps are:

1. Define an *event window* around each intervention: for example, day -1 to day $+1$ around the regulation announcement.
2. Estimate a *normal-return model* for each asset in a pre-event estimation window (for example, 250 trading days before the event). Typical models include:
   - A constant mean return.
   - A market model (regress returns on a market index).
   - Multifactor models (e.g., Fama-French).
3. Compute *abnormal returns* as the realized return minus the predicted normal return for each day in the event window.
4. Aggregate abnormal returns across the event window to obtain cumulative abnormal returns (CARs) for each asset.
5. Average CARs across treated units (or compare treated versus control) and assess statistical significance.

The linkage to DiD is straightforward:

- The normal-return model plays a similar role to unit and time fixed effects: it provides a prediction for what would have happened in the absence of the event.
- Abnormal returns are the counterpart of deviations from the parallel trend.
- When you compare abnormal returns for treated and control assets, you are implicitly implementing a DiD design in return space.

In panel regressions, instead of computing abnormal returns first, we often embed the factor model directly into the DiD or event-study specification by including market and factor returns as controls.

Cross-Sectional Dependence and Robust Inference

A major complication in market data is that assets do not move independently. Shocks are shared across firms, sectors, and countries. This *cross-sectional dependence* matters for event studies and DiD because it can make standard errors far too small if ignored.

Two common sources of dependence are:

- **Common risk factors**: Market, size, value, momentum, and other factors that co-move returns across many assets.
- **Sectoral or geographic shocks**: News specific to a sector (for example, energy prices) or region (for example, regional banking stress).

If you treat each asset-day observation as independent, your inference will be overconfident. To address this, practitioners use:

Clustered standard errors. The most widely used correction is to cluster by unit and/or time:

- Clustering by unit (asset) allows for arbitrary serial correlation within each asset's time series.
- Clustering by time allows for cross-sectional correlation across assets on the same day (for example, a market-wide shock).

In panels with many assets and many days, two-way clustering (by asset and by day) is often appropriate.

Portfolio-level aggregation. Another practical approach in returns-based event studies is to aggregate up to portfolios before running regressions. For example, compute an equal-weight or value-weight average abnormal return for treated and control portfolios each day, and then run the event study at the portfolio level. This reduces cross-sectional dependence within portfolios and focuses on economically meaningful units (e.g., the treated portfolio versus the rest of the market).

Factor adjustments. Including factor returns (market, size, value, etc.) directly in the regression absorbs a large share of the common component, leaving residuals that are closer to cross-sectionally independent. This does not remove the need for robust standard errors, but it improves the signal-to-noise ratio in the estimated treatment path.

For risk committees and trading desks, the takeaway is that standard errors from naive OLS on a large asset-by-time panel are almost always misleading. If your estimated effect looks "precise" only because you ignored correlation across assets and over time, you should treat the result as unproven.

Design, Estimation, and Stress-Testing in Practice

Putting the pieces together, a practical workflow for DiD and event studies in financial markets looks like this:

1. **Clarify the treatment and estimand.** What is the intervention (regulation, index change, fee schedule) and which units are treated when? What outcome matters for your decision (returns, spreads, volumes, volatility)?

2. **Build the panel.** Assemble asset-level or portfolio-level data with consistent time stamps, mark treatment timing for each unit, and track any staggered adoption patterns.

3. **Choose the specification.** Decide whether a simple DiD is sufficient or whether you need a full event-study path. For staggered adoption, favor group-time average treatment effects over a single two-way fixed-effects coefficient.

4. **Model the counterfactual.** Include unit and time fixed effects and relevant controls or factor returns. For classic event studies, estimate normal-return models and compute abnormal returns.

5. **Diagnose parallel trends.** Use graphs, pre-trend tests, and placebo interventions. If pre-trends are strong or placebo effects are large, reconsider the design (for example, refine the control group or restrict to a window where trends are more comparable).

6. **Use robust inference.** Account for cross-sectional and serial dependence via clustering, factor adjustments, or portfolio aggregation.

7. **Stress-test the findings.** Vary the event window, control group definition, and weighting schemes. Check whether results are driven by a single large asset or short subperiod. In trading terms, ask: "Would this effect survive realistic transaction costs and risk constraints?"

By the end of this process you should not only have a point estimate of the treatment effect, but also a nuanced picture of its timing, its heterogeneity across cohorts, and its robustness to alternative specifications. DiD and event-study designs are powerful precisely because they force you to articulate the counterfactual path and then defend it, visually and statistically, against the messy realities of market data.

In the next sections we will extend this logic to designs where treatment is assigned by thresholds (regression discontinuity) and where we must build counterfactuals for a single treated market (synthetic control), but the core idea you have seen here will remain the same: combine time variation with quasi-experimental structure to move from correlation to credible causal claims.

5.2 Regression Discontinuity Designs

In the previous section we used difference-in-differences and event studies to exploit *time* as the key source of quasi-experimental variation. We compared treated and control assets before and after an intervention, under a parallel-trend assumption.

In this section, time largely steps into the background. The quasi-experiment now comes from a *rule*: a threshold or cutoff in some score that determines who is treated and who is not. These threshold rules are common in financial markets:

- Equity indices include firms with free-float market capitalization above a cutoff.

- Margin requirements tighten once an account's risk measure exceeds a limit.
- Regulatory capital or liquidity rules switch tiers at specific size thresholds.
- Collateral haircuts change when a security's rating crosses a rating notch.

Regression discontinuity designs (RDDs) turn these rules into local experiments. The central idea is simple and powerful:

> Units just above and just below a deterministic cutoff are very similar in all respects except treatment status, so differences in their outcomes can be interpreted as causal.

We will first build the basic "sharp" RDD in a single cross-section, then extend to "fuzzy" RDDs where treatment around the cutoff is probabilistic, and finally discuss how these ideas carry over to panel and time-series settings that are typical in trading and risk management.

From Cutoff Rules to Local Experiments

Every regression discontinuity design has three core ingredients:

- A **running variable**: a continuous or finely measured score X (for example, market capitalization rank, risk score, or collateral rating).
- A **cutoff** c: treatment eligibility changes when X crosses c.
- An **outcome** Y: the variable whose causal response to treatment we want to estimate (price impact, spread change, leverage, volume, and so on).

Think of an index-inclusion rule: firms with market-cap rank better (smaller number) than c enter the index; those worse than c do not. The running variable X is the rank; the cutoff c is the inclusion threshold; the treatment is "being in the index."

Now imagine zooming in tightly around the cutoff. Focus only on firms ranked $c-1, c, c+1$, maybe up to a few positions on either side. These nearby firms are similar in size and other fundamentals; they all live in the same part of the cross-sectional distribution. If the rule is strictly applied and not manipulable, exactly at the cutoff the treatment status changes almost as if randomly.

This "as if random" variation near the cutoff is what makes RDD a quasi-experiment:

- Units far away from the cutoff are very different, and comparing them would be confounded.
- Units near the cutoff differ mainly in whether they received the treatment induced by the rule.

The limit we care about is therefore *local*: the jump in the expected outcome Y as we cross the threshold in the running variable X.

Sharp Regression Discontinuity: Treatment Jumps from 0 to 1

A **sharp** RDD is the cleanest case: treatment switches deterministically from 0 to 1 when X crosses c. Formally:

- If $X_i \geq c$, unit i is treated (for example, included in the index).
- If $X_i < c$, unit i is not treated.

There are no exceptions: everyone above the cutoff is treated, everyone below is untreated.

Graphically, we look at a scatter plot of Y versus X around the cutoff. If the treatment has a causal effect, we should see an abrupt jump in the conditional average of Y right at c, even though the underlying trend of Y in X might be smooth. RDD estimation then boils down to two tasks:

1. Estimate the outcome trend in X just to the left of c.

2. Estimate the outcome trend in X just to the right of c.
3. Compare the two at $X = c$.

The difference between these two *limits* is the *local treatment effect at the cutoff*. Because we are only using observations close to the cutoff, this is a *local* effect; it need not equal the average effect for all units.

Near-Threshold Observations as Quasi-Random

Why is it legitimate to treat near-threshold units as quasi-randomly assigned to treatment and control? The crucial assumption is **continuity**: everything that affects the outcome smoothly depends on X near c, except for treatment status itself.

If there were no treatment, the expected outcome as a function of X would be smooth through the cutoff. With treatment, we allow a jump in the outcome's conditional mean exactly at c; this jump is the causal effect.

In financial applications, this continuity condition is often plausible when:

- The rule is applied mechanically by an index provider, exchange, or regulator.
- Market participants cannot precisely manipulate X around the cutoff (for example, they cannot exactly choose their final market-cap rank once prices are set).
- Other policies do not change discontinuously at the same threshold.

In contrast, continuity might fail if, say, banks actively target just-below-threshold size to avoid regulation, or if several rules share the same cutoff, creating multiple jumps.

Because this near-cutoff quasi-randomness is so central, it is helpful to visualize it immediately.

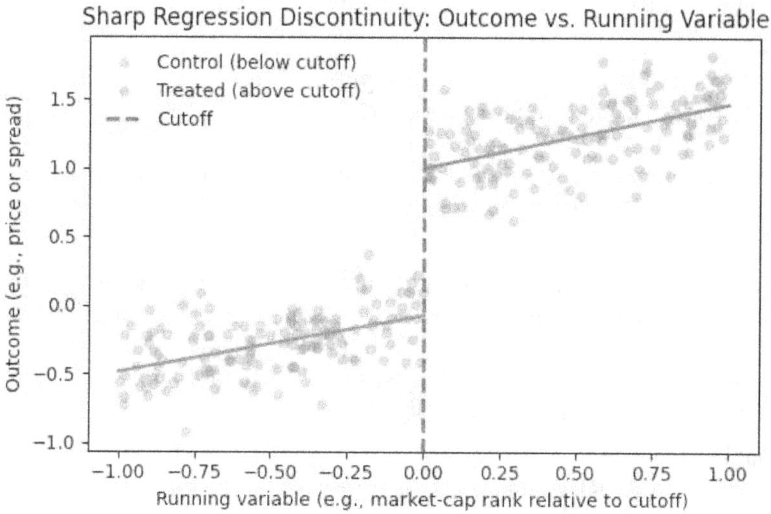

In the figure, the gray and blue points are firms below and above the cutoff. The fitted lines show the local trend on each side. The vertical red line marks the threshold. The jump between the two fitted lines at the cutoff is the sharp RDD estimate.

Practical Estimation: Bandwidth and Local Polynomials

In practice, we do not use all observations in the sample. We restrict attention to those within a *bandwidth* h around the cutoff. Only units with X in $[c-h, c+h]$ enter the RDD estimation. There is a trade-off:

- Smaller bandwidth: observations are more comparable (closer to the cutoff), but we have less data and higher sampling noise.
- Larger bandwidth: more data and lower noise, but a greater risk that the relationship between X and Y is not well approximated by a simple function over the whole window.

Similarly, we choose a *polynomial* order to approximate the smooth relationship between X and Y on each side of c. In modern practice:

- **Local linear** (first-order) polynomials on each side, with appropriate kernel weights, are the default.
- Higher-order (quadratic or cubic) polynomials can easily overfit and introduce artificial wiggles near the cutoff.

For traders and analysts, the right question is: "How complicated does the functional form need to be to capture the smooth variation in Y with X near the threshold?" The answer is usually "not very." A straight line on each side, fitted within a reasonably narrow window, is often sufficient and statistically robust.

Data-driven bandwidth selectors, available in most software implementations of RDD, balance bias and variance using asymptotic formulas. For applied work:

- Start with a recommended bandwidth from such a selector.
- Perform sensitivity checks using slightly smaller and larger bandwidths.
- Report how the estimated jump and its standard error change as you vary h.

If your conclusions flip sign or lose significance when you slightly change the bandwidth, your design is fragile.

Trading Applications of Sharp RDD

Sharp RDDs appear naturally whenever:

- A rule is precisely enforced at a cutoff.
- Treatment is an unambiguous, deterministic function of the running variable.

Some canonical trading-related examples include:

Index inclusion and deletion. Many indices have deterministic inclusion rules based on size, liquidity, or ranking. Near the cutoff, being just inside or outside the index can have large implications for:

- Ownership by index funds and ETFs.
- Liquidity and trading volume.
- Price impact around rebalancing events.

A sharp RDD can estimate, for example, the causal effect of index membership on stock liquidity by comparing firms just above and below the inclusion threshold.

Collar or margin-rule thresholds. Brokerage platforms and exchanges sometimes change margin requirements or collateral haircuts when an internal risk score crosses a threshold. Accounts or securities just above and just below the risk limit can be compared to measure the causal impact of tighter margins on leverage, trading activity, or liquidation risk.

In both cases, the sharp RDD tells you the local impact at exactly the point where the rule bites. For trading, this can inform strategies that position around thresholds (for example, anticipating flows into newly included index members) or risk controls that pay special attention to accounts on the verge of a margin change.

Fuzzy Regression Discontinuity: Probabilistic Treatment Jumps

The sharp RDD assumes that treatment changes deterministically at the cutoff. In practice, financial rules are often implemented with some discretion or noise:

- Index committees override the mechanical rule for some firms.
- Some accounts above a risk threshold negotiate exceptions or delay.

- Not all securities eligible for a new facility actually tap it.

In such settings, the cutoff still matters, but it affects the *probability* of treatment rather than treatment itself. This is the **fuzzy** RDD:

- The probability of treatment jumps at $X = c$.
- Some units below c are treated; some above c are not.

Conceptually, a fuzzy RDD is like an instrumental-variables design where the cutoff indicator (above or below c) serves as an instrument for actual treatment:

- **First stage:** How much does crossing the cutoff change the probability of treatment?
- **Reduced form:** How much does crossing the cutoff change the expected outcome?

The ratio of the reduced-form jump in Y to the first-stage jump in treatment probability gives a *local average treatment effect* (LATE) for units whose treatment status is actually shifted by crossing the threshold (the "compliers" with the rule).

In trading terms, fuzzy RDD answers questions like:

> "For firms whose index inclusion truly depends on crossing the size cutoff—not for those included or excluded regardless—what is the causal effect of inclusion on liquidity or valuation?"

Estimation proceeds much like sharp RDD, but with two key differences:

- You estimate and plot both the jump in treatment probability and the jump in outcomes at the cutoff.
- You interpret the effect as applying to compliers, not to all units near the threshold.

Diagnostics: Manipulation, Donut RDDs, and Placebos

RDDs rely heavily on the assumption that units cannot precisely manipulate their running variable around the cutoff, and that other unobservables do not jump at the same point. Several diagnostics help assess this:

Density tests. If agents actively sort just below or above the threshold, the density of X will be distorted near c. A standard test (often called the McCrary test) examines whether the distribution of X has a discontinuity at the cutoff. A large excess mass just below the cutoff, for example, suggests manipulation (for instance, firms managing their size to avoid regulation).

Covariate continuity. You can treat other pre-determined characteristics (size, leverage, sector) as "placebo outcomes" and run an RDD on them. If pre-determined covariates show sharp jumps at the cutoff, that undermines the continuity assumption.

Donut RDDs. If you suspect manipulation exactly at the cutoff (for example, accounts engineered to be barely below a margin threshold), you can drop observations within a very narrow band around c and re-estimate the RDD using a "donut" window: keeping observations somewhat above and below, but not too close. If the estimated effect remains similar, your results are more robust to small-scale manipulation.

Placebo cutoffs. Another useful robustness check is to repeat the analysis at false thresholds where no policy changes. If you detect large "effects" at these placebo cutoffs, it suggests that your design is picking up smooth nonlinearities in X or general noise, rather than a true discontinuity.

For high-stakes trading or policy conclusions, these diagnostics are not optional. They should be presented alongside the main estimate, not buried in an appendix.

RDD in Panels and Time-Series: Repeated Cross-Sections

So far we have described RDD as a one-shot cross-sectional design. In markets, we often observe the same units over time, and the cutoff-based rule might apply repeatedly (for example, annual index reconstitution, periodic margin reviews, or rolling eligibility for liquidity facilities).

There are two main ways panel structure interacts with RDD:

Repeated cross-sectional RDD. You can apply RDD separately in each period where the rule is evaluated and then average effects across periods. For example, you can:

- Estimate the index-inclusion effect at each annual reconstitution date.
- Stack these event-level cross-sections to increase power.

RDD with fixed effects. If unit-specific unobservables matter and the running variable changes over time, you can embed RDD logic within a panel regression that includes unit and time fixed effects, while still focusing on units near the cutoff in each period. Conceptually, you are running *local* DiD: exploiting within-unit changes in treatment status as the running variable crosses the threshold over time, while maintaining the local comparison around each crossing.

Regardless of implementation, the key remains the same: we only trust comparisons for units that lie close to the cutoff in each episode, and we allow smooth time-varying trends in Y with X around that threshold.

Design Choices for Traders and Risk Managers

From the perspective of someone designing a study to inform trading or risk limits, the main design choices in RDD are:

- **Cutoff definition:** Make sure the cutoff is well-defined and truly governs treatment. Study the rulebook or methodology document; do not rely on an informal description.

- **Running variable measurement:** Use the precise measure that the rule uses (for example, free-float market-cap rank at a specific date, not a rough proxy).
- **Bandwidth and polynomial order:** Default to local linear models with data-driven bandwidths, then perform robustness checks with smaller/larger h.
- **Sharp vs fuzzy:** Carefully distinguish deterministic from probabilistic treatment near the cutoff and choose sharp or fuzzy RDD accordingly.
- **Diagnostics:** Always show density tests, covariate continuity checks, and placebo cutoffs when possible.

When these elements are lined up, RDD provides a highly transparent and intuitive estimate: "Holding everything else smooth in the running variable, what is the discrete jump in the outcome caused by crossing this financial threshold?" That is exactly the question many threshold-based trading and risk decisions hinge on.

In the next section we will move to settings where a single market or asset experiences a unique intervention and there is no obvious control group at all. There, the RDD idea of "local counterfactuals" will reappear in a different guise, via synthetic controls and matrix-completion methods.

5.3 Synthetic Control and Matrix Completion

In the previous sections, we exploited two main kinds of quasi-experiments:

- *Time-based* variation, using difference-in-differences and event studies to compare treated and control assets before and after an intervention.
- *Threshold-based* variation, using regression discontinuity designs where treatment switches at a known cutoff in a running variable.

Both approaches share a common feature: there is a reasonably large pool of untreated units that can play the role of a control group. In many important financial questions, however, this is not true. Sometimes there is only *one* treated unit:

- A single country introduces a new financial-transaction tax.
- One exchange changes its fee structure or tick size.
- A particular bond is moved from over-the-counter to an electronic limit-order book.

In such cases, there is no obvious one-to-one control asset. Yet we still have rich panel data: many other countries, exchanges, or instruments that evolve over time and are unaffected by the intervention.

Synthetic control and matrix-completion methods are designed precisely for this setting. They combine the logic of DiD (compare treated versus untreated paths over time) with a flexible way to build a credible *counterfactual* for a treated unit when no single control exists.

The Synthetic Control Idea: A Data-Driven Twin

Imagine you want to estimate the effect of a new trading-fee schedule introduced on a specific exchange at date T^*. Let:

- Unit 0 be the treated exchange.
- Units $1, 2, \ldots, J$ be other exchanges that did not change fees.
- Y_{jt} be an outcome of interest for exchange j at time t (for example, quoted spreads or depth).

You would like to know what Y_{0t} would have been after T^* if the fee change had not occurred. No single other exchange is a perfect control: each has different market structures, participants, and regulatory environments.

Synthetic control proposes a simple but powerful compromise:

> Construct a weighted average of untreated units whose pre-treatment path closely matches the treated unit. Use this weighted average as a *synthetic* counterfactual after the intervention.

Formally, we choose non-negative weights $w_1, \ldots, w_J$ that sum to 1. These weights define a "synthetic exchange":

$$Y_t^{\text{syn}} = \sum_{j=1}^{J} w_j Y_{jt}.$$

We select $w_1, \ldots, w_J$ so that, over the pre-treatment period $t \leq T^* - 1$, the synthetic path Y_t^{syn} closely tracks Y_{0t}. The closer the pre-treatment fit, the more believable it is that, absent the intervention, the synthetic path would also track the treated unit in the post period.

The estimated treatment effect at time $t \geq T^*$ is then:

$$\widehat{\tau}_t = Y_{0t} - Y_t^{\text{syn}},$$

that is, the gap between the treated unit and its synthetic twin.

Setting Up the Synthetic Control Problem

In practice, we usually work with more than just the raw outcome series. We also incorporate:

- **Pre-treatment outcomes** at different lags (e.g., average spreads in several sub-periods).
- **Predictor variables** (covariates) that influence the outcome (e.g., trading volume, volatility, macro indicators).

We choose weights w_j to minimize a weighted distance between:

- The vector of pre-treatment characteristics for the treated unit, and

- The corresponding weighted average for the donor pool.

This is an optimization problem:

- Objective: minimize some norm (often a quadratic loss) of the difference between treated and synthetic predictors.
- Constraints: weights are non-negative and sum to 1. This keeps the synthetic control within the convex hull of the donor pool and prevents extrapolation outside observed data.

Conceptually, you are asking:

> "What combination of other markets, with non-negative weights, makes the treated market's pre-treatment behavior look as similar as possible?"

If the treated unit is truly unusual in some dimension, the pre-treatment fit will be poor and synthetic control may not be appropriate. Poor pre-fit is not a nuisance—it's a diagnostic that the available donor pool cannot credibly approximate the treated unit.

Interpreting the Treatment Effect Path

Once we have constructed the synthetic control, we compare the treated and synthetic paths over time:

- Before the intervention, the gap $Y_{0t} - Y_t^{\text{syn}}$ should be close to zero if pre-treatment fit is good.
- After the intervention, any systematic divergence can be interpreted as a treatment effect, subject to the assumption that differences in post-treatment behavior are driven by the intervention rather than an unrelated structural break.

Often we summarize the effect by plotting the entire path of $\widehat{\tau}_t$ and then aggregating it into an average over a post-period window (for example, the first year after the policy change). But the time profile itself is informative: it shows whether the effect is immediate, delayed, persistent, or transitory.

To anchor these ideas visually, it is useful to see the treated and synthetic series side by side.

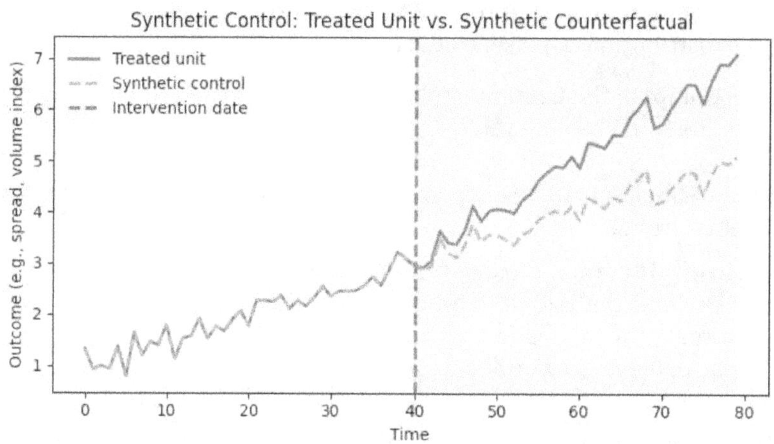

In the figure, the two series track each other closely before the intervention; afterwards, the treated unit gradually diverges upward. The shaded region marks the post-treatment period over which we interpret the gap as a causal effect.

For traders and risk managers, this picture is often more persuasive than a single regression coefficient. It directly answers the question: "How did the treated market behave relative to the best possible composite of other markets that looked like it beforehand?"

Inference via Placebo Tests

Unlike DiD with many units, synthetic control often involves a single treated unit, which makes conventional standard errors less informative. Instead, inference typically relies on *placebo* or *permutation* tests.

Two common strategies are:

In-space placebos. Apply the synthetic-control procedure to each unit in the donor pool as if it were treated at the same time, using the remaining units as donors. For each placebo unit j, you obtain a placebo treatment-effect path. You then:

- Compare the magnitude of the actual treated unit's effect to the distribution of placebo effects.
- Compute the fraction of placebo units whose effect is as large or larger in absolute value; this serves as a kind of p-value.

If the treated unit stands out as a clear outlier, the evidence for a real effect is strong.

In-time placebos. Instead of changing the unit, change the timing. Pretend the intervention occurred at earlier placebo dates and re-estimate the synthetic control. If similarly large "effects" arise at placebo dates where nothing happened, your design is probably capturing unrelated structural breaks rather than the intended policy impact.

From a trading perspective, these placebos are akin to asking: "If I had built the same strategy or story around some other market or some other date, would I have seen a similar pattern?" If the answer is yes, then your apparent edge may be illusory.

When to Use Synthetic Control

Synthetic control is most appropriate when:

- There is a single treated unit (or a small number of treated units) experiencing a unique intervention.
- There is a reasonably rich donor pool of untreated units that share similar pre-treatment dynamics.
- Pre-treatment fit can be made very tight; large pre-period discrepancies undermine credibility.

Examples in finance and trading include:

- Measuring the impact of a new exchange fee schedule on liquidity.
- Assessing the effect of a country's market liberalization or capital-control change on local asset prices.
- Evaluating a unique regulatory reform that affects one jurisdiction or asset class first.

In each case, synthetic control provides a structured way to use all available untreated markets to construct the best possible counterfactual for the treated one.

From Synthetic Control to Matrix Completion

Synthetic control is built around the idea of matching a single treated unit to a weighted combination of other units using pre-treatment data. But modern market datasets are often much richer:

- Multiple units are treated at different times (staggered adoption).
- There may be missing observations in the panel.
- Outcomes often exhibit common factor structures (for example, global and regional risk factors).

Matrix-completion methods generalize synthetic control by viewing the entire panel of outcomes as a large, partially observed matrix:

- Rows correspond to units (stocks, exchanges, countries).
- Columns correspond to time periods.
- Entries are outcomes (returns, spreads, volumes), some of which are unobserved counterfactuals (for example, "treated unit after treatment under no intervention").

The key assumption is that this matrix has a **low-rank structure**, meaning that a small number of latent factors and unit-specific loadings capture most of the variation across time and units. This is closely related to factor models in asset pricing.

Under low rank, we can *complete* the missing entries (counterfactuals) by fitting a low-rank approximation to the observed entries and then using it to predict the unobserved ones. This is the same mathematical machinery that underlies collaborative filtering and recommendation systems.

Matrix Completion as a Panel Counterfactual Tool

Consider again a panel of outcomes Y_{it}, with some cells corresponding to treated units in post-treatment periods. From the perspective of causal inference, these treated cells are "missing" counterfactual outcomes under no treatment. Matrix-completion methods attempt to impute these missing values by exploiting:

- Cross-sectional patterns (how units co-move at a point in time).
- Time-series patterns (how each unit evolves over time).

The typical steps are:

1. Specify a low-rank factor model or regularized objective that penalizes complexity (for example, via nuclear-norm penalties on the matrix of factor loadings).
2. Fit the model using only *untreated* observations and pre-treatment observations for treated units.
3. Use the fitted low-rank structure to impute the missing counterfactual outcomes for treated units in post-treatment periods.
4. Define treatment effects as the difference between realized outcomes and their imputed counterfactuals.

Conceptually, this is a multi-unit extension of synthetic control:

- Synthetic control can be viewed as a special case where you choose unit-specific weights to match pre-treatment outcomes with a convex combination of donors.

- Matrix completion generalizes this to allow for latent factor structures and to handle many treated units and staggered adoption in a unified way.

In finance, this approach is particularly appealing because we already think in terms of factor models: global, regional, sectoral, and style factors that drive returns and spreads. Matrix-completion methods formalize this intuition and apply it to the imputation of counterfactual paths.

Handling Multiple and Staggered Interventions

In modern regulatory environments, interventions often roll out gradually:

- Some countries adopt a trading-tax regime earlier than others.
- Different exchanges phase in new disclosure rules over several years.
- Margin or capital regulations apply to some institutions in one year and to others later.

Matrix-completion and related panel methods are well-suited to this **staggered adoption** setting:

- At any given time, some units are treated, some have not yet been treated, and some may never be treated.
- The low-rank structure is estimated using all units and times where the outcome is not affected by treatment.
- For each treated unit at each post-treatment time, the counterfactual is imputed from the shared factor structure.

This closely complements modern DiD estimators that compute group-time average treatment effects. Whereas DiD focuses on explicit comparisons between treated and control groups at particular times, matrix completion exploits the entire panel's structure to estimate what would have happened absent treatment.

The trade-off is:

- **Pros:** Better use of information when many units are treated at different times, and ability to handle missing data.
- **Cons:** Stronger modeling assumptions (low-rank structure, stable factor loadings) and more complex estimation, which can be sensitive to tuning choices.

For trading applications, these methods can be particularly powerful when you want to understand how a series of regulatory changes or structural shifts across markets have jointly affected prices and liquidity, not just in a single case.

Practical Considerations: Non-Stationarity and Regularization

Real-world market data are rarely stationary. Volatility regimes change, new factors emerge, and correlations shift. This poses challenges for both synthetic control and matrix completion.

Important practical considerations include:

Choice of pre-treatment window. For both methods, you usually select a pre-treatment period over which to fit the counterfactual model. If you go too far back, you risk including data from a different regime; if you use a very short window, you may not have enough information to estimate weights or factors reliably.

Regularization strength. Matrix-completion methods often use regularization (for example, nuclear-norm penalties) to avoid overfitting. Stronger regularization leads to simpler factor structures, which may be more stable out of sample but less flexible in capturing complex dynamics. As always, you should:

- Explore sensitivity to the choice of regularization parameter.
- Use cross-validation on pre-treatment data where possible.

Incorporating volatility and covariance. Markets care not only about average levels (e.g., spreads or returns) but also about volatility and co-movements. In some implementations, you can extend the objective function to give weight to matching not just means but also second moments or factor exposures. For example, you may require the synthetic control to match the treated unit's pre-treatment covariance with key risk factors.

Diagnostics for fit and stability. As with DiD and RDD, diagnostics are crucial:

- Plot pre-treatment fit for treated units: residuals should be small and show no strong drift.
- Check that factor loadings or synthetic weights are economically interpretable (for example, a synthetic exchange built mostly from similar venues, not from unrelated markets).
- Perform placebo and sub-sample checks to see whether inferred treatment effects are robust.

From a risk-committee perspective, you should think of synthetic control and matrix completion as sophisticated but testable modeling choices. Their power comes from combining rich panel structure with clear quasi-experimental timing, but that power must be disciplined by careful validation.

Designing Studies with Synthetic Control and Matrix Completion

To close, it is helpful to summarize how you might decide between these tools in practice:

- Use **synthetic control** when:
  - You have one or a few treated units.
  - A clear intervention date is known.
  - A donor pool exists with reasonably similar units.
  - You want a transparent, visual comparison between treated and synthetic paths.

- Use **matrix completion** (or related low-rank panel methods) when:
  - Many units are treated, often at different times.
  - You suspect a strong factor structure in the data.
  - There is substantial missingness in the panel.
  - You are comfortable imposing and validating stronger modeling assumptions.

Both approaches share the same underlying goal as the rest of this chapter: to construct a credible counterfactual path for what would have happened in the absence of an intervention, using the time-series and cross-sectional richness of financial data. They extend the basic DiD logic into settings where the usual control group intuition breaks down, allowing you to move closer to truly causal answers in complex, evolving markets.

5.4 Instrumental Variables and Two-Stage Least Squares

The methods so far in this chapter—difference-in-differences, event studies, regression discontinuity, and synthetic control—have all shared a common feature: *treatment status was either given by a rule or an external event*. Once you conditioned on time, a cutoff, or an intervention date, you could plausibly treat variation in treatment as exogenous.

In many trading and asset-pricing problems, that luxury disappears. Exposures, leverage, and liquidity choices are often *chosen* by agents who anticipate risks and returns:

- Hedge funds load up on a factor when they expect it to pay off.
- Dealers widen bid-ask spreads when they forecast volatility spikes.
- Banks adjust leverage in response to perceived funding conditions.

In these settings, the key regressor in your model (exposure, spread, leverage) is *endogenous*: it is correlated with unobserved shocks that also affect the outcome. Ordinary least squares (OLS) on such a regression delivers *biased* estimates. If you then build a trading strategy or risk model on top of these biased estimates, you are effectively baking agents' expectations into your "causal" coefficient.

Instrumental variables (IV) and two-stage least squares (2SLS) are designed to solve this problem. They provide a way to recover causal effects when the regressor of interest is chosen in response to information you do not observe, by using additional variables—*instruments*—that move the regressor for reasons unrelated to those unobserved shocks.

Endogeneity in Financial Regressions

Consider a simple example: you want to know how changes in a stock's funding cost affect its return. You might write a regression

$$\text{Return}_{it} = \alpha + \beta\,\text{FundingCost}_{it} + u_{it},$$

where u_{it} captures unobserved news and risk. If funding costs rise in anticipation of bad news (for example, lenders demand higher rates because they foresee trouble), then FundingCost_{it} is positively correlated with u_{it}, and OLS will estimate β as too negative: it will confound "pure" funding effects with the impact of adverse information.

This is a generic pattern:

- Endogeneity arises when the regressor is jointly determined with the error term through some omitted variable, reverse causality, or simultaneity.
- In finance, endogeneity is pervasive because market participants are forward-looking and adjust exposures and prices based on private or hard-to-measure information.

To interpret β causally—"what is the effect on returns of an exogenous change in funding costs?"—we need variation in funding costs that is *not* driven by the unobserved news in u_{it}.

What Is an Instrument?

An **instrument** is a variable Z that helps us isolate exogenous variation in the endogenous regressor X (such as funding cost, leverage, or spread). It must satisfy two core conditions:

- **Relevance:** Z is correlated with X. In other words, changes in the instrument predict changes in the endogenous regressor.
- **Exclusion (validity):** Z affects the outcome Y *only through* X. Conditional on X and other controls, Z is independent of the error term u in the outcome equation.

Put differently, an instrument is a source of *as-if random shocks* to the regressor of interest. It moves X but is otherwise unrelated to the unobserved determinants of Y.

In financial applications, typical candidates include:

- Regulatory or tax-rule changes that alter funding costs or margin requirements for reasons unrelated to a specific asset's news.
- Benchmark or index reweightings that shift investor demand for certain securities.
- Liquidity shocks in upstream funding markets (for example, interbank or repo markets) that affect downstream funding spreads.

The art of IV lies in identifying and defending such instruments, using deep institutional knowledge and careful diagnostics.

Two-Stage Least Squares: Mechanics and Intuition

Two-stage least squares is the standard method to implement IV when you have linear relationships. The idea is simple: instead of regressing Y directly on the problematic X, you first use the instrument to "clean" X, and then use this cleaned version in the outcome regression.

Suppose you have:

- Outcome Y (e.g., returns).
- Endogenous regressor X (e.g., funding cost, leverage, or spread).
- Instrument Z (e.g., regulatory change indicator or benchmark shift).
- Optional controls W (e.g., factors, fixed effects).

First stage: predict the endogenous regressor.

You run a regression of X on the instrument Z and any controls W:

$$X = \pi_0 + \pi_1 Z + \Pi_W W + v.$$

This regression captures how X responds to the exogenous variation in Z (and how it relates to W). From this, you obtain fitted values $\widehat{X}$.

Interpretation:

- $\widehat{X}$ is the component of X that is explained by Z (plus W).
- Because Z is assumed uncorrelated with the error u in the outcome equation, $\widehat{X}$ is also uncorrelated with u.

In other words, $\widehat{X}$ extracts the "exogenous" part of X that comes from the instrument.

Second stage: regress the outcome on the predicted regressor.

You then run a second regression of Y on the fitted values $\widehat{X}$ and the controls W:

$$Y = \alpha + \beta \widehat{X} + \Gamma_W W + \varepsilon.$$

The 2SLS estimator of β is the coefficient on $\widehat{X}$. It answers the question:

> On average, by how much does Y change when X moves in response to changes in the instrument Z, holding W fixed?

Because $\widehat{X}$ is constructed using only exogenous variation from Z (and W), β can be interpreted as a *causal effect* of X on Y for those units whose X is actually moved by Z.

IV as a Ratio of Reduced-Form and First-Stage Effects

There is another way to view 2SLS that is particularly intuitive in quasi-experimental settings: as a *ratio of two differences*.

Suppose Z is binary—for example, an indicator for whether a firm is affected by a regulatory change. Then we can define:

- **First-stage effect:** the impact of Z on X, i.e., the change in funding costs caused by the regulation.
- **Reduced-form effect:** the impact of Z on Y, i.e., the change in returns caused by the regulation, without trying to separate out X.

Under the IV assumptions, the IV estimate of β is essentially:

$$\widehat{\beta}^{IV} = \frac{\text{Effect of } Z \text{ on } Y}{\text{Effect of } Z \text{ on } X}.$$

This has a natural causal interpretation:

> How much do returns change for a given unit change in funding costs, when funding costs are moved by the regulation?

This ratio interpretation is particularly helpful when presenting results to non-technical stakeholders. It clarifies that the identification is driven by the piece of variation in X that comes from the instrument, not from self-selected changes in exposure.

Local Average Treatment Effects in Finance

IV and 2SLS do not generally recover the effect of X on Y for *all* units. Instead, they identify a **local average treatment effect** (LATE): the causal effect for units whose X is actually changed by Z.

In financial terms:

- Some banks may adjust their leverage when margin rules change (compliers).
- Others may maintain their leverage regardless (always-high) or always keep it low (always-low).

The IV estimate captures the effect of leverage on outcomes (such as default risk or funding spread) for banks who adjust their leverage in response to the margin rule change. It does *not* necessarily tell you about banks whose leverage decisions are insensitive to the rule.

For trading and risk decisions, this is a feature, not a bug:

> You are usually most interested in how outcomes respond for units that actually *react* to the policy or instrument.

However, it is crucial to communicate this "local" nature clearly. Extrapolating IV estimates to very different units or regimes (for example, from small illiquid stocks to large blue chips) can be misleading.

Checking Instrument Relevance

Relevance is the mechanically testable part of the instrument conditions: does Z actually shift X in the data?

In the first stage, we require that Z has non-trivial explanatory power for X. A standard diagnostic is the **first-stage F-statistic** for the null hypothesis that the instruments jointly have no effect on X.

Rules of thumb:

- An F-statistic below about 10 is often taken as a warning sign of **weak instruments**.

- Weak instruments lead to IV estimates that are noisy and can be badly biased in finite samples, sometimes worse than OLS.

In financial applications, weak instruments are common:

- Regulatory or index changes may only modestly affect exposures or spreads.
- Market participants can partially offset the instrument's effects (for example, by hedging or shifting to substitutes).

When first-stage strength is limited, you should:

- Report the first-stage coefficient and its F-statistic explicitly.
- Consider alternative instruments or specifications that strengthen the first stage (e.g., more direct measures of the regulatory shock).
- Treat point estimates with caution and emphasize confidence intervals and robustness checks.

Diagnosing Weak Instruments

Weak instruments distort both point estimates and standard errors. Some key symptoms and strategies:

- IV estimates can take implausibly large magnitudes and swing wildly across small specification changes.
- Nominal standard errors understate true uncertainty, leading to over-rejection of null hypotheses.

To mitigate these problems, more advanced diagnostics and methods exist (for example, robust confidence sets or limited-information maximum likelihood), but a simple principle goes a long way:

> If the instrument barely moves the endogenous regressor, do not trust the IV estimate to pin down a precise causal effect.

In trading contexts, where decisions may hinge on whether an effect is economically large, this typically means treating such IV evidence as suggestive at best, not definitive.

Interrogating the Exclusion Restriction

The most delicate assumption in IV is **exclusion**: the instrument affects the outcome only through the endogenous regressor.

Unlike relevance, exclusion is not directly testable. No statistical test can prove that Z does not have some other channel of influence on Y. Instead, we rely on:

- Institutional detail: regulatory rules, timing of announcements, and market structure.
- Design checks: pre-trend analyses, placebo tests, and alternative outcome variables.

Some practical tools:

Overidentification tests. When you have more instruments than endogenous regressors, you can check whether different instruments agree on the estimated effect. Overidentification tests assess whether the residuals are consistent with all instruments being valid. A failure of this test suggests that at least one instrument violates exclusion.

However, passing such a test does *not* prove validity; you could fail to detect mild violations, especially in small samples or noisy financial data.

Placebo outcomes and timing tests. You can examine outcomes that should not be affected by the instrument if exclusion holds—for example, variables measured well before the instrument shifts, or outcomes in markets untouched by the policy. Significant "effects" there call exclusion into question.

Narrow event windows. In some financial IV designs, the instrument is a very short-lived shock, such as a policy announcement. Limiting attention to a narrow time window around the announcement can make alternative channels less plausible (for example, macro conditions are unlikely to change abruptly in that exact minute unless the announcement itself drives them).

Ultimately, as with all quasi-experimental methods, IV demands a convincing story. The statistical machinery adds rigor, but it cannot substitute for a coherent economic argument about why the instrument isolates exogenous variation.

Implementation Details: Panels, Fixed Effects, and Clustering

Most financial IV applications use panel data, sometimes at high frequency. Implementation must account for several practical issues:

Fixed effects. You often include asset and time fixed effects in both stages to absorb:

- Asset-specific average differences (size, liquidity level, business model).
- Common time shocks (macro news, volatility regimes).

The instrument must then vary beyond what these fixed effects soak up—for example, exposure to a regulation that only affects a subset of assets in specific periods.

Multiple endogenous regressors and instruments. You may have more than one endogenous variable (e.g., leverage and margin spread) and multiple instruments (e.g., several regulatory dummies or external shocks). 2SLS generalizes mechanically:

- First stage: regress all endogenous variables on the full set of instruments and controls.
- Second stage: regress the outcome on the fitted values of endogenous variables and controls.

The same relevance and exclusion logic applies, but the interpretation of the resulting coefficients becomes more subtle: they reflect the effect of each endogenous variable for variation jointly induced by the full instrument set.

Robust and clustered standard errors. As in DiD and event studies, financial data exhibit serial correlation and cross-sectional dependence. You should:

- Use heteroskedasticity-robust or cluster-robust standard errors (for example, cluster by asset, by time, or both).
- Recognize that ignoring clustering typically leads to overly optimistic (too small) standard errors.

Clustering is especially important in IV because the effective sample size for identification is determined by how many *independent* instrument-induced shocks you observe, not by the raw number of asset-time observations.

Examples of Financial Instruments

To make the concepts concrete, here are stylized examples of instruments commonly used in trading and asset-pricing research:

- **Regulatory thresholds:** A change in capital or liquidity rules that binds only for banks above a nominal size. For those banks, crossing the threshold can serve as an instrument for leverage or liquidity adjustments, as long as other channels are plausibly ruled out.
- **Benchmark reweightings:** Periodic changes in major indices or benchmark portfolios that alter demand for constituent securities. Changes in benchmark weights can be instruments for holdings or liquidity, if the benchmark methodology is orthogonal to short-run asset-specific news.
- **Funding-market disruptions:** Shocks to interbank or repo markets that are driven by external events (e.g., policy interventions, foreign crises). Such shocks can instrument for changes in funding costs faced by certain intermediaries.

In each case, careful attention must be paid to both relevance (does the regulatory change or reweighting actually move the exposure of interest?) and exclusion (are there other direct effects on returns or spreads beyond the channel you model?).

Interpreting IV Estimates for Trading and Risk

Given the complexity of IV assumptions and diagnostics, how should practitioners interpret the resulting coefficients?

- Treat IV estimates as **local elasticities**: they tell you how outcomes respond when the endogenous regressor is moved by a specific, well-defined shock.
- Be cautious about extrapolation: the effect of a regulatory-driven change in leverage may not equal the effect of a discretionary change by a hedge fund manager.
- Combine IV evidence with other designs: often the most convincing picture emerges when IV estimates align with results from DiD, event studies, or RDD that exploit different sources of variation.

For a risk committee, a well-executed IV study can answer questions like:

> When funding costs rise due to an exogenous regulatory shock—rather than because counterparties fear bad news—how much do spreads widen, and for which institutions?

That is far more actionable than a simple correlation between spreads and funding costs, because it isolates the causal channel of interest.

Instrumental variables and two-stage least squares extend the toolkit of this chapter to settings where treatment or exposure is not externally imposed but endogenously chosen in anticipation of returns or risks. By leveraging instruments that shift exposures for reasons orthogonal to asset-specific news, IV recovers local causal effects that are especially valuable in noisy, forward-looking financial environments.

At the same time, IV places heavy demands on the analyst: instruments must be both strong and plausibly exogenous; diagnostics for weak instruments and exclusion violations must be taken seriously; and inference must respect the dependence structure of market data. When these conditions are met and clearly documented, IV can turn otherwise intractable endogeneity problems into tractable, interpretable causal estimates that meaningfully inform trading strategies and risk management.

5.5 Causal Time-Series and Modern Panel Methods

By now you have seen several ways to construct credible counterfactuals in markets: difference-in-differences and event studies exploit timing; regression discontinuity uses thresholds; synthetic control and matrix completion build data-driven twins. In all of these designs, *time* was present but often treated as a simple index.

In real markets, time is not just an index. Returns and spreads exhibit serial correlation, volatility clustering, structural breaks, and long-run relationships across assets and macro variables. Ignoring these time-series features can produce spurious "effects" or badly mis-stated uncertainty.

This section shows how to integrate time-series and panel-econometric thinking with the quasi-experimental designs you have just learned. We will:

- Revisit basic time-series concepts that matter for causal work.
- Introduce interrupted time-series designs for single-series interventions.
- Connect fixed-effects panels to DiD and event studies.
- Sketch how modern DiD-synthetic-control hybrids and matrix-completion methods sit inside a broader panel-time-series framework.

The goal is not to turn you into a specialist in time-series econometrics, but to give you a structured way to think about dynamics when you apply causal designs in financial data.

Why Time-Series Properties Matter for Causal Claims

Consider three stylized features of financial series:

- **Non-stationarity:** Levels of prices, credit spreads, or macro variables may drift over time or follow unit-root-like behavior. Shocks can have highly persistent effects.
- **Serial correlation:** Returns, order imbalances, and volatility are often serially correlated. Today's noise is not independent of yesterday's.
- **Common factors and breaks:** Many assets share exposure to a small number of factors. Regulatory changes, crises, or technology shifts can produce structural breaks in these dynamics.

If you ignore these features and simply regress levels on treatment indicators, you risk:

- **Spurious correlations:** Two trending series will often move together even if there is no causal link.
- **Biased standard errors:** Serial correlation and common factors make naive standard errors far too small, overstating statistical significance.
- **Misinterpreted dynamics:** A one-off shock may look permanent if your model cannot distinguish levels from trends.

The quasi-experimental designs in earlier sections already mitigate some of these risks: fixed effects soak up persistent differences; time effects absorb common shocks; event-time plots reveal pre-trends. But when dynamics are strong, it is helpful to explicitly model them.

Stationarity, Unit Roots, and Cointegration (At a Glance)

Before turning to causal designs, it is useful to have a minimal vocabulary for time-series behavior:

- A series is **stationary** (in the weak sense) if its mean, variance, and autocorrelation structure are stable over time. Many daily return series are approximately stationary (although volatility may not be).
- A series has a **unit root** if shocks have very persistent effects and the series behaves like a random walk or random walk with drift. Price levels and some macro aggregates often look like this.
- Two or more unit-root series can be **cointegrated** if some linear combination of them is stationary. For example, spot and futures prices or prices of close substitutes can move together in the long run even if each individually trends.

These concepts guide modeling choices:

- For stationary series (e.g., returns, changes in spreads), it is often reasonable to run quasi-experimental regressions directly.
- For non-stationary levels, naive regressions on levels can be misleading unless you control for trends, differences, or cointegrating relationships.

In practice, many causal designs for markets use returns, changes, or log-differences as outcomes precisely to sidestep the worst non-stationarity issues. Still, you should always ask:

> "Is this series roughly stable in distribution over my sample, or is it trending/structurally changing in ways that could confound my design?"

Interrupted Time-Series as a Single-Unit Quasi-Experiment

Interrupted time-series (ITS) designs bring quasi-experimental logic to a single time series that experiences an intervention at a known date—for example:

- A trading halt rule on a specific exchange.
- A new fee schedule for one dark pool.
- A circuit-breaker regime introduced on a futures contract.

The idea is simple: treat the intervention date as an "interruption" in an otherwise stable time-series process, and ask whether there is a discrete change in level, trend, or both.

An ITS setup typically involves:

- A long **pre-intervention** period where the series follows some stable dynamic (often modeled with an ARIMA or state-space model).
- A **post-intervention** period where we allow for:
- A jump in the level at the intervention date (e.g., spreads permanently drop by 2 basis points).
- A change in slope (e.g., the trend in volumes strengthens after the fee cut).

In regression form, you might work with daily spreads and include:

- A time trend for the pre period.
- An intercept shift at the intervention date.
- An interaction of the trend with a post dummy to allow the slope to differ after.

To respect time-series structure, you also include autoregressive terms or use time-series-robust standard errors. In more advanced work, you embed the intervention as a deterministic component in an ARIMA or state-space model.

ITS is conceptually similar to DiD with one treated unit and no explicit control group—the pre period serves as the counterfactual. The key assumption is that, absent the intervention, the pre-intervention dynamics would have continued unchanged. Any deviations in level or trend at the intervention date are then interpreted as causal effects.

In finance, this assumption is strong: other events (macro shocks, market structure changes) may coincide with the policy change. This is why, where possible, you will often want to complement ITS with external controls (other exchanges, securities, or markets) using DiD or synthetic control.

Fixed-Effects Panels as Dynamic DiD

Earlier, we treated fixed-effects panel regressions as a workhorse for DiD and event studies:

- Unit fixed effects capture stable differences across assets.
- Time fixed effects capture common shocks.
- Treatment indicators and event-time dummies capture causal effects.

To bring time-series structure into this picture, you can enrich these specifications in several ways:

Lagged dependent variables. Include lagged outcomes, such as one-day-lagged spreads or returns, on the right-hand side. This allows you to model short-run persistence and adjust for dynamics when estimating treatment effects.

Dynamic treatment effects. Event-study specifications already estimate a path of coefficients at different event times. With panel time-series models, you can go further by allowing effects that depend on past outcomes or past treatments (for example, treatment with decay).

Factor controls. Many panel regressions in finance include factor returns (market, size, value, momentum) as controls. These factor controls impose a specific low-dimensional time-series structure on the cross-section, tying into the factor and matrix-completion ideas discussed earlier.

Interpreted this way, a "static" DiD is just a panel model with:

- No explicit lag structure beyond fixed effects.
- Treatment modeled as a simple on/off indicator.

A "dynamic" panel model for causal questions maintains the DiD structure but overlays a parsimonious representation of the time-series dynamics—through lags, factors, or both.

Dealing with Serial and Cross-Sectional Dependence

In large panels of financial time series, two dependencies are ubiquitous:

- **Serial correlation within units:** Today's spreads or returns depend on yesterday's.
- **Cross-sectional dependence across units:** Many assets move together because of common shocks.

Ignoring these features can give you misleading significance levels for quasi-experimental estimates. Earlier sections emphasized clustered standard errors; here we highlight how this fits into a broader time-series view:

- **Clustering by unit** accounts for serial correlation along the time dimension for each asset.
- **Clustering by time** accounts for cross-sectional correlation at each date.

- **Two-way clustering** handles both simultaneously, which is particularly relevant in panels used for DiD, event studies, and IV.

In more demanding settings (for example, very large cross-sections with strong common factors), you may also use techniques that explicitly model cross-sectional correlation, such as:

- **Factor-augmented regressions:** Include estimated common factors (from principal components) as controls.
- **Driscoll-Kraay-type standard errors:** Robust to both serial and certain forms of cross-sectional dependence.

The conceptual point is that robust inference is not a cosmetic add-on; it is integral to treating financial panels as time series with structure, rather than as a pile of independent observations.

Modern DiD-Synthetic-Control Hybrids

Modern methodological work has recognized that classic DiD and synthetic control are two ends of a spectrum:

- DiD emphasizes parametric structure (fixed effects, linear trends) and uses all controls symmetrically.
- Synthetic control emphasizes flexible matching of a treated unit to a weighted combination of controls, focusing on pre-treatment fit.

Hybrids seek to combine their strengths:

- Allow for unit and time fixed effects (like DiD).
- Construct weights or use regularization to achieve good pre-treatment fit (like synthetic control).
- Permit multiple treated units and staggered treatment timing (like modern DiD).

In practice, these hybrids often look like:

- A regression with unit and time fixed effects, plus unit-specific trends or factors.
- Constraints or penalties that favor solutions achieving good pre-treatment match between treated and control units.
- Estimands defined as group-time average treatment effects, aggregated across cohorts and times with transparent weights.

From a trading or risk-management standpoint, these methods are attractive because they:

- Exploit all available units and time periods.
- Respect quasi-experimental structure (who is treated when).
- Acknowledge—and harness—the factor structure and dynamics of market data.

You can think of them as "synthetic DiD": still grounded in differences over time between treated and comparable controls, but more flexible and data-adaptive in how those controls are constructed.

Matrix Completion Revisited: Time-Series Factor Structure

The matrix-completion methods introduced earlier rest on an explicit time-series view of the panel:

> Most of the variation in outcomes across assets and over time can be captured by a small number of latent common factors and unit-specific loadings.

This is essentially a dynamic factor model. When you use matrix completion to impute missing counterfactual outcomes, you are:

- Estimating these latent factors and loadings from untreated and pre-treatment data.
- Using them to forecast what treated units would have done in the absence of treatment.

Seen this way, matrix completion sits at the intersection of:

- Time-series modeling (factor dynamics over time).
- Panel econometrics (unit-specific loadings).
- Quasi-experiments (treatment windows and missing counterfactuals).

This perspective is useful for several reasons:

- It clarifies the assumptions: you are leaning heavily on a stable factor structure to extrapolate counterfactual paths.
- It suggests diagnostics: check whether factor loadings or factor volatilities shift sharply around the intervention—if they do, your low-rank assumption may fail.
- It aligns with financial intuition: traders already think in terms of factor risk and style exposures; matrix completion simply pushes that framework into counterfactual space.

Interrupted Time Series with External Controls

A powerful way to merge ITS with panel methods is to add external controls—creating what is sometimes called a “controlled ITS” or a single-unit DiD:

- Use ITS structure (level and trend breaks at the intervention date) for the treated unit.
- Include one or more control series (e.g., similar markets without the intervention) to soak up common trends and shocks.

This design is essentially a special case of synthetic control or DiD, but highlights the time-series aspect:

- The treated series is modeled dynamically with pre and post parameters.
- Controls are used to control for non-stationarity and shocks that affect all series.

In markets, you might:

- Model the impact of a tick-size change on one exchange's spreads, using another exchange's spreads as a control.
- Estimate an ITS for a newly regulated bond market, conditioned on spreads in an otherwise similar but unregulated market.

This approach underscores a unifying theme: once you admit dynamics explicitly, the line between "time-series design" and "panel quasi-experiment" blurs. The best designs jointly exploit both.

Balancing Flexibility with Out-of-Sample Stability

A recurring tension in causal work with time-series panels is:

- **Flexibility:** Rich dynamic structures (many lags, unit-specific trends, time-varying factors) can capture complex behavior and improve pre-treatment fit.
- **Stability:** Overly flexible models may overfit noise in the pre period and extrapolate poorly into the post period, distorting estimated treatment effects.

To manage this tension:

- Start with simple dynamic structures (few lags, common factors) and only add complexity when diagnostics indicate clear residual patterns.

- Use cross-validation or out-of-sample checks within the pre period: for example, hold out a block of pre-treatment data and see how well the model predicts it.
- Prefer designs that are transparent enough to explain to a risk committee: a modest set of lags and clear fixed effects is easier to defend than an opaque, high-dimensional model.

Remember that the objective is not to squeeze out every last bit of predictive accuracy; it is to recover credible causal contrasts between treated and counterfactual paths. In many cases, a slightly less predictive but more robust model is preferable.

A Unifying View: Time as an Identification Resource

Across this chapter, time has played several roles:

- As a before/after dimension in DiD and event studies.
- As an index for near-threshold snapshots in regression discontinuity panels.
- As a staging ground for interventions in synthetic control and ITS.
- As a driver of dynamic factor structures in matrix-completion methods.

The unifying perspective is that **time is an identification resource**. It gives you:

- Repeated measurements on the same units, allowing you to control for unobserved heterogeneity with fixed effects.
- Natural variation in policies and market structures, which creates quasi-experiments.
- Rich dynamic patterns, which can be modeled parsimoniously to extract signal from noise and construct counterfactuals.

When you approach a new causal question in markets—about a regulation, a structural change, or a trading rule—ask yourself:

> "How can I use the time dimension, together with cross-sectional variation, to approximate the experiment I wish I had?"

The methods in this chapter—DiD, event studies, RDD, synthetic control, IV, ITS, and modern panel hybrids—are different ways of answering that question. They are not mutually exclusive; the strongest empirical work often combines several, checking that conclusions are consistent across designs that rely on different assumptions and exploit different facets of the time-series and panel structure of market data.

Chapter 6

Policy Learning, Evaluation & Robust Deployment

You've estimated causal effects-now what? This chapter shows how to convert them into trading policies that can be tested without touching capital, tuned to real-world constraints, deployed with controlled exploration, and monitored so that when markets shift, you notice in time. The goal is not just higher backtest Sharpe, but a disciplined loop from causal insight to robust, auditable decision-making in live markets.

6.1 Offline Policy Evaluation

In earlier chapters we focused on estimating causal effects: what happens to returns, costs, or risk if we change an execution parameter, a hedge, or a signal activation rule. That work lives at the level of *treatments*: turning a knob from 0 to 1 and asking for the expected causal impact.

In a live trading business, however, desks rarely deploy a single treatment in isolation. They deploy *policies*: systematic rules that map states of the world to actions. For example:

- "If bid–ask spread < 1 tick and volatility is low, use a passive limit order; otherwise, cross the spread."
- "Only apply the value signal when macro risk is low and liquidity is high."
- "Reroute client orders to the fast venue when predicted slippage improvement exceeds 2 basis points."

This section explains how to evaluate such policies *offline*, using historical data generated under a different strategy or benchmark, without immediately risking capital in live markets. The key tool is a family of *importance sampling* estimators adapted from statistics and reinforcement learning. We will:

- Show why naive backtests can seriously misprice the value of new policies when they reuse data from an existing strategy.
- Introduce the main offline policy evaluation (OPE) estimators: inverse propensity scoring (IPS), self-normalized IPS (SNIPS), and doubly robust (DR).
- Discuss practical issues in trading: estimating propensities from logs, extreme weights, clipping, and stabilization.
- Explain diagnostics and confidence intervals that tell you *when to trust* OPE and how to translate estimates into go/no-go and sizing decisions.

Throughout, you should think of a policy as a function that takes a context (market and portfolio state) and outputs a trading action, and of OPE as a way to answer the question:

> *If we had followed this new policy in the past, using the historical market paths we observed, what would our average outcome have been?*

Why naive backtests are not enough

Suppose you have detailed execution logs from the last year, generated by your current execution policy π_0. For each order or decision time i, you have:

- Context X_i: features like order size, spread, volatility, venue, time of day.
- Action A_i: which execution style or venue you actually chose.
- Outcome Y_i: realized implementation shortfall, slippage, or P&L contribution.

Now you design a new policy π_{new} (for example, a smarter routing rule). A tempting idea is:

> Filter the historical data down to the decisions where π_{new} happens to agree with what we *actually* did, then compute the average outcome over that subset. Use that as the estimated performance of π_{new}.

This "agreement subset" approach is intuitive but fragile:

- **Selection bias.** The subset where π_{new} matches π_0 is not a random sample of market states. Your historical policy might have chosen aggressive orders mostly in high-liquidity contexts, while π_{new} would choose them in different conditions.
- **Data inefficiency.** You throw away any decision where π_{new} would differ from what actually happened, precisely those cases where you most want to know the counterfactual outcome.
- **Confounding by design.** If the old policy concentrated certain actions in particular regimes (for example, passive orders only in calm markets), the outcomes you observe for those actions are entangled with the conditions under which they were taken. Simply re-using them as if they applied to all regimes is misleading.

Full historical simulation—replaying the entire environment with the new policy—would be ideal, but in markets we typically cannot do that: we observe only the realized trajectory, not all possible price and order-book paths that could have occurred under different actions.

Offline policy evaluation tries to bridge this gap. It uses logs from a *behavior policy* (your existing strategy) to estimate the expected outcome under a *target policy* (the one you are considering), by reweighting observed samples so that they resemble what you would have seen under the target.

Behavior policy, target policy, and propensities

Formally, we distinguish:

- The **behavior policy** $\pi_b(a \mid x)$: the probability that your historical system chose action a in context x. This is the "data-generating" policy. It may be deterministic (always chooses the same action in a given context) or stochastic (for example, some randomized exploration).
- The **target policy** $\pi_t(a \mid x)$: the new policy whose performance you want to estimate. It maps contexts to a probability distribution over actions; it may also be deterministic.
- The **propensity** of an action under a policy: simply the probability of taking that action, given the context.

The key idea is that if an action taken in the past was *unlikely* under the behavior policy but would be *likely* under the target policy, then that sample tells you a lot about how the target would behave and should be up-weighted. Importance sampling formalizes this reweighting.

Concretely, for each logged decision i we can, in principle, compute:

- $\pi_b(A_i \mid X_i)$: how likely was the historical policy to choose the actual action we took?
- $\pi_t(A_i \mid X_i)$: how likely is the target policy to choose that same action, in the same context?

The *importance weight* for sample i is then:

$$w_i = \frac{\pi_t(A_i \mid X_i)}{\pi_b(A_i \mid X_i)}.$$

You can read w_i as: "How much more (or less) often would the target policy take this action in this context, compared to what actually happened?"

If w_i is greater than 1, that sample represents a decision the target would take more often than the behavior policy. If w_i is less than 1, it represents a decision the target would take less often. If w_i is zero, it means the target would never take that action in that context, so this sample tells you nothing about the target's behavior.

Inverse Propensity Scoring (IPS)

The simplest importance-sampling-based estimator of the target policy's average outcome is **inverse propensity scoring**.

Imagine you want to estimate the average implementation shortfall under the target policy. Under mild conditions, the IPS estimator takes the form:

$$\hat{V}_{IPS}(\pi_t) = \frac{1}{N} \sum_{i=1}^{N} w_i Y_i,$$

where N is the number of logged decisions and Y_i is the observed outcome for decision i.

Intuitively:

- You keep all samples, not just those where the target and behavior policies agree.
- Samples that the target policy would encounter more often are up-weighted; those it would encounter less often are down-weighted.
- If the behavior policy happens to be equal to the target policy, then $\pi_t/\pi_b = 1$ and IPS reduces to the usual simple average.

In a trading setting:

- π_b is your legacy execution algorithm or signal activation rule.
- π_t is a candidate new algorithm: perhaps one of a family of routing policies parameterized by a risk-aversion parameter.
- Y_i might be minus implementation shortfall (so higher is better), or a risk-adjusted P&L contribution.

IPS has an important theoretical advantage: under appropriate causal identification assumptions (no unmeasured confounding, correct propensities, enough overlap between behavior and target policies), it is *unbiased.* In expectation, it recovers the true average outcome under the target policy, even though the data were generated under a different policy.

In practice, however, IPS can have very high variance, especially in markets.

Weight instability and variance

The difficulty is that w_i can be very large if the target policy puts substantial probability on actions that were rare under the behavior policy. In markets this is common:

- Your historical policy might have used aggressive orders only rarely during extreme volatility, while the new policy would use them more.
- Your desk may have explored alternative hedges only in certain regions of the state space.

Large w_i values mean that a few observations can dominate the IPS estimate. If those happen to be noisy or extreme outcomes (for example, a few trades during a flash crash), your estimated policy value becomes unstable.

To manage this, we need refinements of IPS that trade some bias for lower variance and better stability.

Self-Normalized IPS (SNIPS)

Self-normalized IPS (SNIPS) modifies IPS by normalizing the weights so that they sum to one. Instead of averaging $w_i Y_i$ directly, SNIPS uses:

$$\hat{V}_{SNIPS}(\pi_t) = \frac{\sum_{i=1}^{N} w_i Y_i}{\sum_{i=1}^{N} w_i}.$$

You can think of SNIPS as forming a weighted average of outcomes:

$$\hat{V}_{SNIPS}(\pi_t) = \sum_{i=1}^{N} \tilde{w}_i Y_i, \quad \text{where } \tilde{w}_i = \frac{w_i}{\sum_{j=1}^{N} w_j}.$$

This normalization does two helpful things:

- It makes the estimator less sensitive to the overall scale of the weights.
- It reduces variance in finite samples, because the normalized weights cannot "blow up" the sample average as easily.

The trade-off is a small bias: SNIPS is not exactly unbiased anymore, particularly when sample size is small or weight variability is extreme. In practice, for trading applications where stability and risk control matter, this bias–variance trade-off is often acceptable, and SNIPS is widely used.

Doubly Robust (DR) Estimators

IPS and SNIPS rely heavily on correct propensities. If you mis-estimate π_b or mis-specify the behavior policy, the importance weights will be wrong and your policy value estimates can be biased.

A complementary approach is to build a predictive model for the outcome given context and action, say $\hat{m}(x, a) \approx \mathbb{E}[Y \mid X = x, A = a]$. This kind of model is similar to the treatment-effect and outcome models you fit in earlier chapters.

Doubly robust estimators combine both strategies:

- They use an outcome model $\hat{m}(x, a)$ to directly predict what would happen under the target policy.
- They use importance weights to correct for residual mismatch between the distribution of actions in the data and in the target policy.

A typical DR estimator for the average value of π_t can be written (conceptually) as:

$$\hat{V}_{DR}(\pi_t) = \frac{1}{N} \sum_{i=1}^{N} \left[\hat{m}(X_i, \pi_t) + w_i \big(Y_i - \hat{m}(X_i, A_i) \big) \right],$$

where $\hat{m}(X_i, \pi_t)$ denotes the predicted outcome when we apply the target policy in context X_i (for deterministic policies, this is simply $\hat{m}(X_i, a_t(X_i))$).

The structure is worth unpacking:

- The first term, $\hat{m}(X_i, \pi_t)$, is a direct model-based estimate of how the target policy would perform in that context.
- The second term, $w_i\big(Y_i - \hat{m}(X_i, A_i)\big)$, is an importance-weighted residual. It adjusts for the difference between what actually happened and what the model predicted under the observed action.

The crucial property of DR estimators is:

> If either the propensity model is correct *or* the outcome model is correct (not necessarily both), the estimator is still consistent for the true policy value.

This "two chances to be right" feature is particularly appealing in financial applications, where both models are imperfect. DR estimators often achieve lower bias and variance than pure IPS or pure model-based approaches, especially when combined with techniques like cross-fitting to avoid overfitting.

Estimating propensities from trading logs

All three estimators above rely on propensity scores or their ratios. In some systems, you know the behavior policy exactly: for example, a smart order router that flips a fair coin between two venues when spreads are equal. In many trading systems, however, the historical policy is a complex piece of code that has evolved over time.

As a result, you often have to *estimate* $\pi_b(a \mid x)$ from the logs themselves. Typical approaches include:

- **Supervised classification.** Treat the action as a categorical label and fit a multinomial logistic regression, gradient boosted trees, or a random forest that predicts A from X. The predicted probabilities are your estimated propensities.
- **Segmented policies.** If you know that different desks or time periods used different decision rules, fit separate propensity models within each regime.
- **Hybrid approaches.** Combine known business rules (for example, "never use venue B when spread > X") with statistical modeling for the remaining variation.

Quality of propensity estimates is critical. Overconfident models that output probabilities near zero or one can create extreme weights and unstable IPS estimates. It is often better to use deliberately *smoothed* models that avoid assigning vanishing probabilities to any action that actually occurred.

Clipping and truncation: controlling extreme weights

Even with careful propensity modeling, financial data are heavy-tailed. Some contexts will receive very low propensity under the behavior policy yet high probability under the target policy, leading to huge w_i.

A common safety practice is to *clip* or *truncate* importance weights:

- Define a maximum allowed weight W_{max} (for example, 10 or 20).

- Replace w_i with $\min(w_i, W_{max})$ before computing IPS, SNIPS, or DR estimates.

This introduces bias—you are effectively saying, "I refuse to let any single observation speak more than W_{max} times louder than an average observation." But it dramatically reduces variance and guards against rare but catastrophic mis-estimation of propensities.

In practice, you might evaluate policy value estimates for a range of clipping thresholds. If results are broadly consistent across reasonable thresholds, your conclusions are more robust.

Diagnostics: when to trust offline evaluation

Offline policy evaluation is powerful but not magic. Before acting on an OPE estimate, you should ask: *Is the data actually informative about this target policy?* Several diagnostics help answer this.

Support and overlap checks

Offline evaluation assumes that the behavior policy gives you some coverage of the states and actions that the target policy will use. Formally, if $\pi_t(a \mid x) > 0$ but $\pi_b(a \mid x) = 0$ for some (x, a), then the importance weight is infinite, and you have no direct information about that part of the policy.

In practice, you can:

- Check, for each decision rule in π_t, whether the corresponding actions were ever taken under similar contexts historically.
- Plot the distribution of importance weights w_i for each candidate policy. Heavy tails or a mass at zero indicate poor overlap.

If the target policy makes frequent use of actions that were *never* or *almost never* taken under the behavior policy in certain regimes (for example, aggressive orders in stressed markets), offline evaluation may be unreliable there. You may need additional experimentation or a more conservative rollout strategy.

Effective sample size

A convenient summary of how informative the data are for a given target policy is the **effective sample size** (ESS). For normalized weights $\tilde{w}_i$ (for example, from SNIPS), the ESS is often defined as:

$$\text{ESS} = \frac{1}{\sum_{i=1}^{N} \tilde{w}_i^2}.$$

You can think of ESS as the number of "independent, equally weighted" samples that the reweighted data correspond to. If all weights are equal, ESS is N. If a few weights dominate, ESS can be much smaller than N, even though you technically have many observations.

In a trading context, you might compute ESS:

- For each candidate policy π_t you are comparing.
- Within key market regimes (for example, split by volatility quintiles or by asset class).

Low ESS—say, a few hundred samples for a policy evaluated over millions of decisions—is a sign that your offline estimate is driven by a thin slice of history. You should respond by either simplifying the policy (bringing it closer to the behavior policy) or by gathering more diverse data through exploration.

Uncertainty quantification and confidence intervals

Point estimates of policy value are not enough for serious capital decisions. You also need measures of uncertainty.

For IPS, SNIPS, and DR, you can approximate variability in several ways:

- **Asymptotic variance formulas.** Under regularity conditions, importance sampling estimators are asymptotically normal, and you can derive closed-form expressions for their variances based on the sample. This is fast and often adequate when ESS is large.

- **Bootstrap.** Resample your logged decisions with replacement, recompute the OPE estimator for each bootstrap sample, and form empirical quantiles of the resulting distribution. This is more computationally intensive but flexible, and it tends to work well even with complex estimators and clustering.
- **Block bootstrap.** In markets, observations are time-dependent. A block bootstrap, where you resample contiguous time blocks instead of individual trades, respects serial correlation and regime structure better than naive bootstrapping at the decision level.

Once you have a standard error or empirical distribution, you can construct confidence intervals (for example, 95% intervals) around your estimated policy values. These intervals support concrete decisions:

- **Go/no-go.** Require that the lower end of the confidence interval for the new policy exceeds the current policy's estimated value by a minimum margin, before approving a full-scale rollout.
- **Sizing.** Scale the initial capital allocation or order-routing share proportionally to a measure of statistical confidence, phasing in larger deployment only as more data accrue and intervals tighten.

From estimates to deployment decisions

Offline policy evaluation sits between pure historical backtesting and full online experimentation. It is strongest when:

- The target policy is not too far from the behavior policy, so overlap is good and weights are stable.
- You have accurate or conservative propensity models.
- Effective sample size is reasonably large in the regimes you care about.
- Confidence intervals are narrow enough to distinguish materially better from materially worse policies.

When these conditions are met, IPS, SNIPS, and DR give you a principled way to rank candidate policies, discard clear losers before they ever touch the market, and justify your choices to risk and governance teams based on causal reasoning rather than pure correlation.

When diagnostics look poor—extreme weights, low ESS, wide intervals—you should treat OPE as a warning sign and fall back on more cautious strategies: restricted live experiments, cluster-randomized rollouts, or simpler policy changes closer to existing behavior.

In the rest of the chapter we will build on these offline evaluation tools to *learn* policies directly from estimated effects, incorporate constraints and risk, and then deploy and monitor causal strategies in a robust, governance-friendly way.

6.2 Policy Learning and Uplift Optimization

In the previous section we learned how to *evaluate* a proposed trading policy offline, using importance-sampling estimators such as IPS, SNIPS, and doubly robust methods. That answered the question:

> "Given a candidate policy, how well would it have performed on our historical data?"

We now shift to the complementary problem:

> "Given historical data and estimated *causal effects*, how can we *construct* a good policy in the first place, subject to our real-world limits on capital, risk, and operational capacity?"

This is the realm of *policy learning* and *uplift optimization*. Rather than hand-crafting many candidate rules and testing them one by one, we can use our conditional treatment effect machinery to directly design rules that decide:

- When to turn a signal on or off for a given asset.
- When to switch execution style for a particular order.
- When to add or remove a hedge from a portfolio.
- Which clients or orders should receive a more intensive service level.

The unifying object here is the **conditional average treatment effect** (CATE), which you met earlier. For a given context X (describing the trade, instrument, time, and market state), the CATE tells you the expected causal *uplift* in some outcome Y (for example, P&L, implementation shortfall, or a risk metric) when you take action $A = 1$ instead of $A = 0$.

From CATE to decision rules

Suppose you have an estimate of the treatment effect $\hat{\tau}(x)$ for each potential decision. For concreteness, think of:

- Treatment $A = 1$: "apply the signal" or "use the aggressive execution style".
- Control $A = 0$: "do not apply the signal" or "use the passive style".
- Outcome Y: improvement in basis points relative to a benchmark.

The CATE $\tau(x)$ is then:

> Expected improvement in Y if we take the treatment instead of control, *for trades or times with features* x.

If you had perfect knowledge of $\tau(x)$ and no constraints, an idealized decision rule would be simple:

> Take the treatment whenever $\tau(x) > 0$; otherwise, do not.

This corresponds to a policy that always chooses the option with higher expected causal value. In reality, three complications arise:

1. **Estimation error:** $\hat{\tau}(x)$ is noisy, especially in sparse regions of the state space.
2. **Resource limits:** you may not be able to treat every eligible trade (for example, capacity limits on a certain venue, risk limits on a hedge).
3. **Risk and governance:** you may require a margin of safety before acting on an estimated effect.

Policy learning is about turning noisy estimates of uplift into practical rules that respect these realities.

Simple threshold rules on estimated uplift

A natural starting point is to act when estimated uplift exceeds a threshold. For example, define a policy

$$\pi_\theta(x) = \begin{cases} 1 & \text{if } \hat{\tau}(x) \geq \theta, \\ 0 & \text{otherwise,} \end{cases}$$

where θ is a positive constant (measured in basis points of improvement, or in expected Sharpe ratio units, etc.).

This rule has an intuitive interpretation:

- $\theta = 0$ means you act whenever the treatment is estimated to be better than control on average.
- Larger θ means you require a stronger signal of positive uplift before you intervene. You are trading off *coverage* (how many trades you treat) against *confidence* per treated trade.

In practice:

- Execution desks might set θ to 1–2 basis points of expected shortfall improvement before switching to a more complex or potentially disruptive routing option.
- An asset manager might require, say, a 0.1 increase in expected risk-adjusted return before adding a hedge that consumes scarce balance sheet.

Threshold rules are easy to communicate and implement. They also provide a natural handle for controlling turnover and operational load: raising θ shrinks the treated set, reducing the number of policy changes.

Ranking and budgeted uplift optimization

Thresholding assumes you can treat all trades with $\hat{\tau}(x) \geq \theta$. Often this is unrealistic. Two common constraints are:

- **Budget constraints:** You can only commit a limited amount of capital, balance sheet, or risk to a given strategy at a time.
- **Capacity constraints:** A venue, strategy, or service channel can only process a certain number of orders or clients concurrently.

In these settings, it is more natural to think in terms of *ranking* and *allocation*:

> You have a list of candidate interventions, each with an estimated uplift and resource cost. You want to choose a subset that fits within your budget and maximizes total expected uplift.

Formally, consider N candidate decisions indexed by i (trades, orders, or client requests). For each i you have:

- Estimated uplift $\hat{\tau}_i$.

- Resource cost c_i (for example, notional, risk weight, or an internal capacity unit).

You also have a total budget B (for example, maximum capital or risk you are willing to allocate to this treatment at a given time). The budgeted uplift optimization problem is:

> Choose a binary action $a_i \in \{0, 1\}$ for each i to maximize the sum of expected uplift $\sum_i a_i \hat{\tau}_i$, subject to the resource constraint $\sum_i a_i c_i \leq B$.

At this level, this is just a knapsack-like optimization. A simple and often near-optimal strategy, when c_i is similar across trades, is:

1. Rank candidates by $\hat{\tau}_i$ from largest to smallest.
2. Treat in that order until you exhaust the budget.

When resource costs differ, it is better to rank by *uplift per unit cost*, $\hat{\tau}_i/c_i$, just as you might in portfolio optimization:

1. Rank candidates by $\hat{\tau}_i/c_i$.
2. Treat from top to bottom while respecting $\sum_i a_i c_i \leq B$.

This is the essence of *uplift optimization*: you treat those trades where each unit of scarce resource "buys" you the largest expected causal improvement.

Individual-level vs segment-level policies

So far we have described decisions at the level of individual trades or orders. In many organizations, decisions must also be interpretable and stable across *segments*, for example:

- Client segments (retail, small institutional, large institutional).
- Instrument classes (liquid large-cap equities vs micro-caps).

- Regions or time zones.

In these cases, you may want a policy that operates at segment level:

> For segment s, either always apply the treatment, never apply it, or apply it under a simple condition on a few key features.

You can still use CATE estimates to drive such policies. One approach is:

1. Aggregate CATE estimates within each segment (for example, average $\hat{\tau}_i$ across all trades in segment s).
2. Consider a small menu of segment-level rules (for example, "treat all trades in segment s when volatility is low" vs "never treat"), and estimate the uplift for each via offline policy evaluation.
3. Choose the segment rule that gives the highest expected uplift subject to any fairness or operational constraints.

Segment-level policies may sacrifice some granularity compared with fully individualized rules, but they are often easier to explain to stakeholders and more robust to estimation noise, since they aggregate information across many observations.

Dealing with estimation uncertainty

All of the above assumes that $\hat{\tau}(x)$ is accurate. In financial data, this is rarely true everywhere. If we act on noisy estimates too aggressively, we risk *overfitting in decision space*: we choose actions that look good in-sample because of noise, not because of true causal uplift.

There are several practical ways to guard against this.

Margins and conservative thresholds

Instead of treating when $\hat{\tau}(x) > 0$, require:

$$\hat{\tau}(x) - \lambda \cdot \widehat{\sigma}(x) > 0,$$

where $\widehat{\sigma}(x)$ is an estimate of the standard error of $\widehat{\tau}(x)$, and λ is a tunable parameter (for example, 1 or 2). In words:

> Treat only when the lower end of an uncertainty-adjusted interval for uplift is positive.

This is analogous to requiring statistical significance before acting. It tends to focus treatment on regions where you have both high estimated uplift and relatively precise estimates.

Shrinkage and regularization

You can also shrink noisy estimates towards zero or towards a segment-level mean before using them in policies. For example:

- Hierarchical or multi-level models can automatically pull extreme treatment-effect estimates towards a group average when data are sparse.
- Post-hoc shrinkage rules (for instance, multiplying $\widehat{\tau}(x)$ by a factor less than one when its standard error is large) reduce the amplitude of noisy signals.

Regularization of the underlying CATE model (for example, through penalization, depth limits in trees, or early stopping in boosting) also reduces variance and, indirectly, stabilizes downstream policies.

Policy cross-validation

In predictive modeling, you use cross-validation to compare models. In policy learning, a similar idea applies, but the object of interest is the *policy* itself.

A typical workflow is:

1. Split your historical data into K folds by time or by instruments.
2. On each training fold, fit a CATE model and derive a candidate policy (for example, a threshold or ranking rule).
3. Evaluate each policy on the corresponding validation fold using an offline policy evaluation estimator (IPS, SNIPS, or DR).

4. Compare average validation performance across folds and select the policy class or hyperparameters that perform best.

This process directly measures how well a policy generalizes, not just how well the effect model fits. It guards against subtle forms of overfitting where a model captures patterns that do not translate into robust decisions.

Encoding practical constraints

Trading policies live within a web of constraints: risk limits, regulatory requirements, client mandates, and operational capacities. Fortunately, many of these constraints can be expressed in simple mathematical forms and built into the policy learning process.

Some common examples:

- **Turnover caps:** Limit how many times per day or per week a policy is allowed to change an instrument's position or execution style. This can be expressed as a constraint on the number or size of treated trades over a time window.
- **Exposure limits:** Limit sector, factor, or region exposures resulting from treatments (for example, only allow additional hedges that keep sector weights within bands). When treatment decisions are associated with known exposure changes, this becomes a set of linear constraints on total treated exposure.
- **Inventory bounds:** For market making or options books, ensure that applying a treatment (for example, quoting tighter spreads) does not push inventory outside a safe corridor. The policy must respect these state-dependent bounds.

In many cases, the problem reduces to:

> Maximize total expected uplift over a set of decision variables, subject to linear or convex constraints on their aggregate costs, risks, and exposures.

This is structurally similar to portfolio optimization, except that the "returns" are causal uplifts on specific actions rather than asset returns. The same optimization tools—linear programming, quadratic programming, or simple greedy heuristics—can be reused, as long as you are careful about how you estimate and interpret risk.

Examples: routing and hedging decisions

To make these ideas concrete, consider two short examples.

Example 1: Routing latency-sensitive orders

Imagine a broker that can choose between two venues for client equity orders: a "fast" venue that often yields better prices but has limited capacity, and a "standard" venue with essentially unlimited capacity.

From past experiments, the broker has estimated a CATE model that predicts, for each incoming order and market context, the expected improvement in implementation shortfall (in basis points) if the order is routed to the fast venue instead of the standard one.

- The treatment is: "route to fast venue".
- The uplift $\hat{\tau}_i$ is the predicted improvement in shortfall for order i.
- The resource cost c_i might be a measure of the order's size or the proportion of fast-venue capacity consumed.

Fast-venue capacity is limited: the broker can only allocate up to, say, 20% of total daily volume there without degrading performance.

A policy-learning approach would:

1. Compute $\hat{\tau}_i$ for each order as it arrives.
2. Rank orders by uplift per unit capacity, $\hat{\tau}_i/c_i$.
3. Route to the fast venue in that order until the capacity budget is reached.

4. Optionally impose a minimum uplift threshold so that only orders with estimated improvement above some level are ever considered for fast routing.

Offline policy evaluation, using past logs where some orders went to each venue, can estimate the expected shortfall reduction and its uncertainty under this ranking-based policy before full deployment.

Example 2: Selective hedging in a factor portfolio

An asset manager runs a factor-based equity portfolio. They consider adding index futures hedges to reduce downside risk during turbulent periods. Hedges, however, consume capital and may reduce upside in calmer markets.

Using historical data (including past hedging episodes and unhedged periods), the manager estimates a CATE model for each rebalance date and current state:

- Treatment: "add the hedge position" versus "no hedge".
- Outcome: risk-adjusted P&L over the next month.
- Context features: volatility measures, macro indicators, portfolio tilts, and liquidity.

For each date, the model produces $\hat{\tau}(x_t)$: the estimated change in risk-adjusted P&L if hedging is applied.

The policy could be:

- Apply the hedge when $\hat{\tau}(x_t)$ exceeds a threshold and implied volatility indicates stressful conditions.
- Limit the notional hedge exposure to a maximum fraction of portfolio NAV (a budget constraint).

Again, this can be viewed as a budgeted uplift optimization: among all possible hedge levels across time, choose those periods where the expected causal uplift of hedging, adjusted for risk and cost, is highest, subject to exposure limits.

Summary and outlook

In this section we have moved from *evaluating* fixed policies to *learning* them directly from causal-effect estimates. The key steps are:

1. Use CATE and uplift models to estimate the incremental effect of treatments at the level of trades, orders, or segments.
2. Convert these estimates into decision rules via thresholds, rankings, and budgeted optimization.
3. Incorporate practical constraints and estimation uncertainty through margins, regularization, and policy cross-validation.
4. Maintain interpretability by aggregating to segment-level policies when appropriate.

The resulting policies are not just predictive rules; they are *causally informed trading rules* designed to use scarce resources where they have the highest expected causal impact on P&L or risk.

In the next section we will deepen this connection by explicitly framing policy learning as a portfolio-style optimization problem. There we will integrate capital, turnover, and risk constraints more formally, and we will see how mean–variance, tail-risk, and robust optimization concepts can be adapted to causal treatment effects and uplift-based strategies.

6.3 Budget, Constraints, and Risk-Aware Decisions

In the previous section we treated policy learning as an uplift maximization problem: estimate the causal effect of each potential intervention, then choose actions that deliver the largest expected improvement in P&L or trading cost. We largely ignored what every practitioner knows is central in real trading:

- Capital and balance-sheet are limited.

- Turnover, transaction costs, and operational capacity must be controlled.
- Risk constraints on volatility, drawdown, and factor exposures are binding.

This section integrates these realities directly into causal policies. We will:

- Recast policy learning in a portfolio-style framework where each treatment is a "mini-asset" with an estimated causal return (uplift) and risk.
- Introduce mean–variance policy optimization based on treatment effects.
- Extend to tail-focused criteria such as Conditional Value-at-Risk (CVaR).
- Discuss robust optimization when treatment effect estimates are themselves uncertain.
- Show how capital, turnover, and exposure limits become constraints in these optimization problems.

The key idea is simple but powerful: once you have a set of candidate interventions with estimated causal uplifts and risk contributions, you can treat them like a portfolio. Instead of allocating capital across stocks or bonds, you allocate *capacity to intervene* across trades, hedges, or execution changes.

Treatments as portfolio assets

Consider a cross-section of N candidate treatments indexed by i:

- Each i might be "apply signal S to instrument j today", or "route this order to venue A instead of venue B", or "add this hedge to the portfolio at this time".

- From previous causal modeling, you have an estimated uplift $\hat{\tau}_i$ for each treatment, measured in the same units (for example, expected extra basis points of return, or improvement in implementation shortfall).
- Around each $\hat{\tau}_i$ you also have an estimate of variability or risk, based on residual variation in outcomes or scenario analysis.

A policy corresponds to choosing an action level w_i for each treatment:

- For some problems w_i is binary: 1 if you apply the treatment, 0 if not.
- For others w_i can be fractional: how much size to allocate to a trade, how much notional to hedge, or what proportion of orders to route via a given protocol.

Collect the w_i into a decision vector w. Then:

- The **expected policy uplift** is approximately a weighted sum $\sum_i w_i \hat{\tau}_i$.
- The **risk** of the policy can be summarized by a variance or volatility measure, or by tail-risk measures like CVaR, using the distribution of uplift across scenarios.

This is structurally identical to portfolio allocation, with $\hat{\tau}_i$ playing the role of expected return and the distribution of treatment effects playing the role of risk.

The benefit of this viewpoint is that it lets us bring familiar optimization tools to causal policy design, while staying grounded in treatment-effect estimates.

Mean–variance optimization with causal uplift

Mean–variance portfolio theory trades off expected return against variance of return. In the context of causal policies, we adapt this to:

> Choose treatment intensities w_i to balance higher expected causal uplift against higher uncertainty in that uplift.

To make this concrete, you need:

- An estimate of the *expected uplift vector*: $\hat{\tau} = (\hat{\tau}_1, \ldots, \hat{\tau}_N)$.
- An estimate of the *covariance matrix of uplift*: Σ, where Σ_{ij} measures how the realized uplift of treatment i co-moves with that of treatment j across time or scenarios.

Given a decision vector w, you can define:

- Expected total uplift: $U(w) = w^\top \hat{\tau}$.
- Risk (variance of uplift): $R(w) = w^\top \Sigma w$.

One canonical mean–variance problem is:

> Maximize $U(w) - \frac{\gamma}{2} R(w)$ subject to budget and operational constraints, where γ is a risk-aversion parameter.

Here, larger γ penalizes risk more heavily and produces more conservative policies. The constraints encode capital, turnover, and exposure limits, which we will discuss shortly.

This set-up captures several intuitions:

- Treatments with high estimated uplift and low variance are naturally favored.
- Correlation in uplift matters: if two interventions tend to succeed or fail together in the same scenarios, combining them does less to diversify policy risk than if they are weakly correlated.
- You can directly control the aggressiveness of your policy via γ, much like you control portfolio risk appetite.

In many trading problems, especially at the mark-to-market level, a quadratic mean–variance objective with linear constraints leads to a convex optimization problem solvable quickly at each decision time.

Tail-risk and CVaR-aware policies

Variance is a symmetric measure: it penalizes upside and downside fluctuations equally. Trading organizations, however, are typically much more concerned about the left tail: scenarios where treatments backfire and cause significant losses or slippage.

To reflect this in policy learning, we can use tail-focused criteria such as Conditional Value-at-Risk (CVaR). Think of CVaR as:

> The average loss (or shortfall in uplift) in the worst α fraction of scenarios.

For example, you might consider the average shortfall in the worst 5% of days (or rebalances) under a candidate policy. A tail-risk-aware causal policy problem might look like:

> Maximize expected uplift $U(w)$ subject to a constraint that CVaR of uplift at a chosen confidence level does not exceed a specified loss limit.

Operationally, you would:

- Construct a set of historical or simulated scenarios (days, weeks, or regimes).
- For each scenario and treatment i, estimate or simulate the realized uplift under treatment vs control.
- For a candidate policy w, compute the distribution of total uplift across scenarios, then its CVaR.

Then you solve for w that offers an attractive trade-off between expected uplift and tail protection.

This is particularly important in settings with skewed payoffs:

- Options trading, where certain hedges may lose small amounts in normal conditions but prevent catastrophic losses in crashes.

- Illiquid assets, where treatments that seem beneficial on average may amplify losses in stress scenarios due to liquidity spirals.

By building CVaR into policy design, you ensure that your causal interventions are not just good in expectation but also acceptable in the worst plausible states of the world.

Robust optimization under effect uncertainty

Up to now we have treated $\hat{\tau}$ and Σ as known inputs. In practice they are estimates with uncertainty. If you optimize aggressively against a single point estimate of uplift, you risk *optimizing on noise*: tilting heavily toward treatments whose uplifts are overestimated by chance.

Robust optimization makes this explicit. Instead of taking $\hat{\tau}$ as the truth, you define an *uncertainty set* $\mathcal{T}$ of plausible treatment-effect vectors consistent with your data and standard errors. For example:

- An interval per treatment: $\tau_i \in [\hat{\tau}_i - \delta_i, \hat{\tau}_i + \delta_i]$.
- An elliptical set around $\hat{\tau}$ defined by the covariance of the effect estimates.

A robust policy problem then becomes:

> Choose w to maximize the *worst-case* expected uplift across all $\tau \in \mathcal{T}$, subject to constraints.

In words:

> Find a policy that performs well even if the true treatment effects are at the less favorable end of what our estimation uncertainty allows.

This tends to shrink allocations away from treatments with uncertain or unstable estimates, even if their point estimates are high. It is especially valuable early in a strategy's life, when sample sizes are modest and CATE estimates are volatile.

Encoding capital, turnover, and exposure limits

Mean–variance, CVaR, and robust objectives tell you how to trade off uplift and risk. To make causal policies implementable, you must also encode your *constraints*. Most trading constraints can be expressed as linear or convex conditions on w.

Capital and balance-sheet constraints

Capital constraints specify how much notional, margin, or balance sheet you can commit to a set of treatments. If c_i measures the capital consumption of treatment i (for example, trade size times margin rate), a simple constraint is:

$$\sum_i c_i w_i \leq B_{capital},$$

where $B_{capital}$ is your capital budget for this policy at the current decision time.

You can also introduce:

- Desk-level budgets: separate constraints for equities, credit, FX, etc.
- Client-level budgets: limits for each account or mandate.

These constraints ensure your policy does not accidentally over-allocate to attractive but capital-hungry interventions.

Turnover and transaction-cost constraints

Aggressive causal policies may change positions or execution styles frequently, creating high turnover and transaction costs. You can:

- Include an explicit *penalty* for turnover in the objective (for instance, subtract a term proportional to expected trading cost).
- Impose an explicit *constraint* on total turnover or the number of changes relative to the current policy.

For example, if d_i measures the expected incremental turnover induced by treatment i, a basic turnover constraint is:

$$\sum_i d_i w_i \leq B_{turnover},$$

limiting how much you allow the policy to change holdings or routing decisions at this step. This encourages the optimizer to concentrate interventions where the causal uplift justifies the additional trading cost.

Exposure and risk-factor limits

Most institutions operate with factor and sector exposure limits. Treatments can change exposures, for example:

- Adding a hedge alters beta to equity or rates factors.
- Re-weighting stocks changes sector and style exposures.
- Changing execution style may shift realized exposure to intraday volatility.

If f_{ik} denotes the change in exposure to factor k if treatment i is applied, and E_k^{max} is an allowed bound, you can enforce:

$$\left| \sum_i f_{ik} w_i \right| \leq E_k^{max} \quad \text{for each factor } k.$$

This ensures that, in aggregate, the policy's interventions keep the book within desired factor corridors. The same approach extends to sector weights, country exposures, and liquidity buckets.

Putting it together: a generic optimization template

With these building blocks, many causal policy problems can be expressed in a common template:

> Choose w to maximize a risk-adjusted causal objective (mean–variance, CVaR-constrained, or robust uplift), subject to linear constraints that encode capital, turnover, and exposure limits.

Symbolically, for a mean–variance example:

$$\max_{w} \quad w^\top \hat{\tau} - \frac{\gamma}{2} w^\top \Sigma w$$

subject to

$$\sum_i c_i w_i \leq B_{capital}, \; \sum_i d_i w_i \leq B_{turnover}, \; \left| \sum_i f_{ik} w_i \right| \leq E_k^{max}, \; \text{and } w \in \mathcal{W},$$

where $\mathcal{W}$ encodes sign constraints (long-only or box constraints), integrality conditions (for binary treatments), or other implementation rules.

In many cases this optimization is small and tractable enough to solve at each rebalance or decision time, using standard quadratic or convex programming solvers.

Worked example: selecting trades with uplift and VaR limits

Consider an equity long/short strategy that generates a nightly list of 500 potential incremental trades (position changes). For each candidate trade i, your causal modeling pipeline provides:

- $\hat{\tau}_i$: estimated uplift in expected alpha (per unit of size) if you execute the trade.
- σ_i: estimated standard deviation of the incremental alpha.
- Factor exposures f_{ik} to a small set of style and sector factors.

You also know:

- A capital budget $B_{capital}$ for additional gross exposure.
- VaR and factor exposure limits that the overall portfolio must respect.

A simple policy design exercise is:

- Treat the trade sizes w_i (in normalized units) as decision variables.
- Approximate the covariance matrix of incremental alphas as diagonal, with entries σ_i^2, plus a factor component derived from f_{ik} and factor covariance.
- Formulate a mean–variance objective based on $\hat{\tau}_i$ and this covariance.
- Add constraints ensuring that:
  - The incremental contribution to portfolio VaR is below a pre-specified limit.
  - Factor exposures remain within bands after the trades.
  - Turnover (sum of absolute w_i) is under a threshold.
- Solve for the vector of trades that maximizes risk-adjusted causal uplift.

Note the important difference from classical portfolio optimization: here the "return" input is the *causal uplift* from making a specific change relative to control, not the total expected return level of each instrument. This keeps the optimization grounded in incremental, policy-driven reasoning rather than static predictive forecasts.

Worked example: capacity-constrained execution improvements

As a second example, suppose your execution team has identified a new algorithm that can reduce implementation shortfall for certain order types. However:

- The algorithm uses a limited high-speed infrastructure, so only a fraction of daily volume can pass through it.

- Risk management wants assurance that, in volatile days, applying the algorithm more broadly will not inadvertently increase tail slippage.

From historical experimentation, you have:

- For each order i, an estimated uplift $\hat{\tau}_i$ in shortfall if you use the new algorithm vs the baseline.
- Scenario-based estimates of how this uplift behaves across volatility regimes, from which you compute a CVaR measure for any policy that chooses fractions w_i of orders to treat.

A CVaR-aware causal policy could be:

> Maximize expected aggregate shortfall improvement subject to:
>
> - A capacity constraint on total notional routed via the new algorithm.
> - A CVaR constraint ensuring that, even in the worst 5% of volatility days, total shortfall is not worse than a stipulated threshold.

This optimization will typically:

- Allocate capacity first to orders with high uplift and stable performance across scenarios.
- Allocate less (or zero) to orders whose uplift is highly uncertain or deteriorates in stress regimes.

The result is a deployment plan that uses causal evidence to improve average execution quality while embedding explicit guardrails on tail outcomes.

Causal policy learning becomes practically powerful only when it respects the real constraints of a trading business. By:

- Treating treatments as assets with causal returns and risks,
- Using mean–variance, CVaR, and robust optimization to trade off uplift and risk,
- Encoding capital, turnover, and exposure limits as constraints,

you obtain policies that are not only causally justified but also capital-efficient, risk-aware, and implementable at scale.

In the next section we will move from one-shot or static policy optimization to sequential settings. There we will see how contextual bandits and reinforcement learning can adapt policies over time, while still honoring the causal logic and risk constraints developed so far.

6.4 Causal Reinforcement Learning and Sequential Experimentation

Up to this point, our focus has been on *static* decisions. We learned how to:

- Estimate causal treatment effects (uplift) for individual trades or positions.
- Build policies that choose actions based on these effects, subject to capital and risk constraints.
- Evaluate candidate policies offline before deployment.

In real trading, however, decisions are not one-shot. Today's actions affect *tomorrow's* data, market conditions evolve, and strategies must be improved continually. This is where *sequential* decision making enters: we repeatedly observe the market, choose actions, see rewards, and update our policies.

This section connects that sequential learning problem with causal thinking. We will:

- Introduce contextual bandits as a natural extension of uplift-based policies.

- Explain how exploration strategies (epsilon-greedy, Thompson sampling, UCB) relate to causal concepts like overlap and confounding.
- Discuss market-specific complications: non-stationarity, delayed rewards, and interference.
- Outline design patterns for sequential experimentation in markets, including safe exploration and guard-rail policies.
- Contrast full reinforcement learning with simpler bandits, and explain when each is appropriate in trading.

The unifying theme is that **learning a better policy over time is itself a causal experiment**, and must be designed with the same care we applied to static causal estimation.

From static uplift to contextual bandits

In earlier chapters we considered a cross-section of decisions: for each trade or order with features X, we compared the causal effect of actions $A = 1$ vs $A = 0$. Conceptually, we asked:

> If we were to take action a in context x, what would be the expected outcome?

A **contextual bandit** formulates this question in an online, sequential way. At each decision time t:

- You observe a context X_t (market state, order attributes, portfolio state).
- You choose an action A_t from some set (for example, execution style, venue, or hedge on/off).
- You observe a reward R_t (P&L impact, shortfall, fill probability) that depends causally on (X_t, A_t).
- You update your policy, aiming to improve future decisions.

The goal is to learn a policy $\pi(a \mid x)$ that maximizes the *long-run* expected reward, while still exploring enough actions to correctly identify what works.

You can see how this connects directly to uplift:

- The conditional treatment effect $\tau(x)$ between two actions reflects the *instantaneous advantage* of one arm over another in a given context.
- A contextual bandit problem is about learning and exploiting $\tau(x)$ while you are still collecting data.

The new difficulty is that you no longer have a fixed historical dataset to analyze offline. Instead, the data are being generated on the fly by the very policy you are trying to improve. This makes causal thinking even more important.

Exploration as enforced overlap

In static causal inference, we insist on *overlap*: for each region of the context space, there must be some variation in actions, or we cannot identify treatment effects. In observational data, lack of overlap leads to reliance on modeling assumptions and extrapolation.

In sequential decision making, you actually *control* the action assignment. This gives you a powerful lever: by injecting randomness into your policy, you can enforce overlap and make later causal estimation more reliable.

This is exactly what standard exploration strategies do, though they are often described from a purely predictive or regret-minimization point of view. Let us reinterpret them causally.

Epsilon-greedy

An epsilon-greedy strategy works as follows:

- With probability $1 - \varepsilon$, choose the action that currently looks best according to your estimates (highest predicted uplift or reward).

- With probability ε, choose an action at random (or according to a broad distribution).

From a causal perspective:

- The exploitation part focuses on what you currently believe has the highest causal effect.
- The exploration part deliberately creates randomized variation in actions, maintaining overlap across arms and contexts.

If ε is too small, you stop learning: certain actions will almost never be tried in some contexts, and you lose identifiability. If ε is too large, you waste performance by exploring clearly inferior actions too often.

In trading, you might:

- Use higher ε during an initial rollout phase of a new algorithm to rapidly learn its effects.
- Gradually reduce ε as evidence accumulates ("annealing"), but never take it all the way to zero, preserving some minimal level of variation for monitoring and drift detection.

Thompson sampling

Thompson sampling maintains a *distribution* over plausible reward or effect parameters for each action, given the data so far. At each step it:

- Samples a set of parameters from these distributions.
- Chooses the action that is optimal under that sampled parameter realization.

Causally, you can think of this as:

> At each step, imagine a plausible world consistent with the data, then choose the action that would be best if that world were true.

Because different actions have different uncertainties, Thompson sampling naturally explores more where you are less sure and exploits where evidence is stronger. It can be combined with prior knowledge about likely treatment effects (for example, from backtests or domain expertise).

Upper Confidence Bound (UCB)

UCB methods take an optimistic view of uncertainty:

- For each action and context, compute an upper confidence bound on its expected reward: estimate plus a multiple of the standard error.
- Choose the action with the highest upper bound.

The method thus favors actions that are either known to be good or are less certain but could plausibly be good. It is exploration by optimism: you try actions that are promising or under-explored, but you do not waste as much time on arms whose upper bounds are definitively low.

In causal language, UCB ensures that:

- You keep collecting data where potential uplift is high but uncertain.
- Eventually, as uncertainty shrinks, you converge to arms with truly higher causal effects.

In practice, all three families (epsilon-greedy, Thompson, UCB) can be adapted using *uplift* estimates as inputs rather than raw predictive rewards, aligning exploration tightly with causal questions.

Market-specific complications

Classical bandit theory assumes that the environment's response distribution is stationary and that each arm's reward depends only on its own action. Financial markets violate both assumptions in important ways.

Non-stationarity and regime shifts

Markets go through regimes: low-volatility grind, high-volatility crisis, liquidity crunch, policy changes. The causal effect of a treatment (for example, a particular execution style or hedge) can change dramatically across regimes.

If you fit a single global model ignoring this, your bandit may:

- Overestimate the value of treatments learned in a bull market once conditions turn bearish.
- Under-react to new opportunities when a structural change makes an action more effective.

To handle non-stationarity causally, you can:

- Include regime indicators (volatility, spreads, macro variables) in the context X_t, so you estimate treatment effects conditional on regime.
- Use *time-decay* in your estimation, giving more weight to recent data.
- Implement *change-point* or drift detection to trigger re-initialization or more aggressive exploration when evidence suggests the effect surface has shifted.

The goal is to maintain a policy that is not just optimal in the average historical environment, but adaptive to the current causal structure of the market.

Delayed rewards

Many trading actions have delayed consequences:

- A trade's full P&L impact may unfold over days or weeks.
- A hedge's benefit is realized primarily in stress events that are rare.
- A liquidity-provision decision affects both immediate spread capture and longer-term adverse selection.

In a pure bandit, the reward is observed right after the action. When rewards are delayed, naive credit assignment can mislead:

- You may attribute a loss to the most recent action, while it was caused by a trade opening days earlier.
- You may treat as independent rewards that are actually linked along a path-dependent trajectory.

There are two complementary ways to respond:

- **Design rewards to be as local as possible.** For example, in execution, measure implementation shortfall over a relatively short window and treat longer-term P&L as outside the bandit's scope.
- **Move to full reinforcement learning (RL) when necessary.** RL frameworks explicitly handle multi-step credit assignment, modeling the state dynamics of the portfolio and market.

For many intra-day execution or micro-structure decisions, contextual bandits with carefully defined short-horizon rewards are sufficient. For long-horizon portfolio or risk-overlay decisions, RL becomes more appropriate.

Interference and market impact

Interference occurs when one unit's treatment affects another unit's outcome. In trading:

- Your decision to send more volume through one venue affects prices and liquidity, altering the rewards of subsequent orders.
- Multiple desks experimenting with execution changes can crowd into the same liquidity, changing each other's realized effects.

This violates the no-interference assumption common in simple causal and bandit models.

To mitigate interference:

- **Cluster randomization:** Randomize actions at the level of larger groups (instruments, time blocks, clients) rather than per-trade, so that interference is mostly within clusters you can model.
- **Group-level bandits:** Treat each cluster (for example, symbol or sector) as an arm, and learn policies over clusters rather than tiny individual units.
- **Rate limiting:** Cap the total experimental volume in any venue or instrument to avoid crowding and large market impact during learning.

These practices respect the reality that your own actions can change the environment, and they align experimentation with how impact and liquidity actually propagate.

Design patterns for sequential experiments in markets

Beyond the abstract bandit algorithms, trading organizations need concrete patterns for rolling out experiments while staying within risk and governance bounds. Several patterns are particularly useful.

Staggered rollouts

A staggered rollout gradually increases the fraction of flow under a new policy:

- Start with a small share of volume or a subset of instruments under exploration.
- Use causal and bandit methods to evaluate performance relative to control.
- If results are favorable and diagnostics look healthy, expand coverage; if not, roll back.

This acts like a time- and size-scaled bandit, with a high baseline of safe control behavior and growing experimentation only where justified.

Cluster-level randomization

Instead of randomizing at the level of individual trades, you may:

- Randomize entire symbols to treatment or control conditions.
- Randomize client groups, regions, or time windows.

Within each cluster, you may run a simple static policy; across clusters, you use bandit or experimental logic to compare outcomes. This makes interference and spillovers easier to reason about, since most cross-impact is partitioned by cluster.

Guard-rail and conservative bandits

Safe exploration is crucial in trading. You rarely have the luxury of large regret during learning. Conservative bandit strategies formalize this by maintaining a *baseline policy* π_0 with known acceptable performance and constraining experiments to stay close to it.

In practice:

- You may require that, at any time, at least a fixed fraction of flow (say 70–90%) goes through π_0.
- Experimental arms can only be allocated the remaining fraction, and their cumulative performance is monitored closely.
- If an experimental arm underperforms relative to baseline by more than a pre-set tolerance, it is automatically shut down (a stop-loss in policy space).

This combination of allocation caps and performance-based stopping rules creates a form of "bandit with safety constraints", aligning with regulatory and risk expectations.

When to use full reinforcement learning

Contextual bandits handle one-step decisions: you pick an action, observe a reward, and there is no notion of a state that persists beyond what is encoded in the context. Full reinforcement learning (RL) generalizes this to multi-step dynamics:

- There is a state S_t that evolves over time according to your actions and external randomness.
- Rewards at time t depend on the current state and action.
- Your objective is to maximize the discounted sum of future rewards.

In trading, RL becomes attractive when:

- Actions have long-lived effects on the portfolio or inventory (for example, market making with inventory risk, or dynamic hedging).
- Constraints and risk metrics are path-dependent (drawdown, time-varying leverage).
- You cannot define a clean local reward that captures the full effect of a decision.

However, RL comes with significant challenges:

- It is more data-hungry than bandits, requiring many observed trajectories.
- Off-policy evaluation becomes harder, since counterfactual state trajectories are unobserved.
- Causal identification of long-horizon effects requires stronger assumptions and more careful design.

For these reasons, a practical recommendation is:

- Use contextual bandits (and the static causal tools from earlier chapters) for localized decisions with short feedback cycles: execution, micro-routing, small signal switches.
- Reserve full RL for problems where dynamics and multi-step credit assignment are clearly central, and where you can afford the complexity (for example, large-scale market making desks with rich simulation environments).

Even in RL settings, the causal mindset still applies: you must think carefully about the mapping between actions and counterfactual trajectories, the assumptions behind your simulators, and how to validate them with real data.

Sequential decision making is the natural next step after static causal policy optimization. In this section we have:

- Framed contextual bandits as an online extension of uplift-based policies.
- Interpreted exploration strategies as ways to enforce overlap and avoid confounding in the data you collect.
- Highlighted market-specific issues—non-stationarity, delayed rewards, interference—that complicate naive bandit approaches and demand causal care.
- Described practical sequential experimentation patterns, including staggered rollouts, cluster randomization, and conservative bandits with guard-rails.
- Clarified when the added complexity of full reinforcement learning is justified, and how causal thinking continues to guide its use.

Taken together, these tools let you not only design and evaluate a single causal policy, but also *adapt* that policy over time in live markets, learning from experience without sacrificing safety or interpretability.

6.5 Robustness, Monitoring, and Governance

By now we have moved from estimating causal effects, to learning policies that exploit those effects, to adapting policies sequentially. All of this work rests on a crucial, often uncomfortable fact:

> Our causal models are approximations, built on imperfect data and assumptions that may fail over time.

If we deploy causal policies in production without robust checks and ongoing monitoring, we risk:

- Acting on spurious effects caused by unobserved confounding or data leakage.
- Overreacting to noise or regime shifts and destabilizing portfolios.
- Violating risk, regulatory, or client constraints in subtle ways.

This section focuses on keeping causal policies *safe and explainable* once they are live. We will:

- Revisit identification assumptions in production via stress tests and falsification checks.
- Quantify uncertainty at the policy level and use it to temper decisions.
- Address data and pipeline issues that can silently break causal validity.
- Design monitoring and alerting for both performance and assumptions.
- Wrap everything in a governance loop with clear ownership and review.

The emphasis is practical: what you need in place so that causal policies enhance, rather than surprise, your trading organization.

Re-checking causal assumptions in production

In earlier chapters we emphasized identification assumptions: no unmeasured confounding (conditional on covariates), correct timing, and no forbidden feedback loops. Those checks were done on historical data before deployment. Once a policy is live, the data-generating process changes:

- New features may be introduced to support the policy.
- The policy itself changes which trades or clients receive which actions.
- Market structure and liquidity conditions evolve.

It is therefore essential to re-run identification diagnostics on *production* data.

Placebo and falsification tests

Placebo tests look for patterns that *should not* be present if your causal story is correct. Examples include:

- **Pre-treatment trends:** In a before/after or staggered rollout, if your treatment is assigned at time T, outcomes before T should not systematically differ across treated and control groups, after conditioning on covariates. Large pre-trends suggest confounding or anticipation effects.
- **Future-outcome prediction:** If current treatment variables help predict *past* outcomes (controlling for covariates), that indicates leakage or bad timing in your feature engineering.
- **Placebo treatments:** Construct a "fake" treatment variable (for example, random assignment, or a shifted version of the true treatment) and verify that your pipeline does not find strong effects where none should exist.

These tests can be automated and run regularly. A spike in placebo effect size or pre-treatment imbalance is an early warning that your identification assumptions may no longer hold.

Overlap and support drift

When a policy is deployed, it may change the distribution of contexts that receive certain actions. For example:

- A successful uplift policy may concentrate a particular execution strategy in specific volatility regimes.
- A sequential bandit may increasingly favor a subset of venues or hedges.

If this process continues unchecked, you can lose *overlap*: some regions of the state space may no longer see both treated and control actions. That makes future effect estimation and monitoring harder and eventually impossible.

To detect this:

- Track the distribution of actions across key covariates (volatility, spread, time of day, instrument type) over time.
- Monitor effective sample size (ESS) for offline policy evaluation, split by regime and segment.
- Establish thresholds below which ESS or overlap metrics trigger a review or an increase in randomized exploration.

In other words, monitoring is not just about performance; it is also about preserving the conditions needed for continued causal learning.

Sensitivity analysis and robustness to unobserved confounding

Even if identification holds approximately, there may still be unobserved factors that bias your effect estimates. Sensitivity analysis asks:

> How strong would unobserved confounding need to be to overturn our policy conclusions?

In deployment, you can:

- Compute sensitivity metrics for key effects or policy differences (for example, how large an unmeasured confounder's correlation with treatment and outcome would need to be to reduce the estimated uplift to zero).

- Present these metrics alongside policy performance, so risk and governance teams can judge whether the required confounding level is plausible.
- Revisit sensitivity whenever you extend a policy to new assets, regions, or client types.

Sensitivity analysis does not remove confounding, but it quantifies the fragility of your decisions. If only a very small unmeasured factor could explain away your uplift, then you should be cautious and perhaps constrain the policy or demand stronger experimental evidence.

Policy-level uncertainty and confidence bands

In earlier sections we constructed confidence intervals for the value of a policy using offline evaluation (IPS, SNIPS, DR, bootstrap). Once a policy is live, you should continue to track:

- **Rolling estimates** of policy performance (for example, over 1-month or 3-month windows).
- **Uncertainty intervals** around these estimates, accounting for serial correlation and regime changes.

Instead of just asking, "Is the new policy better than the old one on average?", you ask:

> Given the data observed so far, what range of performance is consistent with our uncertainty, and is that consistent with our risk appetite and business case?

Practical ways to use policy-level uncertainty:

- **Graduated scaling:** Tie the share of flow or capital allocated to a policy to the lower bound of its confidence interval relative to baseline. As evidence strengthens, you scale up.

- **Stop-loss rules:** If the upper bound of the policy's performance interval falls below a minimum threshold for a sustained period, automatically de-scale or deactivate the policy and trigger a review.
- **Dashboard visualization:** Display point estimates and bands over time, broken down by segment (asset class, region, client type) to spot where performance is strong, weak, or uncertain.

The key mindset shift is to treat the policy itself as a stochastic object with uncertainty, not a fixed black box.

Data and pipeline robustness

Causal policies are only as good as the data and timing on which they rely. Common failure modes in production include:

- Missing or delayed data feeds.
- Changes in feature definitions or vendor data.
- As-of joins that accidentally use future information.
- Silent shifts in universe (for example, delistings, new listings) that break transportability.

To protect against these, you need explicit **data and pipeline controls**.

Causal timing and as-of joins

Causal validity depends critically on using only information available at decision time. In production systems:

- Enforce as-of joins where features are built as of a clear timestamp, with hard checks that no future data can leak in (for example, by comparing decision timestamps with data timestamps).

- Maintain versioned feature definitions, so that if you backfill history or change a calculation, you know exactly which versions were used when.
- Implement unit tests that intentionally shift timestamps forward to detect whether a feature would change (indicating time leakage).

These practices make the "no future information" assumption concrete and testable rather than implicit.

Missing data and measurement error

Live feeds will occasionally fail or degrade. When that happens, a naive policy might extrapolate aggressively based on incorrect or partial inputs.

Best practices include:

- **Graceful degradation:** Define fallback behaviors when key features are missing or stale (for example, revert to a conservative baseline policy).
- **Feature quality flags:** Track freshness, completeness, and anomaly scores for each input feature, and expose them to the policy so it can adjust or abstain.
- **Input monitoring:** Alert when the distribution of key features shifts abruptly (for instance, a volatility measure becomes constant due to feed issues).

Handling measurement error is harder; sensitivity analysis and simulation can help you understand how noisy inputs propagate into treatment decisions and outcomes.

Reproducible logging and audit trails

For both internal review and external regulators, you must be able to answer:

> Why did the policy choose this action for this trade, at that time?

This requires detailed logging:

- The context features X_t used at decision time, ideally hashed or summarized if sensitive.
- The action A_t taken, including any exploration randomization (for bandits).
- Key intermediate quantities (for example, estimated uplift, propensity scores, confidence scores).
- The realized outcome Y_t once available.
- Model and feature versions in effect at the time.

Logs should be structured so that an investigator can reconstruct, at least in principle, the decision logic and re-run evaluation code later. This is essential for root-cause analysis when things go wrong and for building institutional trust in causal methods.

Monitoring: performance, assumptions, and operations

A robust monitoring setup for causal policies spans three layers.

Performance monitoring

This is the most familiar layer:

- Track realized P&L contributions, implementation shortfall, or risk-adjusted return attributable to the policy.
- Compare against benchmarks: the prior policy, a naive baseline, or a randomized holdout.

- Break down performance by segment (instrument, region, client) and regime (volatility, liquidity).

These metrics tell you *what* is happening.

Assumption monitoring

Assumption monitoring asks *whether the causal story still makes sense*. Key items include:

- Overlap metrics and effective sample size, as discussed earlier.
- Placebo and falsification test statistics over rolling windows.
- Stability of estimated treatment effects over time and across subgroups.
- Drift in covariate distributions and in the mapping from covariates to actions.

Alerts from this layer may not immediately harm P&L, but they indicate that your ability to reliably measure and control the policy is degrading.

Operational monitoring

Finally, you need operational health indicators:

- Data freshness and availability.
- Pipeline latency and failure rates.
- Model scoring uptime and error rates.
- Compliance flags (for example, whether limits and thresholds are respected).

Clear, pre-defined escalation paths are important: who gets notified when overlap collapses, or when falsification tests light up, or when a model begins to ignore certain segments? Monitoring is only as useful as the actions it triggers.

Governance and organizational processes

Technical robustness is necessary but not sufficient. Causal policies sit in a broader organizational context of model risk, compliance, and business ownership. Governance answers questions like:

- Who owns this policy and its performance?
- Who can approve changes to the model or features?
- What review is required before scaling up risk or capital?

Key elements of a governance framework include:

Clear ownership and accountability

Each causal policy should have:

- A *business owner* (for example, head of a desk) accountable for economic performance and alignment with strategy.
- A *model owner* (for example, a quant lead) responsible for technical correctness, data, and code.
- A *risk and compliance contact* who reviews limits, fairness, and regulatory issues.

Responsibilities for monitoring, responding to alerts, and initiating reviews should be documented.

Change management and release cycles

Causal policies should not change arbitrarily day to day. Instead:

- Adopt a release cycle (for example, monthly) for material changes to models, features, or decision rules.
- Require model validation and sign-off before each major change, including an offline evaluation, stress tests, and, where appropriate, shadow runs.

- Maintain version control and release notes describing what changed and why, along with expected impact.

This reduces the risk of accidental breaks and facilitates post-mortem analysis if a release correlates with performance degradation.

Model risk and compliance review

Many institutions have centralized model risk management (MRM) and compliance functions. Causal trading policies should feed into these existing structures, with some causal-specific content:

- Documentation of identification assumptions and their empirical support.
- Sensitivity analysis results and interpretation.
- Description of exploration mechanisms (for bandits) and how they respect risk constraints.
- Evidence from offline policy evaluation and, where available, controlled experiments.

Regulators increasingly care about explainability. Causal framing is an asset here: you can articulate in plain language how and why the policy changes outcomes, rather than just pointing to opaque predictions.

A lifecycle view

It is helpful to picture causal trading policies as following a lifecycle:

- **Data and assumptions:** Collect and clean data, check identification assumptions, and build CATE or outcome models.
- **Policy design:** Learn uplift-based policies with capital and risk constraints.
- **Offline evaluation:** Use OPE methods to estimate policy value and uncertainty.

- **Guarded deployment:** Roll out gradually with exploration and conservative bandits.
- **Monitoring and stress tests:** Track performance, assumptions, and operations; run falsification and sensitivity analyses.
- **Review and adaptation:** Periodically review policies, adjust or retire them, and feed new data back into the modeling loop.

To emphasize this, we include a schematic governance and monitoring loop.

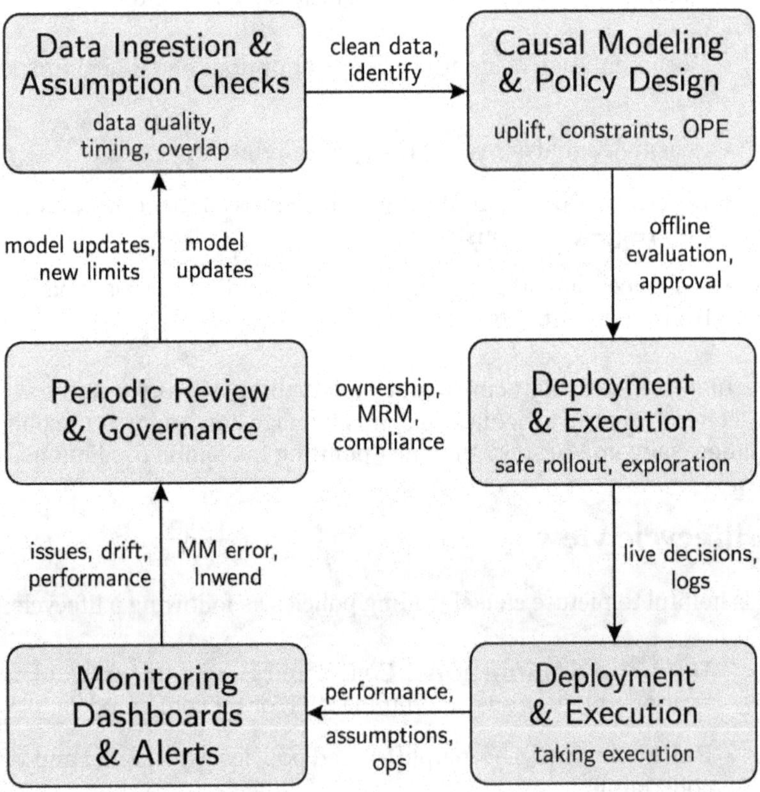

Robustness, monitoring, and governance close the loop on causal trading policies. They ensure that:

- Identification assumptions are not just checked once, but revalidated as policies and markets evolve.
- Uncertainty is acknowledged and used to scale and stop policies responsibly.
- Data and pipelines respect causal timing and maintain auditability.
- Monitoring covers performance, assumptions, and operations, triggering meaningful responses.
- Governance assigns clear ownership and embeds causal models in existing model-risk and compliance frameworks.

With these elements in place, causal inference moves from a research exercise to an operational capability: a disciplined way of designing, deploying, and sustaining trading policies that truly aim to answer, and keep answering, the question, “What happens if we change our actions?”

www.ingramcontent.com/pod-product-compliance
Lightning Source LLC
LaVergne TN
LVHW052033200926
848481LV00005B/1659